DRONE WARRIOR

DRONE WARRIOR

AN ELITE SOLDIER'S INSIDE ACCOUNT OF THE HUNT
FOR AMERICA'S MOST DANGEROUS ENEMIES

Brett Velicovich and
Christopher S. Stewart

DEY ST.
An Imprint of WILLIAM MORROW

HarperCollins books may be purchased for educational, business, or sales promotional use. For information, please email the Special Markets Department at SPsales@harpercollins.com.

FIRST EDITION

Designed by Renata De Oliveira

Library of Congress Cataloging-in-Publication Data has been applied for.

ISBN 978-0-06-269391-4

17 18 19 20 21 DIX/LSC 10 9 8 7 6 5 4 3 2 1

CONTENTS

AUTHOR'S NOTE

L et's get one thing straight up front: I am not a hero; I don't deserve praise for doing my job; but this story needs to be told.

I was fortunate enough to be part of a new generation of warfare, a generation that has forever changed the way future wars will be fought. Every soldier has his or her role, and this was mine.

Except for public officials and well-known individuals and/or entities in the public domain, the names of individuals involved in the operations mentioned in this book have been changed in order to conceal their identities. Most of my former colleagues are still involved in this work, taking the fight to the enemy day in and day out.

Similarly, the terrorists referred to in this book have been given fake names, with the exception of well-known public terrorist figures. I have changed the methodologies we used to look for different terrorists with drones to ensure that no current tactics, techniques, or procedures are compromised.

This manuscript was submitted to the Defense Office of Prepublication and Security Review and authorized for public release. It has been vetted and reviewed by organizations within the government most people don't even know exist. This exhausting U.S. government review process to publication took longer to complete than it took me to write the actual book. Certain details of my work and the highly classified missions I was a part of have been redacted from the text at the request of the U.S. government. The views expressed in this book are those of the author and do not necessarily reflect the official views, policies, opinions, or positions of the United States government, including but not limited to the U.S. Department of Defense.

Even though the book has been vetted and cleared for publication by the government, this is my story. The events that happened are true, recounted from the best of my recollection. I've reconstructed dialogue from memory, which means that it may not be word for word. But the essence of what was said is accurate.

A few people have asked me why I'm writing this book. I'm writing it because I want my experiences and knowledge to help people and to provide much-needed perspective on a central feature of life, business, and war in the twenty-first century. I'm writing this book so that people understand what drones are actually about, and to show how they save lives and empower humanity, contrary to much of the persistent narrative that casts them in a negative light.

WHEN I FIRST STARTED IN THE ARMY, THERE WERE VERY FEW DRONES. HAVING *ONE* available was a luxury. During the hunt for Saddam Hussein after the invasion of Iraq, most people were fighting over a single Predator for the search.

By the time I left the Army, nearly a decade later, my team alone was directing the movement of three Predator drones over individual targets, stacking them on top of each other in the airspace to watch our prey from multiple angles.

That's why I called them our unblinking eyes; our drones saw everything and they never slept.

When you look at how wars were waged before my generation, aerial support was essentially about cover and bombardment. Infantry units would go on long missions in the field blind, and just hope the airpower had softened up the resistance for them. Or they would navigate urban warfare terrain with little to no clue as to what was around the corner of that building, or behind that door, or poking through that window.

Now, especially within the special operations community, missions don't happen without drones overhead. That's how valuable they are. You can bet that of any mission you see happening overseas—a SEAL team raid in Yemen, a hostage rescue in Syria, a terrorist snatched from a compound in Somalia—none of them take place without a drone. Before, during, and after the mission.

It is astonishing how rapid this change has been: already, many in the military—particularly those who began their careers in the post-9/11 era—wonder how we even functioned without drones in the sky. Their importance cannot be overstated.

I often think about all the missions of the men who came before me, and how many lives could have been saved if they'd had an armed Predator or Reaper watching over them. I think about the targets we could have taken out, people whom we might have stopped before they visited ruin on the world.

But drone warfare is not always about nailing the bad guys. In fact, it's not about that most of the time at all. It's about finding the things that some of the most dangerous people alive don't want you to see. It's about connecting networks of individuals, families, money, matériel, and plots.

My team and I lived in a Box in the hottest war zones of the war on terror. No one outside our black ops community really knew what we were doing. I doubt many would have believed it even if they did. We were high-tech detectives unlike any the world had ever seen, and our work represented a profound evolution in warfare.

The drones we had allowed us to save lives. They reduced collateral damage. They gave our soldiers intel, allowing us to peer into the future on their behalves, predicting what would occur rather than simply letting it.

This is the greatest beauty of drones. The ability to be proactive instead of reactive, to take the fight to the enemy before they can take it to us. With drones, we became faster than the terrorists, thinking a few steps ahead. Our targeting and raiding teams were built to ensure that we never gave those we hunted a moment's rest.

Conventional militaries have boundaries. All the enemy has to do is simply jump outside that boundary, slipping away or disappearing within a new one. But my team didn't have boundaries. We moved like the enemy moved; we were as mobile as they were. We became the shadows that haunted them.

Drone warfare will continue to evolve, as groups like ISIS start getting their hands on commercial drone technology and attaching grenades and bombs to them in order to conduct their own drone strikes. And we will have to use and develop technologies to combat them.

Our new leaders in Washington are the same guys who helped build this drone revolution. General Michael Flynn, although he resigned from the National Security Council, was a significant driver of that revolution. General James Mattis, certainly.

I have no doubt that the current administration will increase the use of drones and strikes overseas, because these were the leaders who saw firsthand the benefits they bring to the warfighter. Organizations like Joint Special Operations Command are the only groups bringing the fight to the enemy every day, and they need more drones at their disposal.

When President Donald Trump was running for office one of his basic arguments was that we need to be more proactive against groups like ISIS and Al Qaeda, to be on offense, and to use the tools at America's disposal to destroy them. It falls in line with exactly what unmanned aerial vehicles (UAVs) are good for, and that is projecting strength and striking the enemy, no matter where they are hiding.

It is also worth noting that leaders like Mattis saw with their own eyes what happened when we reduced the pressure on those we were hunting: it gave us ISIS.

The Trump administration by now surely understands the importance of the technology. I am guessing President Trump himself has been astonished by it, as most of what we are capable of (and have done) is completely off the books, highly classified.

Most members of Congress and the intelligence committees still have no idea how, exactly, my team and I did our work. Occasionally members of my team were asked to visit and debrief officials on successful operations against terrorist targets, but those on the other side of the table never really understood or were allowed into the day-to-day of how our targeting machine really worked.

That is what this book is about. An entirely new form of warfare that has emerged over the course of the last decade, my role in it, and the committed and forever-bound individuals who risked their lives to make it a reality.

PART ONE

ARGET 3

1

SHOULD WE KILL HIM?

I was wired on Rip It energy drinks, heart pounding, eyes glued open to the bright screens as we followed a white bongo truck for miles as it drove south, kicking up dust from the Syrian border through the open desert.

"Raise altitude and switch to thermal sensors," I called over to the team. "If this guy spots us in the air, we're done."

It was midday, September 2009, and I was in the Box, a secret windowless bunker at the edge of an undisclosed military base south of Mosul, Iraq, not far from the Syrian border, staring at eight flat-screen TVs on the wall, stacked in two rows of four, the shittiest Best Buy you've ever seen.

Some of the screens streamed live camera feeds from the Predator drone: current altitude, speed, missile laser target designator system, and detailed map of the land below. Others flashed pictures of our targets, their families, and their complex terrorist networks, which spanned the globe. Much of this came courtesy of experts from the CIA, Defense Intelligence Agency (DIA), National Security Agency (NSA), and FBI operating along my side.

I was Delta, special ops, and my specialty was high-level capture and kill missions. My weapon was mainly Predator MQ-1 drones, equipped with two laser-guided AGM-114P Hellfire missiles. My job was to hunt down the most dangerous terrorists in the world. If I was chasing you, you never saw me.

The room was sweltering from the computer servers and lit by blinking screens. A low hum of machinery was a constant in the background and stayed in our heads. When you walked outside the Box, you'd never know that behind the door was one of the world's most technologically advanced operation centers, run by some of the best minds in the business of war. Some of the technology we had wouldn't be publicly known for years to come.

My team of six, a mix of elite military intelligence personnel with different specialties, was called when a terrorist needed to be located. I have no doubt that we could find anyone in the world, no matter how hidden they think they are. I prided myself on tracking down even the most senior terrorist leaders, people who others considered ghosts.

Our target's name was Abu Bashir. We'd been looking for him for weeks—until we got a tip on the ground that he was heading in our direction, south from the Syria–Iraq border. Bashir was an explosives expert for the group Al Qaeda in Iraq (AQI).

Mostly undetected, he moved the material and components for heavy bombs into Iraq, along with foreign fighters and suicide bombers waging war against the United States. His trip was going to end badly, with another attack against either innocent civilians or U.S. military personnel stationed at a base nearby.

A fleet of helicopters were on call nearby if we needed them to intercept a target fast. We sat in a cramped room with cement floors, working off a makeshift desk built out of plywood. Jake, an Air Force tactical controller, sat next to me; he was my shadow. We had our laptops out, running a sophisticated chat program that allowed us to have about twenty different classified conversations with every intelligence agency running at once, including the CIA and NSA, our ground force elements, senior officials in the U.S. government, and the technical side of the operations in Iraq and across the globe.

As I called out instructions—zoom orders, latitude, longitude, altitude, vehicle pursuit directions—Jake chatted everything to a camera sensor operator and Predator pilot, two Air Force personnel sitting next to each other in a trailer in Nevada who actually flew the drones at my every command.

The bongo truck, similar to a pickup truck but with a wider body, was heading southeast now from the Syrian border—fast. They were definitely transporting something. We'd picked him up about an hour before in a desolate place in the desert that I'd been able to narrow down based on an analysis of his earlier movements.

"Jake, why does every terrorist in Iraq that we track seem to own a white bongo?"

"Groupon."

On the monitors, the bongo was kicking up dust everywhere and creating a huge signature visible from the sky. We had the bird at a two-nautical-mile standoff from the target, trailing at around 12,000 feet to keep it out of sight. If our target ever heard the drone's engine or somehow caught sight of it, he'd abandon his mission and go underground—phones tossed, email accounts abandoned, everything gone. Months of our intelligence work destroyed.

The road wasn't much of a road, just some zigzagging tracks

worn into the hard-packed sand for hundreds of miles. It was mainly no-man's-land, with some dots of villages here and there, ten to twenty people at most to a village.

The guys coming across the Syrian border usually followed a predetermined smuggling route, moving explosives or suicide bombers between the villages on the way to their ultimate destination.

Sometimes the first stop was the nearest major town, where the vehicle would be used to blow up the closest U.S. military convoy.

I had been up now for twenty hours. This was when I would fight to keep my eyes focused. The empty Rip It cans were piled at my elbow.

What's he doing? Where's he going?

It was another twenty minutes before the vehicle came to a stop outside a village.

"Zoom in," I said. "I need to see who's inside the truck."

Kill or capture was always on the table, but we needed visual confirmation of Abu Bashir before we made the call, which most times didn't get made until the very last minute. *These life-and-death decisions would change people's lives in the blink of an eye, even my own.*

Two people exited.

"Looks like two military-aged males, wearing white dishdashas," Jake said.

"Confirm for me: no women or children," I said.

Jake went back and reviewed the drone feed, like a replay on ESPN, showing full views of both sides of the truck.

"Confirmed."

"Zoom in two times. What are they waiting for?"

"Prayer time, maybe."

"No, not for another hour."

Suddenly, the passenger began to walk out of view of our camera and into the open desert, while the driver walked around to the back of the bongo.

"Stay with the driver," I called.

"Roger."

The driver began digging into the bed of the bongo and now I could see there were barrels in the back with a bunch of garden-size hoses sticking out.

"You see the passenger anywhere?" I asked. "Zoom out."

I had them switch the camera from electro-optical, or daytime, TV, which shows everything in brown and gray, to infrared view. Both men were now on the monitors. Their bodies were suddenly a bright, ghostly black against the white fall desert. When the passenger lit a cigarette, a huge light exploded, like a house on fire.

Why didn't he want to smoke near the truck?

Within a few minutes another white bongo pulled up and three men climbed out. I took note of how they greeted the others. All of them kissed the hands and hugged the driver of the first truck: Bashir.

The men began cautiously offloading thick jugs about three or four feet tall to the first truck. Just like the ones already in the back.

Now, a normal analyst might discount this because we couldn't ever confirm 100 percent what those thick jugs were from the air. Maybe the first truck was just getting gas or maybe he was transporting the village water source. In the years I've spent hunting and watching in the cesspools of the Middle East, I have found that people do funny things. These guys could simply be locals not connected to the Al Qaeda network at all.

What set our team apart was knowing that nothing in this business is a coincidence. These were explosives and, knowing

Bashir, they could be rigging the truck to blow up like the Fourth of July.

AT TWENTY-FIVE YEARS OLD I HAD THE POWER TO DECIDE WHETHER A MAN LIVED or died. That wasn't an easy decision, even with hundreds of missions to my name and top-of-the-line intelligence networks at my disposal.

I was part of a handful of people in the American military at the time with the responsibility to pick drone targets and order their deaths. I created a kill list—people in Al Qaeda in Iraq network or in ISIS whom we had prioritized for capturing or taking out—and acted on it day and night. We had to move faster than our enemy did, and we kept the pressure on, striking over and over again so they never felt at ease.

Few had knowledge that our elite task force even existed. Delta was part of the Army but worked alongside other special elite forces like DEVGRU, a highly specialized SEAL team. To the rest of the world and even to most within our own government, we were officially off the books, and that was how we liked it.

We took out the worst of the worst. But we had a broader mission in Iraq: attacking and destroying Al Qaeda in Iraq and its predecessor, the Islamic State of Iraq. We became one of the deadliest drone targeting teams in the military. Within the terrorist network, my focus was on taking out critical nodes—senior members who played key command and support roles that allowed the organization to function. Taking down one member led us to another, like one big puzzle, as we methodically connected the dots and made our way to the top.

At the time, AQI was morphing into the Islamic State of Iraq, or ISI, which would later become the ISIS we know today after the group moved its operations into Syria due to increased U.S. pressure. We used the names AQI and ISI interchangeably at the time. Few in the public knew the group yet, but we'd been watching them closely for years. They were the biggest threat to the Iraqi government and stability in the region—and to the United States, as we'd soon find out.

"Page Max in now," I said.

Max was the assault team commander for our task force—the stealth ground soldier, the finishing half of our special ops group. When things got bad, or when we wanted to grab our target, Max and his team of soldiers headed for the choppers stationed outside our door.

Less than a minute later, he swooped into the room, already kitted up with body armor. He had a dip packed in his lip, as usual. He was tall and ripped, what you expected these legendary operators to look like.

"We gotta shut these guys down now," I told him, pointing to the bongo on the big screen.

On the monitors, Abu Bashir's bongo with all the explosives was now speeding southeast in the desert, while the other vehicle had departed in the opposite direction.

Time was not on our side. Bashir was traveling fast toward the large city of Tikrit. Camp Speicher was there, with thousands of American forces and even more Iraqi civilians.

"Max, my assumption is he's either moving a large amount of explosives to be used for an attack or he's going to use that bongo itself as the detonation device."

We had about twenty minutes now before Bashir reached Tikrit with the explosives. At that point he'd be too close for us to do anything if he decided to immediately detonate.

"Good," he said, "we're going."

He paged the rest of his team to get ready.

Our fleet of helicopters was warming up, their blades thrumming the hot air. According to standard operating procedure for our outfit, there were two MH-60s—we called them

Little Birds—along with a few Black Hawks, all fully armed with machine guns and missiles. These weren't simply some usual military aircraft. They were designed just for our kill/capture missions.

Missions are about options—we'd make the decision about whether to strike Bashir with a missile or try to grab him on the ground on the scene.

When the drone was armed, our screens turned into one red crosshair. Hellfire missiles are powerful and extremely precise. We could hit a car in traffic without scuffing the paint off any of the other cars.

I briefed Max on the target's current status and gave him an intelligence packet with printed photos of the target and interrogation cards with questions to ask anyone captured alive.

Minutes later, Max and his team, dressed in desert-colored camouflage, armed to the teeth with Heckler & Koch 416 automatic assault rifles and customized sidearms, were flying away in the helos.

As everything spun up, I began to worry that Bashir would get away. I also worried about the assault team. What if they tried to intersect and the bomber exploded just as they came into contact? What if I was wrong?

There was no turning back now. I played out the various scenarios in my head. Did I miss something?

Bashir was responsible for murdering hundreds of civilians with his explosives. He had brought into Iraq foreign fighters who blew themselves up in market centers, killing kids, families, and U.S. soldiers. I kept that in the back of my mind. I knew what was about to happen to him was just a matter of how.

Did we need to kill him?

This was always the question that came up in the last seconds. Sometimes there was no choice.

I sent the file of Abu Bashir to my superior, who was at an

interagency command center away from the kill zone to get his read on the situation.

His opinion came back in seconds. He wanted to hold off on a Hellfire strike and see how it played out on the ground. We could use this guy alive, if he wanted to stay alive.

"Your assault team is en route to the target and has an opportunity for possible capture," he said on the chat.

"Roger," I shot back.

The drone was to keep watch, playing cover, if anything went wrong.

C'mon guys, get there.

On my headset, I heard the assault team over the radio. "Five minutes TOT [time on target]."

My eyes were locked on the TV screens, looking for anything out of place, the drone camera with its day-TV lens switched on, watching the bongo move through the desert and waiting for the choppers to suddenly flash into view.

I wondered what it must be like to be talking to the guy next to you in your car driving down the road, chatting about what you are going to do that weekend, and then, the next second—you're gone.

Our bird's camera was showing the bongo about a minute away from the city's perimeter. And I couldn't tell if our team would get there in time.

"Thirty seconds before the vehicle reaches the population center."

Then the bullets came.

THE BULLETS RAINED DOWN ON THE DESERT FLOOR IN FRONT OF THE BONGO, SO close to the truck and with such intensity that sand was spraying up in clouds onto the bongo's hood.

A second later, two helicopters with the assault team came

screaming across the hood of the truck, causing the vehicle to slam on the breaks and come to a full stop.

The Black Hawks were a few seconds behind and things started to blur into violent action. We set the drone's course to orbit the scene.

"In the picture," a radio operator said over the wires, notifying everyone that U.S. troops were now confirmed within view of the drone's camera feed.

The assault team dropped out of the choppers hovering over the ground, goggled and guns pointing at the target. Because the truck could be rigged to blow at any moment, the guys moved slowly, weapons ready.

When the two men finally stepped out of the bongo, the assault team was locked in on them, ready to kill if either made a wrong move. The men were standing there in shock, sand swirling all around them from the rotary winds of the choppers nearby.

My heart was blasting around in my chest. It hurt.

Split seconds in these situations were not like other people's split seconds. It was like a car accident when time slows down right before impact.

I had done everything to make sure that one of the men in that truck was Abu Bashir, my target. But there's always the gut check, and the reality wasn't so clear-cut: in my world you can never be 100 percent sure.

Second guesses always creeped up at the very end of every operation. What if it wasn't him? What if those weren't explosives in the back of his truck? What if we killed an innocent? What if troops were killed, too?

Finally, the two men stepped away from the bongo and dropped to the desert floor. I could see their hands go behind their heads. And then a few seconds later the assault team commander's voice came over the radio.

"Romeo, zero one," Max said. "We have confirmed Jackpot."

2

WHERE WERE YOU WHEN THE WORLD STOPPED TURNING?

I was in my college apartment, half-asleep, on September 11, 2001, with the windows shut tight. The air smelled of a mix of old milk and unwashed socks and the plastic fan made annoying clicking sounds as it wobbled on the table next to my head. I squinted back a cracking headache, my memory still fuzzy from the frat party the night before. The digital red glare of the clock: 7:54 A.M.

Why the hell was I up so early? The floor was a mess of Keystone Light beer cans and *Maxim* magazines. I had given myself the day off from class. Maybe I'd take the rest of the week off just to be sure I fully recovered. The apartment was dead quiet, my two roommates out cold. In my head, I could still hear the thumping rap music. We had some of the guys over after the party for a late-night session: drinking, pounding away at Halo on Xbox, and talking about the hot girls we'd met the night before.

I was a typical freshman at the University of Houston, figuring myself out, but mostly partying, drinking, pledging frats, and cramming in study sessions. I had grown up in a little town called Katy, Texas, and dreamed of trading stocks on Wall Street, working for a big finance firm like Goldman Sachs or becoming a lawyer like a lot of my pals were doing. All of my friends had their lives pretty much mapped out from start to finish, as if they were working from a blueprint. I was the same way, until things swerved. That morning.

I didn't understand any of it at first. I was too young and narrow-minded. I didn't even know what the World Trade Center symbolized. I didn't know anything about Muslims, the Middle East, or why Islamic radicals I'd never heard of had so much hate for us.

Before 9/11, I thought my life was heading in a mostly straight line.

Then my mother called me frantic after the second tower fell. I told her not to worry. I was, after all, nowhere near New York.

Days after the attack I started to digest things. The event seemed to wake me up, jolt me. The world I lived in suddenly seemed offensively superficial, the path I was on too safe. My life was a college apartment, frat parties, the drinking, the drugs, the girls. Over and over the same scenario played out nightly, and now it was a broken record that wouldn't have had any meaning even if it played.

I was missing something. That's the best way I can put it. A lot of people came to the same conclusion in those months.

The confusion of it all led me to the campus library, a little cubicle on the top floor, far away from anyone, where I pored over a mountain of books about terrorism, Islam, Al Qaeda. Stories of these pockets of groups who were forming around the world, intent on killing Americans.

The stories of terrorism sucked me in, wouldn't let me alone: One about the October 2000 bombing attack on the USS *Cole* in a harbor in Yemen, which killed seventeen American sailors; another about the truck bomb blasts against the U.S. embassies in Tanzania and Kenya in August 1998, which killed more than two hundred innocent people. I skipped hanging out with my friends and drinking at the frat. I made excuses not to party, embarrassed a bit, instead returning to the cubicle stinking of dust and old books. This wasn't me. Something nagged inside, like a mysterious tap on the shoulder. When I finished one book, I went back for another.

Weeks passed like this. Soon I was reading about all the intelligence services, what they did, which ones were in charge of finding terrorists. I read about the first drone strike the CIA did in Afghanistan that same November. I became obsessed with the Office of Strategic Services—the World War II group, led by the famous Wild Bill Donovan, that would later become the CIA. I spent weeks in the book stacks. One night I got locked in the library. I became enamored with the sacrifices that Army soldiers had made and the early intelligence networks that disrupted plots against the United States. A lightbulb turned on and I knew what I needed to do.

It went fast. By late November, I was standing in front of an Army recruiter at a nearby strip mall, explaining that I wanted in. I wanted to be in the military intelligence corps. I told him that college and everywhere it led to felt meaningless. Everyone around me in school was doing the same thing, trying to go after the same degrees, that same boring life. The 9/11 attack opened me up and made me see for the first time just how small my life had been. I wanted something larger than myself, something outside of Texas. I wanted to serve my country and I wanted to be in the world of intelligence. This rushed out of me like I had been holding it inside for years.

"I want to go to war," I said.

"I DON'T SEE WHY YOU'RE DOING THIS," MY MOM SAID, ANGRY AS I WALKED THROUGH the front door. It was mid-2002 and months had passed since I entered the recruiter's office. At first I didn't know what she was talking about and started to say, what? But she cut me off.

"An Army recruiter came looking for you," she said. I could tell by the look on her face that all kinds of horrid thoughts of war swirled in her head. The recruiter had told her everything, that I had enlisted, that I was going into the Army. "Is it true?" she asked.

I nodded. "Don't worry," I told her, as she began to cry.

I hated anything that hurt her. I tried to tell her that people in Army intelligence never went to the front lines. That there was no way I was going to war. But none of it seemed to make sense. She kept shaking her head, as the tears rolled down her face, as if all she could ask was why. Why would someone who never talked about the military suddenly join—and not even tell her?

We were close. My mom brought me up alone in Katy, Texas, a tiny town not far from Houston. Few ever strayed very far and the town was obsessed with only two things: guns and football. The pride of the place was the Katy High School football team, which won the state championship almost every year that I was there. The Tigers. Our stadium was nearly as big as some professional teams'.

My dad split when I was three. Who knows where he went. He'd call in every once in a while but then disappear for years at a time. He spoke five languages and constantly traveled around the world, and for a long time I thought he was a spy. Maybe a part of me hoped he was something more than a father who cared only about himself, more like what the other families had around me. *Maybe his wandering vagabond thing was somewhere deep inside me.*

We lived in a one-story house in a small suburb of Katy. Mom had been proud to take me out of the small apartments we'd bounced around as she chased jobs. The backyard felt like a football field and the front yard had a single tree, about six feet tall, put in the day we moved there. That tree never grew any taller in all the years I lived there, like it was just wasting away its life, praying for some water to rescue it.

My mom was slim and athletic and her brown hair was always cut short. She worked as a computer programmer for big oil companies and had her own business on the side. I'm sure I didn't appreciate all that she did at the time—her constant work put some distance between us—but I have a lot of admiration for her now. She always talked about the importance of respecting others, of having strong character and being a gentleman. Being a gentleman was an especially big deal to her. She made me read books about it and gave me gift certificates for classes on proper etiquette for when I would eventually meet a girl. Except that she always hated the girls I brought home. None of them ever seemed to live up to her standards. So at some point I just stopped bringing them around.

I got a job at fifteen stocking shelves at a clothing store because my mom was laid up after a car accident and we needed money. But the good part was that I got my driver's license, which meant I was cruising Katy's main street for girls a year before my friends could get behind the wheel.

During the times my mom had to play the dad, she knew how to lay down the law, even if it hurt. One time in ninth grade she caught me drinking beer and smoking cigarettes at a neighbor's house and the belt came out. That was the kind of discipline she knew growing up while living on a farm outside Buffalo, New

York. "Sorry," I kept saying, to no effect. That evening I caught her crying in the bathroom.

The day I told her that I was dropping out of college to join the Army, she cried for what seemed like hours. But she never tried to discourage me. Not that day or the days after, even though all of her friends told her she was crazy to let me go to war. The rest of the family told her she was a terrible mother for it and to let the degenerates of the country go risk their lives.

My mom wasn't alone in trying to figure me out. My friends didn't know what to make of it, either. One even said that I was too smart for it. "The Army is for people who have nothing better to do, who can't get real jobs." My other friends were never outright rude, but I knew they looked down on me for not finishing college and enlisting. I didn't blame them—but I didn't care.

I WAS EIGHTEEN WHEN I SHIPPED OFF TO BASIC TRAINING AT FORT JACKSON, SOUTH Carolina, in 2002. We called it "Relaxin' Jackson." All veterans have their own basic training story—the push-ups, the running, all the shit-talking. It was a waste of time. I just wanted to go to war.

Twelve weeks later I headed to intelligence school in Fort Huachuca, Arizona. It was January 2003, two months before the war started in Iraq. The invasion in March took us all by surprise. We thought Afghanistan was our focus, but recently things had shifted to Iraq and we heard only about Saddam Hussein and his weapons of mass destruction. The night the Army invaded Iraq, everyone was called together and the head of the program told us to be prepared for what was to come. "Whether it's Afghanistan or Iraq, be ready. You will all likely find yourselves in a combat zone soon."

Fort Huachuca was a huge place, high in elevation in the middle of what felt like a desert. We were close to the Mexican border, so close we could see the Customs and Border Patrol blimps always positioned high in the air watching for illegals. I thought Texas was hot, but Huachuca was a stifling furnace.

I scored high enough on the Army entrance exams to qualify for any intelligence job I wanted—cyber, interrogation, source handler, signal intelligence, whatever. I chose intelligence analysis because they did it all.

Intelligence school was like college at an accelerated pace, lots of studying and late-night cramming sessions. In order to qualify for a job I had to pass a bunch of tests along the way at a superior level or else risk getting washed out. I was in the analysis school but we shared the same dorms with the interrogation school, source handling, and electronic warfare.

We got up as a class—sixty soldiers from various backgrounds—at 6 A.M. every weekday and worked out as a group, running miles through the desert trails that wrapped around the massive base, then headed to classes all day. Lights were out at 9 P.M. The ones who couldn't cut it were quickly sent home in the first couple weeks. If you failed a test, which might happen simply if you missed one or two questions, you had one chance to learn the material and take a retest. If you failed again, you were gone, no exceptions. The trainers singled me out as a platoon leader. That meant leading early morning workout sessions, marching the soldiers to class, and leading intelligence meetings in class.

Every week there was another class on a new intelligence subject, but most of the material felt outdated. They were literally still training us to fight the Russians and communists in big battlefield situations, with tank battalions and thousands of men. Morse code was still being taught. Some days we all crowded around a table map, where we placed pieces on the board, our

army versus the Russians. We'd talk about how we would maneuver around them like it was a game of Risk.

There was absolutely no training in counterterrorism techniques or how to target terrorist networks and small, compart-
mentalized terror cells. Nothing about unconventional warfare,
which was what war was these days—not massive battlefield
showdowns. When I asked about it, the instructors just said this
was standard training.

The one thing I learned very well was how to read a map, use
a compass, and quickly get coordinates for a certain area. If I got
lost in a jungle, I could find my way out faster than others. I also
had a knack for picking out anomalies in intelligence reports, pin-
pointing the details necessary to destroy hidden enemy forma-
tions in our made-up war scenarios.

On one of my last nights of intel school, I met a pilot learning
how to fly drones. He was part of a brand-new training course in
the military's broader drone program, which had hardly gotten
off the ground at the time, 2003. I was intrigued by drones but
knew very little about them. Few did. Drones were still a very mi-
nor part of the military. I had read recently about one of the first
drone strikes in Yemen in late 2001, targeting Al Qaeda leader
Qaed Senyan Abu Ali al-Harithi, who was behind the USS *Cole*
bombing. Al-Harithi had disintegrated after the missile from the
drone penetrated the four-door sedan he was driving through the
countryside; he and the other terrorists in the car with him never
knew what hit them.

The first armed drones had only started to hit the skies in
Iraq and Afghanistan and their actions were more rumor than
real, which got me curious. I was fascinated by the possibilities of
unmanned aircraft. Still, it seemed light-years away. The pilot lamented that he was one of only a very few training to fly drones at
Fort Huachuca at the time. To him it felt unimportant among the
other programs ramping up for battle. He wanted to fly Apache

helicopters. Because of the limited drone fleet, the pilot said he didn't even know if there was going to be enough work for him. "Who knows what I'll end up doing," he said, a little hopelessly. "I probably won't even get to the war."

I got my deployment orders shortly after graduating with about forty others who made the cut; I was one of only three soldiers selected from the group to support the special forces because of the high scores I obtained at the school. While the rest of them shipped off to Alaska to form a new Army brigade and freeze their asses off, I was headed to Afghanistan. My official orders said I was to report to the 3rd Battalion, 1st Special Forces Group, a unit of the Green Berets stationed in Washington State.

Before leaving, I did a three-week stint at the Airborne School at Fort Benning, Georgia, where I parachuted out of airplanes—and then had a bit of a reckoning. In all the time I'd spent training, I hadn't actually been able to think much about what I'd gotten myself into.

3

NEW GUY

m I going to have to run out of this helicopter shooting? Are there going to be Taliban everywhere trying to shoot at me when I land? Fuck, I had less than a week of training on old M-16 assault rifles in intel school. No place for a laptop in a war zone. I'm not ready for this.

I sat alone on a helicopter transport heading straight to the front lines.

The Chinook was flying me to my new home, a camp outside Jalalabad, in the very eastern part of Afghanistan. It was 2005, after about two years of training and bureaucratic delays.

I was twenty years old and this is where I would begin my first deployment. It also happened to be one of the most treacherous places in the world: the last place Al Qaeda leader Osama bin Laden had been spotted before he disappeared after 9/11. The news channels had made it sound savage—heads being lopped off, women stoned to death, children raped by their own parents. I didn't know what to expect when I landed. I just assumed there were Taliban everywhere.

Afghanistan is a beautiful country when you forget about all the death and destruction. I was used to big cities back home, nice houses with rooftops. There was little of that here. It was mostly windswept ridgelines, mountains with occasional mud huts. I could see people being pulled on carts by donkeys along the main road, families bathing in the small rivers, chickens and cattle scattering across the countryside as the Chinook whipped past.

We flew over high mountains and threaded valleys, the pilots and crew keeping watch for Taliban or signs of surface-to-air missiles. Even with the earplugs I had been given, the thump of the Chinook's rotors kept me from hearing my own thoughts. The door gunner sat on the edge looking out into the barren landscape as we edged around hilltops. I turned to my right and peered out the small circular window inside the helo as we flew over a group of sheep herders walking alongside their flock, in what seemed like miles from any form of civilization, and who no doubt heard us soaring in their direction from miles away. I watched the land zip past, one finger on my rifle trigger. I wondered if my old friends would even believe that I was seeing this. This was a long way from Katy.

As an intel analyst, I would work closely with the Green Beret team deployed in the area. I was meant to be their eyes on the ground, analyzing and collecting whatever intelligence I could about threats to our small team, making sure they knew anything that was going on. I would help build their understanding of the human terrain by collecting intelligence reports from spies operating through the countryside and formulating recommendations about where our team needed to go. I spoke to the local tribes, making sure I understood everything about them before our larger group sat down with their elders. The tribes were also my sources on the movements of Taliban we were hunting. Mainly we were there to win hearts and minds, which meant making friends with the elders who were the keys to it all.

It was a pretty monumental task considering we were a team

of fifteen Americans surrounded by hundreds of thousands of Afghans. We were on our own, the nearest big military base hundreds of miles away.

An hour before Jalalabad came into view, the Chinook flew over the city and then descended miles outside in an empty field, with nothing around it except a crush of mud huts and buildings, with patches of farm, and big towering mountains of snow in the background. Jalalabad proper had more civilization than other parts of the country; some called it the Palm Springs of Afghanistan. I never imagined Palm Springs to be anything like this.

Two desert-camouflaged Humvees, no doors or windshields, skidded to a stop when I stepped out of the helo. A team of ten Green Berets jumped out. There was a force of another twenty or so locals wearing Afghani garb, gray beards, packed into two Toyota Hilux 4x4 trucks, all armed with AK-47s and rocket-propelled grenades (RPGs)—extra security.

The Green Berets looked like badasses, huge muj beards, like they'd just survived a Taliban prison. Some wore NYPD ball caps. They were armed to the teeth, guns painted different colors of camouflage, with scopes. The only thing missing was the horses I heard they rode to help them blend in with the locals. *Look tougher and less like a nerdy intel guy . . . everyone is staring at you,* I thought.

One of the guys ran over and asked, "You the intel guy?"

"Yeah," I yelled over the departing Chinook.

I stuck out: clean-shaven, fresh haircut, brand-new fatigues, packing grease still on my new gun.

"Welcome to the team, we're happy to have you," he said. Then with a big smile, "Start growing your hair out. This isn't basic training."

Along with the fifteen of us, there were about eighty Afghan security guards. We were one of the first to occupy the Jalalabad airfield, which was littered with blown-up Russian tanks and planes from decades before. They lined the main airstrip. Rocks painted red—signifying live mine fields—were still everywhere around us.

I thought it was a joke when the guys introduced me to my new home, an underground prison that had once been home to Al Qaeda and the Taliban. It was hidden under the old airfield terminal. My jail room? Made of concrete, yellow paint peeling, with a flimsy plywood door and claw marks still on the wall, somewhere you'd imagine many had lost their minds.

Over the next few months I began to learn what it meant to be an intelligence specialist. I grew out my beard, and ditched my uniform for a shalwar kameez and a kufi skullcap. We traveled to remote villages, meeting with locals and tribal leaders while gathering intelligence. Sometimes the people couldn't distinguish us from themselves. It felt a little like being an explorer, going places few if any Americans had ever been before. Some areas of Afghanistan had been so cut off from the world that the people thought the Russians still controlled parts of the country. For the first time during these travels and seeing how others lived, I realized how fortunate I was to be an American.

I turned twenty-one in Afghanistan. The team celebrated with me and in my honor chugged a few "near beers," basically drinks that gave you the taste of Bud Light but without the alcohol (it was illegal for U.S. troops to consume). Other friends my age back home couldn't have imagined the feeling of turning twenty-one without an epic drunken night on the town to commemorate the occasion. Maybe it was better they didn't know the feeling. Maybe this was the reason that soldiers like me and others were out fighting a war on the other side of the world: so they didn't have to feel that.

IT WAS THE FIRST TIME I EVER ENCOUNTERED A DRONE. I'D NEVER SEEN ANYTHING like it. The "Raven" was lightweight and designed to launch by hand and get a quick view of what's over the horizon. It had roughly a sixty- to ninety-minute flight time, a typical operating altitude of anywhere from one to five hundred feet, and couldn't travel much more than six miles out. The price tag was more than a couple years' worth of my Army salary.

"Want to see something cool?" asked Garth, the Green Beret who'd brought the drone to our camp. That day our team had all decided to take a break and grill out.

Garth threw it up and it started buzzing off into the bright sky. The one thing that caught my attention right away was how loud it was, really loud, like a swarm of bees in my ear. No way this thing was sneaking up on the enemy. Even when it disappeared into the horizon, I could still hear it.

Like a video game, he worked the drone with a remote control. It reminded me of an old-school, handheld Sega Genesis with the video screen in the middle and two joysticks on either side, one for the drone camera, the other to adjust altitude.

I was in awe.

"Can you guys see it? I can hear it, but I can't tell where it is."

Garth laughed. "I'm flying it up and down the airstrip. Look on the map."

On the ground there was a small laptop, with mapping software that showed the location of the aircraft over the terrain below. It was turning back to us now.

As he flew it over where we were standing, I could see us on the drone camera on his handheld remote. I waved at the drone.

"Want to try it?" he asked.

Of course I did. I grabbed the controls and he gave me a few pointers about how to turn it: very slow with the joystick, don't do many big movements with your thumbs or it could lose altitude, just be easy with it.

Around the screen there was a small flap that protected the screen from any glare from the sunlight, so you basically had to stick your face right up into the screen, like you might do when you are looking through binoculars.

I looked into it and started watching the feed of the ground below and moving the joysticks on either side of the screen with my thumbs.

I turned the Raven slowly and did a racetrack in the air a few times up and down the airfield, staying at the same altitude.

The one thing that stood out was how wobbly the camera was. It was like a video taken while riding a horse. When you think of a 747, you think about how stable it is in the air. But because this was such a small plane and very light, the winds knocked it around and made the camera feed sway.

The feed also wasn't very clear, although I was still very impressed because it was the first drone footage I had ever seen. Years later I'd figure out that these camera optics were shit, like the difference between a digital camera and a Polaroid.

This went on for only a short time before Garth wanted to call it quits and get to the grill.

"Let's bring it back down for a bit . . . just land it close to where we're standing."

I had no fucking idea how to land this thing.

I lowered the altitude and steered the Raven toward our location. My plan was to do a nice landing, just like any commercial airline pilot, but I lost control of it and the drone entered into a straight nosedive.

The Raven slammed hard into the ground, breaking into several pieces. The nose cone broke apart from the base station and both wings went flying, along with the tail. I blinked hard to make sure this was happening. It was. The Raven lay scattered across the cement.

Fuck, I've just destroyed government property worth tens of thousands of dollars.

"Man," said Garth. "This is not good. You fucked up my Raven!"

I must have had a horrible look of discomfort on my face, like I was about to vomit. I thought I was going to have to pay for this.

That's when Garth broke out laughing. "Got you, man!"

Turned out the Raven was created specifically to break apart in a bunch of pieces on impact so the enemy couldn't get their hands on it. A built-in security mechanism to trick the unaware. It had worked at my expense.

Garth continued to laugh hysterically as he picked up the pieces and walked back to the spot where the rest of the team was still grilling.

Any opportunity to screw with the new guy.

4
CAMP PIZZA HUT

"Allahu Akbar, Allahu Akbar."

I was bent down, barefoot. My hands, knees, and forehead were pressed against the small short-haired rug on the concrete floor.

"Allahu Akbar, Allahu Akbar."

The sun was just creeping up over the horizon as I recited the Muslim prayer in Arabic, line after line. I continued to press my forehead against the rug and then stood, facing the direction of the holy city of Mecca, just as I was taught.

Others prayed around me in the large empty room, voices echoing off the walls. My Koran lay on the ground behind me.

After I finished praying, I planned to rejoin my group to begin laying out our attack on a convoy transporting a high-ranking VIP from the United States. My group was as extreme as they came. Other believers of Islam didn't understand that we were the true descendants of Allah. The ones who didn't understand us had to die.

We only had a short window to get the attack right. Our brothers told us that the American VIP and his armed security escort would be traveling south along a dirt road close to our village. Our ambush had to be planned carefully.

"You must understand the mindset of the terrorist," an instructor said later, shaking me from a brainwashed daze. I'd been hearing this all week—this was mirror-image training in secret in the backwoods of North Carolina.

I wore a full head scarf to protect my identity; others could only glimpse my eyes. This was terrorist training, designed specifically to teach a select few of us how to be just like the enemy, so that we could fight them.

Every day started at dawn, running speed laps around the building and reciting verses from the Koran. The rest of the day we were Islamic terrorists planning attacks, praying, firing foreign weapons like AK-47s, rocket-propelled grenades, heavy shotguns. We conducted mock ambushes on convoys, planned kidnappings of high-ranking officials, and plotted our own suicide missions.

One day we learned how to pack a suicide vest with ball bearings for maximum carnage against civilians in our path. When I picked it up, I was surprised by its lightness. It felt like a hunting jacket. It would be easy to move around with the vest in a heavily populated area undetected and squeeze the trigger, maximizing the death toll.

Sometimes it was easy to forget whose team you were on: the United States or Al Qaeda. The sleeplessness added to that. You spend enough time obsessively thinking and doing things like someone else and you become that someone else.

The propaganda videos they made us watch only fuzzied that

line more. These were videos found on YouTube and parts of the Dark Web. In them they made it seem like U.S. soldiers were personally going out and killing innocent civilians. I remembered one montage of a U.S. Army soldier shooting his M-16 that quickly cut to a clip of an injured child, making it look like the soldier had shot him.

It was one of the strangest training camps I'd ever been to. In part, they were brainwashing us, just like Al Qaeda brainwashed its recruits in order to convince them it was their duty to kill as many Westerners as possible. Hearing enough of it myself day after day, I could see why a terrorist would think that way if an elder or religious figure they trusted fed them those lies. Those barbarians cursing our country had grown up unable to understand anything else.

"Why do they hate us so much?" I asked one of the instructors.

"Because they have a perverted view of Islam," he said.

I didn't get it. I wasn't taught to view others with so much hate. I hadn't done anything to our enemies, quite the opposite in fact. When we were in Afghanistan, our special forces group brought food and medical supplies to families in need. Once we even called a helicopter with U.S. medics on board to our base to assist a little Afghani child who couldn't walk.

A former FBI agent came in and showed us videos of suicide bombers. One opened with the grainy image of a crowded market in a city somewhere in the Middle East. The terrorist's associates had videotaped the scene from a rooftop nearby. Soon a seemingly innocuous truck pulls up next to a crowded café as if it is going to drop someone off. After a couple seconds, the vehicle explodes, killing dozens. "This is the evil that exists in the world," the agent told us. "These are the people you're after."

I began to feel hate inside my heart for them, their way of life threatening America's very existence. The hatred was unsettling, but it emboldened me.

A FEW MONTHS LATER I WAS HEADING OFF ON MY NEXT DEPLOYMENT, THIS TIME TO Iraq. It was a September night when my C-17 transport plane circled down fast in a steep approach, headed for the Baghdad runway. Insurgents were known to shoot planes out of the sky, so we wore full body armor, weapons in hand, locked and loaded, helmets on. I was ready for the worst.

Two thousand five had been a deadly year in Iraq. The insurgency had produced a full-fledged bloodbath: at least 844 American service members were killed, about half of them by homemade bombs planted on the roads. Many more were wounded. It was sometimes hard to keep track. Saddam Hussein had been captured two years before and the United States had trusted the country to an interim Iraqi government. But the place was still a murderous thunderdome of nationalist and Muslim groups fighting for supremacy.

Each group wanted a piece of Iraq, fighting each other and U.S. forces spread across the countryside. Saddam's Ba'athist party had its own gang. Shia Muslim gangs with connections to Iran were sometimes deployed to fight against U.S. forces. Radical Sunnis formed their own gangs and others still were simply warring in the name of jihad—the mujahideen. Al Qaeda in Iraq was winning that war, out of sheer brutality. They believed they were killing for Allah, and even fellow Sunni Muslims wouldn't stand in their way.

As our plane settled down on the runway, I imagined bunkers of bad guys lined up with RPGs and automatic weapons waiting for the doors to open. Brace yourself, I thought, gripping my M4 carbine assault rifle.

But the plane landed without incident. And when the tailgate came down to let us out, there was no one firing. There weren't even armored trucks on the runway. Four or five white buses, caked in dust, pulled up to take us off the plane. We threw our bags underneath. *What the hell is this?* It was like some kind of chartered adventure.

It was bizarre, and it only got weirder. Our buses pulled out of the airport and I watched as the city streets passed. The streets looked barren and almost ghostly, fully lined with barbed wire and three-foot-tall cement barriers to protect unauthorized civilians from entering the camp.

Why isn't the driver at least driving fast? What about snipers?

"Are you kidding me?" I said to the soldier next to me as a strip mall came into view. A Pizza Hut passed. Then a Burger King. And a Cinnabon. A sign in front of one building advertised salsa dancing lessons on Friday night.

"Isn't this supposed to be a war zone?" I asked, incredulously. He shrugged.

This was Camp Taji, a huge base built at the site of one of Saddam's old chemical weapon facilities. The Army had retrofitted most of the buildings and built its own as well, so little was left of the old palace. It might as well have been Toledo.

ABOUT TWENTY OF US INTEL GUYS WORKED OUT OF A SMALL HOT ROOM IN ONE OF the newer buildings on campus. I built target packets on the enemies—basically, digital folders containing documents our special forces teams had gathered from the field on local enemy leaders or militia groups we wanted captured or dead.

Some targets had files hundreds of pages long, while others were more mysterious, with just a few pages. The elaborate packets included everything from an enemy's personal and terror history, to maps of the area where he lived or operated, and any notable physical characteristics, such as a prominent mole on the neck or a nose that had been broken ten times.

Most of the targets were not well known and often it was unclear what role they actually played in the larger terrorist world. Sometimes I wondered if they were actually even bad and if sources were feeding us flawed intel. But there were few ways to tell.

Even at this stage of the war, there was no real rhyme or reason to how we did anything. Pretty much anyone whose name was mentioned in the field went into some sort of packet.

You can imagine all the reports. We became basically an intel factory. And for what? The problem was that few of our reports were actually acted on in time. Many commanders just waited and waited after we'd sent files, saying they needed time to prepare for an actual mission. They'd spend three days just talking about the mission without action. Did they think any of these terrorist fanatics worth their salt in street cred would actually stick around long enough in one place to be captured?

We had a name for this kind of self-defeating work: "the self-licking ice cream cone." It meant creating intelligence for the sake of creating it. Busywork. And over time, we probably lost dozens of guys because of this.

Nightly, I sat on my cot, itching to go somewhere else. You couldn't do real intelligence work from a computer room behind the front lines. It made me question my self-worth—had I gone through years of training to let it all go stale while the terrorists plotted their next attack?

Days passed and soon I couldn't take it anymore. I blew up.

I was on the phone with a special forces captain in the north of Iraq when things turned heated. Our analysis section had the exact location of a bad guy's house, which was a Humvee ride away from this commander's group.

The target was a notorious weapons maker, deft at making and planting the improvised explosives that were killing so many of our guys.

Three weeks had passed since we'd given the commander the packet on the bomb maker. And I was pissed.

"Why are you sitting on this guy?" I said. The commander outranked me, but I didn't care. "What's taking you guys so long?"

"You got to slow down," he said, explaining that they were still planning an assault, but there were a lot of moving pieces. "You don't understand how these things work."

He was cordial about it. But I knew what the commander was really thinking: You're at headquarters with those nice air-conditioned offices, while I'm sitting here in tents with no showers. Stay out of my business and go back to your fucking Pizza Hut.

5

SPY GAME

would have done anything to get out of Camp Pizza Hut, so when a secret intelligence unit came calling in late 2006 I jumped at the opportunity to see a different side of the intel world.

I flew back to the States from Iraq that winter before the deployment officially ended. A couple of planes later I was at a classified base in the Northeast. I threw my bag down on a twin bed in a three-story building. Even though my head was still spinning from the trip, there wasn't much time to catch my breath. I headed to some orientation events that day and then to the common bar on campus, where fifty of us drank. Many of us only knew about the life of spies from the movies.

I had been recruited by a special organization within the military that sends a small group of U.S. military members from different branches every year to spy training. The specific details around my recruitment are classified. I was being trained and certified as an operative, a case officer as they are known in our circles. This was the doctorate of spy training.

"It's very rare for someone to get this opportunity," one of the instructors told us that first night, crowded among dozens of recruits or students in a mess hall. "You're the best and brightest of your generation, but this is a very difficult course." Most of the instructors were civilians, but some were military intelligence officers. They were there to break our asses and teach us spy tradecraft. We were about to become part of an elite and clandestine class of men and women. "You are the next generation of spies," he told us. "Welcome to the Farm."

That's what they called this place: the Farm.

When I got back to my room that night, I worried about cameras. I looked behind the mirror on the wall and along the edges of a landscape painting. I was sure that they'd begun to watch me—and judge every move. I was being a little paranoid, but that's the feeling the camp created inside all of us.

For weeks the camp was just like one big game of spy versus spy, played out across a midsize U.S. city around us—with the local population often in the dark about what we were doing. Our missions involved spotting, assessing, and recruiting foreign assets who could provide the United States with important information.

I wore a lot of disguises. Makeup artists taught me how to appear a lot older than the twenty-two-year-old I was at the time. They gave me wigs with gray hairs, taught me how to alter my walk and posture to appear older, how to color and trim fake mustaches. After practice, I had a couple of different disguises that I could put on within about ten minutes of prep and even my own mother wouldn't have recognized me.

Still, the disguises took some getting used to. Every time I looked into a rearview mirror on a mission, I felt a bit ridiculous in a colored wig, like I was a grown-up playing Halloween out of season. But locals didn't seem to notice. I walked into a convenience store and paid for a cup of coffee and the guy at the register didn't take a second look at my hippie ponytail. I ate lunch at a local diner and the waitress looked at me like I was just another dude with a handlebar mustache.

The Farm opened my eyes to a kind of invisible world that unfolded around us. When you were inside of it, it felt a bit like the Matrix, where only a lucky few truly saw what was going on behind the daily routine of the world. Ever notice a chalk mark on a random wall in a shopping center? Or a group of cars all of a sudden breaking formation with others in a crowded intersection and driving erratically? I would never be the same after the Farm.

I was taught for the first time how to tie a tie, tailor my suits, and order a glass of Scotch for a particular occasion. In some ways, the Farm taught me what my father never did growing up, which was how to become a man.

At night I attended mock cocktail parties where I learned to "bump" foreign personnel who had special access and placement in different levels of government—a general, a foreign ambassador, a socialite. It wasn't much different than a typical businessman trying to make connections at a social event.

Human intelligence, or what we called HUMINT, was all about figuring out another's weakness—and then being able to turn that weakness to your advantage. Did the source need money? Did he have a weird sex habit? Did he want to help his country?

The reports were the worst part. I had to write them up after any interaction: who I talked to, what streets I drove down, exactly what the source said, what he didn't say, what I thought he was thinking, my plan for the next meeting, descriptions of any people or cars I thought were following me. There were nights that I was up until well after midnight writing about some meaningless interaction.

I knew it was a big deal for me to be at the Farm. At twenty-two, I was the youngest there.

BUT AS THE WEEKS PASSED, I BEGAN TO REALIZE THAT THE FARM WASN'T EXACTLY James Bond. Before arriving, I wasn't stupid enough to think that all I was going to be doing was driving fast cars, dining beautiful women, and assassinating people. But I was twenty-two. And I thought I would at least enjoy it.

The thing I began to learn, though, was that life as a spy was incredibly boring.

About 10 percent of it was sexy, with cool gadgets you've seen in the movies, like water-dissolving paper, hidden compartments in briefcases, and plenty of fake documents like passports, driver's licenses, and credit cards. But the other 90 percent—driving around all day masking your trail, and document writing—completely sucked. This started to nag at me after a while. Did I really want to be a spy? Was there something different out there?

I got my answer one day.

An instructor brought us into a dark room and flipped on a video. "This is for motivation," he said. The video was shot from a drone, which was orbiting an Al Qaeda training camp in some deep, hidden corner of the Middle East. The camp was dusty and Spartan, with dozens of men with weapons walking around. At one point the trainees sat down and appeared from the drone camera to be listening to the instructor talk.

Then out of nowhere, a Hellfire missile came blasting down from the drone. In one great flash of whiteness, the missile obliterated the camp—and everyone in it. There had to be more than a hundred people there. Pieces of the main hut within it were thrown up in the air, almost floating up in slow motion as the drone camera changed angles to view the full devastation. When the white receded, we could see that there were bodies on the ground.

I had never seen a drone attack.

Up until then, I'd felt ambivalent about what I was going to do in the intelligence world. But seeing the drone video focused me. Those were terrorists, and they were dead. I wanted to be a part of that.

But I had no idea how to get there. What I did know was that the agency was probably not going to work out. I had three more years of my contract with the Army. Which meant that anything I did for the agency had to be through the Army. The agency didn't fly its drones through the military; they did it alone. So I'd never get to work with drones through this path as far as I could tell. What I was destined for instead at the agency was a life of recruiting sources and gathering human intelligence for the military, probably stuck at some embassy. Which meant writing reports. Lots of them.

When I told one of the instructors that I wanted to leave, he looked at me like I had two heads. In the Army we're trained not to quit anything. It isn't in our blood and even thoughts of quitting make you feel weak. The head instructor came in to see me that night. "Why go now?" he asked, telling me that I was making a big mistake. "You have two weeks left before you graduate."

He spent the next two days trying to convince me to stick around. His final attempt came early one morning at an Italian restaurant on the bottom floor of a high-end hotel. It was in the middle of one of our last spy games. I was staying at the hotel under a cover identity, in the middle of sourcing and gathering intelligence on a plot against a foreign country.

The spy took off his overcoat and hat, then sat down. He was an old-school, Cold War spy, with a thick mustache. He'd been at the job for decades.

He didn't waste any time. There were few others around. "Not many people get this chance," he said in a low voice that he'd clearly cultivated over his years in the service.

I nodded, because I knew it was true.

"You're meant to do this work and we think you need to reconsider. Why don't we give you a few more days' rest to think it through? We'll keep this all between us."

We talked for about thirty minutes. But I had already made up my mind. I knew what had to be done, where I wanted to go. "I'm sorry," I said.

The last thing I remembered was him shaking my hand. He stood up from the table, put on his overcoat and top hat, and walked straight out toward the sunny foyer. He never looked back.

I got on a plane that night and checked into a shitty motel in Maryland.

I waited there for my next assignment in a haze of uncertainty about what would come next. Beer bottles and pizza boxes were scattered everywhere. I had the DO NOT DISTURB sign on the door for over three weeks.

6

THE SHITBOX/ GARBAGE CITY

I woke up on a musty old cot to the sound of screaming.

"*Incoming, incoming!*" a soldier yelled from somewhere in the four-story building. I blinked awake. Dust filled my nostrils from the early morning air. Before I could sit up, a mortar slammed into the roof.

The building shook with the blow, followed quickly by twelve more, each whistling in before it hit, which I counted out like the long seconds on a clock.

Around me were twenty other soldiers laid out on rusty cots. Some, like me, had been having trouble sleeping and were just lying there, eyes open, staring up at the plywood ceilings as the dust fell from between the cracks with each mortar impact, and probably wondering when it was all going to come sinking down like a cake.

It was only 6 A.M., another whole day of mortar rounds ahead of us. The local residents turned enemy had been hitting us all week, one after another, surrounding us like sharks, with little that we could do to retaliate. And even though our men could have struck back, the military rules of engagement at the time didn't allow it. A nice gift to the enemy from headquarters far-away from the fight, who worried that the militants were firing from houses occupied by innocent civilians. But we took comfort in knowing that these mortars weren't strong enough to break through the building. At least not yet.

Three months before, I'd gotten the call in that Maryland motel that I'd been assigned to do intelligence work for the 82nd Airborne. Now I was just outside Baghdad's Sadr City, northeast of the Green Zone—combat outpost Callahan.

The rooms we lived in stunk of mold and sweat and somedays it was like being stuck in a shitbox, the smell so bad at times that it pinched your stomach and bunched up your nose. It was like prison—or worse. Our cots were thin and lumpy and the pillows were about what you get on an airplane. There were no working lights. When we wanted to see what we were doing at night, we flipped on our headlamps. Just like miners.

Our building was about the size of a Walgreens and originally designed to withstand dust storms and heavy winds, not enemy fire. About four hundred soldiers were jammed in across four floors. Before it was abandoned, the building had been a mall. When the Iraqis leave a building behind, it's not a place you want to be. Dried shit had been smeared across the interior walls by the squatters who'd called it home before us.

My diet was MREs (Meals, Ready to Eat—aka field rations), along with the one Hickory Farms sausage and cheese box my aunt Linda had sent from New Jersey. I bathed using water bottles because we had no showers. Going to the bathroom was a struggle. We had a row of porta-potties just outside the building, but we had to wear full body armor and a helmet to get there.

I always had my gun locked and loaded. Every soldier's worst fear was getting killed by a mortar in the john, pants around his ankles.

When the mortars slowed down, other threats replaced them: snipers, stray rounds, car bombs. Even the sheik from the local mosque was against us. He used the loudspeakers in the city to instruct the people to attack all Westerners, which became a nightmare soundtrack that you couldn't turn off.

I'd been told that my deployment was only going to be six months, but that turned into a year and then fifteen months, a kind of low-grade fever that I couldn't kick. "Welcome to hell" was how others greeted new soldiers when they came in. This was the beginning of the Surge, the strategy whereby President George W. Bush shipped over thirty thousand more U.S. troops at the request of General David Petraeus and other senior military strategists back home, keeping their fingers crossed that the chaos would end.

SADR CITY WAS THE MOST DENSELY POPULATED SLUM IN THE COUNTRY, WITH SOME two million people jammed into eight square miles. The streets were rubble, streaming with sewage and crammed with two- and three-story buildings that all seemed to be falling down.

A Shia cleric named Muqtada al-Sadr ran the slum. Being in this area meant that we weren't just fighting Shia extremists. We were also fighting Iran, which was using trained locals who shared similar religious ideology and goals to wage a proxy war against us.

The Surge was initiated earlier in the year as Iraq slid deeper into violence, with different armed groups fighting each other and U.S. troops. The monthly body count of U.S. soldiers killed in battle was at its highest level in the Iraq War. The new prime minister of Iraq, Nouri al-Maliki, hadn't worked out as planned. As a

Shia, he had quickly shut out most of the other religious groups. And the U.S. troops had largely spent their time at big protected bases across the country, making little meaningful interaction with the local population. The Surge was meant to change that.

Most of the thirty thousand new soldiers were deployed deep within neighborhoods around Baghdad. Our mission was basically to clean up the neighborhoods and make them safer. Clear out the guns and root out the extremists.

At combat outpost Callahan, I was one of about eight intelligence analysts. We spent our days in a small, windowless room behind computers, putting together intelligence packets on the local bad guys, a kind of who's who of the neighborhood. The information came in bits and pieces from the field, mostly from people we'd interviewed or taken prisoner, but it tended to be unreliable or hard to verify.

Soon our walls were covered with targets, lines drawn showing how each was connected to the other, like one expansive planetary system. The main boss of our unit's assigned neighborhood was an old bastard named Hajji Jawad, part of a Shia group called the Jaysh al-Mahdi, or Mahdi's Army.

Hundreds of men reported to him. He ran extortion rackets. Many in the neighborhood, including the market, paid his men protection money. His men's singular objective was simple: to kill us. Every bomb that hit our building came because of him.

Early on, I went on a patrol with infantry guys to get a lay of the land. I was curious in particular about the main market, where Hajji Jawad's militias plotted, traded weapons, and extorted money. We drove in a convoy, eyeing the road for improvised explosives in the piles of garbage. The crowds swelled around us as we passed, like something pulsing in a blender.

At the market, the carts and storefronts were suffocatingly close and trafficked in everything from electronics and housewares to kebobs. Sewage and meat and something rancid hung in the air. Men with guns sat in a Toyota pickup, keeping a close watch on us as we stopped and climbed out of our Humvees. We knew about these guys from our intelligence reports. They were the eyes of the market.

I took photos and walked around, taking note of stores that our intelligence reports had connected to Hajji Jawad. I had imagined him hanging out with his guys, plotting attacks like Tony Soprano and his men at their meat market. But it was strangely ordinary, calm even. Despite the crowds and the Toyota, the market was just a market like any other.

When we got intel on his men, we passed it along to the infantry guys who conducted raids. But those raids were never very precise and rarely ended with us getting our target. We seldom had specific houses, which led to a lot of mistakes. The worthless sources within the city usually gave us two or three addresses at a time, so we raided all of them. If we thought a militant was located in one house, the infantry guys would raid not only that house, but also the places on either side. And when the soldiers arrived in their convoy, many times the enemy was ready. They saw us coming from miles away, their intel better than ours. Other times, the men inside didn't turn out to be the targets we believed we were going after. In one raid, the man firing on us turned out to be just a homeowner protecting his house—he'd thought he was being robbed by local thugs. Civilians were dying partly because of our mistakes, the fog of war at its worst.

Over those months near Sadr City, we just didn't have enough information and know-how to target the enemy embedded among the populace with pinpoint accuracy. We trusted the wrong sources, who turned out to be giving us fake information for the money, no doubt some even working directly for the enemy to gather information on us. We also detained local citizens in the area when they probably shouldn't have been detained. We were imprecise. It was either us or them and I think it pissed off everyone involved.

On our side of it, the consequence was that a lot of our men died along the way. They were shot up in the streets or hit by IEDs on patrol. For a stretch, it seemed like we lost a man every week. One afternoon I looked through the camera that faced out our front gate as a small convoy of vehicles transporting our infantrymen returned from patrol, only to see a massive explosion erupt from a telephone pole as they drove by. The battered vehicle stopped right in its tracks. That year was one of the deadliest of the war for U.S. troops. There were nights when I wondered if I might be next.

It's hard to shake that feeling when it hits you—that you could die at any moment and don't have any choice in the matter. Being in a constant state of danger gets to you, a compulsive thought you can't stop. It's one thing to feel fear for a few minutes, maybe when you're walking through a tough neighborhood late at night or for a few hours after a terrible car accident. But it's another thing entirely to feel that fear for weeks, months, and even years at a time.

Every soldier feels this way at some point, whether they admit it or not. You either go crazy thinking about it all day long or you just accept the fact that when your time is up, it's up. Maybe a higher power has a plan for you, which is a nice way to deal with that fear, and there is nothing else left to do. But the soldiers who learn to push the fear way down inside and cover it up are the ones who get by best.

I began to feel an extreme hatred for the locals and the Iraqi people, even for those in the country who didn't mean us harm. It wasn't like me to hate so much and so broadly. It wasn't the way my mother raised me. I began hating these people whom I didn't even know because they clearly had so much hate for me. That hate started to manifest itself, slowly taking me over.

"What the fuck are we doing here?" I said one night to Jay, the analyst next to me at our bay of computers, as we scrolled through a list of shitheads that just kept getting longer and longer.

"This is bullshit."

"Just sitting behind these damn computers, and for what? It's not like the intelligence is going anywhere."

"We can't even leave this damn building."

We had a version of this conversation regularly. All of us did.

"They're just firing at us," he said.

"We're sitting ducks."

MY ONLY REFUGE WAS THE DRONE ROOM. I WENT THERE DURING BREAKS. IT WAS A tiny office—basically a closet—on the second floor, with one small laptop that streamed footage of the Army's Predator RQ-1 drone that orbited the city day and night, its pinlike camera capturing the hundreds of thousands of people on the streets. Someone had told us how to log into the system and the guys had set up the room to watch for our entertainment.

There were no chairs, so we sat on piles of MRE boxes—and hours passed there. It was my first real taste of a drone in action since my fuckup in Afghanistan with Garth, and my first education in how it was being used the wrong way.

The big Army HQ in the Green Zone controlled it. Because it was only being used to collect information, it wasn't armed. But we were lucky to even have it flying over our area for the few hours a day that it did. There were so few Predators operating at the time, and even fewer military units with the power to control them. It flew along roads that our convoys traveled but mostly it did route scans and searched the city streets for pieces of trash that might be roadside bombs.

The hope was that the drone's thermal sensors would pick out improvised explosive devices radiating heat in a pile of trash.

But the scans were completely ridiculous. The street trash was oceanic. Parts of Baghdad felt like a giant Dumpster—the garbage was all over—and the drones never, in all the hours I spent watching, found an IED.

Sometimes I'd open up the chat function on the monitor streaming the live video feed as the drone looked at a pile of rocks or some paper in the road and I'd see the pilots chatting back and forth. The conversations were always the same.

"Hey, I think we got something hot here," one chatted to another. I could see the camera on the drone from 4,000 feet up staring down at a white plastic bag in the road that looked no different than the sea of other white plastic bags floating through the garbage-laden streets like giant jellyfish.

The drone circled the plastic bag for thirty minutes, sniffing out an angle that might give light to what was hidden under it. Soon the pilot looped in the infantry commander of the unit in the area. "We got something," the pilot messaged to him. "It's hot!"

Hot garbage was dangerous garbage.

Soon after, the commander would send out a convoy with ordnance soldiers to dismantle the IED. I watched the camera feed as the convoy slowly approached the bag and then a soldier in a big, bomb-protective suit that looked like the Michelin Man climbed out and went to examine it.

"There they go again," I said to Jay.

"Garbage patrol," he said.

Sure enough, when the ordnance soldier turned over the bag, there was nothing there.

The thing is, even if the drone ever did spot an IED during a convoy, the pilot didn't have the ability to talk directly to the 82nd Airborne convoy commander in the field. His warning would have to go through multiple channels before it even got to him. And by that time, it would likely be too late.

"Burning holes in the sky," I said to Jay. "That's all these drones do."

It sounded like a song. But it was a sad song. The military was using multimillion-dollar machines to hunt for garbage, while we were dying.

DURING THOSE MONTHS THERE WERE SO MANY EXTREMIST GROUPS IN THE CITY VY-ing to get their licks in. We were simply target practice for them.

The worst I can recall came around four o'clock one morning, and I was starting to drift off at my computer in the back corner of our office. I had been clicking through different enemy photos and reading intelligence reports for the last couple hours. It was turning into another all-nighter. The whole outpost was nearly pitch-black and unusually silent, except for the standing fan rattling through the dusty air.

Thinking that I needed a walk to clear my mind, I got up and headed for the computer lab upstairs, where I could jump on Facebook and see what my friends were up to back home, in Katy, Texas. That's what most of the guys did with downtime, anything to escape the prison of this place.

Then it happened.

Halfway down the hallway: a gigantic, blinding flash of light out of nowhere, like someone had suddenly hit the hall with a giant blowtorch, and then in the same second, while my eyes were burning and trying to adjust, *boom*! An object came crashing through the concrete right in front of me like the front end of an eighteen-wheeler, slamming into a sleeping area, where twenty or so soldiers were racked out.

It all seemed to happen in slow motion. Concrete and rebar collapsed around me and the explosion threw me to the ground, the heat of it all over my body, like when the door to an incinerator is suddenly thrown open. Sparks were flying everywhere as small chunks of debris from the wall struck me. The ringing in my ears was in stereo. Then suddenly everything went dark and for a second it was just dust and smoke and then nothing at all. Was I dead? I tried to blink. I tried to look down the hall and get a view of what happened, but I couldn't even tell if the building was still standing.

I don't know how long that lasted, but slowly my feeling came back. I had arms and legs again as I used the wall next to me to get up. A throbbing started in the deep part of my eardrums and it hurt like hell, like something burrowing in. The ringing, too, like a gun had gone off next to my face. Damn. I tried to blink it away. I squeezed my eyes shut and then opened them. My head felt like it was going to come off.

I began to stagger around, trying to hold on to the wall. But the explosions came again, one and then two, and then another, like they were being dropped from directly above.

I must have slipped into a haze again because at some point as I stood there, trying to hold on to whatever wasn't falling around me, another soldier appeared.

He shook me.

"GET YOUR BODY ARMOR ON NOW!"

"What?"

"GET YOUR ARMOR NOW!"

It took a second to snap back into reality. Patting myself down head to toe to see if my body was still whole, if I'd been hit.

I was alive.

I'd find out later that others weren't as lucky that morning. Twenty Katyusha rockets had torn holes into the building. They'd been launched from a massive flatbed truck parked parallel to our building on the street out in front.

Blood was everywhere, like many overturned paint buckets. I remember seeing a young soldier with his legs torn off, lying there in the mess, partly clothed in his uniform, as others yelled for medical help. Exactly how many people were hurt that day, I don't remember. Maybe I blocked it out of my mind. But I would always remember that soldier. He came to represent how bad things had become. He made me want to raze the whole country, until there was nothing left. I never hated anything that much before. I wanted to kill every last one of them, but I was power-less.

It was in the hours that followed that I learned how close others had come to dying. One soldier had been on the top floor quietly reading his Bible when two rockets blasted right past him, punching two big holes in the building, one hole on either side of where he sat. Miraculously, not a scratch on him. Just some dust on his clothes.

Maybe he was lucky. Maybe that meant there was a God. I don't know. I just knew that the war was at its worst and I was more afraid than I'd ever been before.

I CALLED HOME AFTER THAT MORNING. THERE WAS A LINE OF US WAITING TO DO THE same. I hadn't yet changed out of my dirty, ripped-up clothes. I needed to hear my mother's voice. I needed to escape the war. Just talk about anything else.

"Tell me about your day," she said.

I called her every couple months, just to check in. Usually I didn't talk much about all the danger. I didn't want her to worry. I didn't want her to know that just a few more steps down that hall and I could have easily been killed. I asked about all the regular stuff—how the family was doing, what she was up to. I tried to keep it upbeat.

But I felt myself cracking this time. I couldn't muster the usual enthusiasm. "Things are good," I said. "The usual."

"What's the usual?"

"It's nothing."

"Something happened, didn't it?"

There was a long silence. And then I broke. "I'm not sure if I'll live through this," I said, my voice stuttering as the fear I had kept inside took over. I told her about the missile attack. "It's just a matter of time before it's my turn."

I could tell she was taken aback because she didn't say anything at first. She'd assumed life wasn't that dangerous. That I was safe.

She began to cry.

"I'm sorry, Mom, it's bad here."

"You shouldn't talk like that," she said. "You shouldn't do that."

"Mom."

"Everything will be okay."

But we both knew we'd entered a place that neither of us had been before.

NATURALLY, ALL THE ATTACKS MADE US ANGRIER AND MORE DRIVEN TO STRIKE back. Thoughts cycled through about what I could do differently, what power I had to change things, to fight back.

I immediately thought of our sporadic Predator flights.

I chatted up the drone pilot on daily garbage patrol and asked if he'd try a different route. Instead of a route scan, I asked him to fly over the houses that we'd targeted to raid. "We could use some support seeing what our infantry guys on the ground can't before a raid," I chatted him on the secure line. "We're dying down here."

From then on, the drone group began supporting us once or twice a week for two- or three-hour stretches. Even as the military was starting to get more birds out to support missions, as part of a broader policy shift, they were still scarce in the skies—at least for us. We had to share one drone with three or four nearby Army units. Which still wasn't very practical. But we made the most out of it.

The new drone strategy worked as well as it could. The soldiers suddenly had visibility on whatever house they were raiding, whether there were any gunmen perched on rooftops, suspicious lurkers, and how many people might be waiting inside the house. There were always firefights when our guys took to the streets inside Sadr City and the drone helped become their extra eyes in the sky.

It was hard to actually quantify the shift. But the advantage felt like it mattered. And we started bringing in more militants, with fewer soldiers in our outpost getting killed. The new targeting also seemed to scare Hajji Jawad some. One day we got intelligence that he'd moved deeper into the slum and had stopped moving around as much, fearing that we were getting closer. I didn't see him for a long time after that. Years later, the Seals would send me a picture of him rotting in a Baghdad jail.

IT WAS AROUND THIS TIME, FROM OUT OF NOWHERE ONE NIGHT, THAT I RECEIVED A cell phone call.

"Hello," the voice said.

"Who's this?"

"This is Mr. White."

7

THE DOOR AT THE END OF THE HALL

Mr. White never told me his first name. It was only Mr. White. On the phone, he said that he'd heard a lot about me, but he didn't say what he'd heard or who had told him anything. He wanted me to try out for a new job.

What was it? He wouldn't say. I flew home anyway.

The command at 82nd didn't like it at all. They had tried to stop me from going, but the top brass told them they couldn't get in the way, and everyone quickly fell in line.

I traveled to an undisclosed location in the United States in early 2007 and met Mr. White for the first time. He was waiting for me the morning after I arrived.

There was something about him that made me feel anxious whenever we crossed paths. Like he already knew the answer to all the questions he asked me. I got the sense right away that asking too many questions of anyone when I got there would get me into trouble—an uneasiness no doubt by design. This was part of the selection process.

About that: the U.S. government won't let me say much about how I was recruited into the unit or the gauntlet of mental tests that only a few pass to gain entry into what is hands-down the most elite organization in the military.

I can't tell you about where I went, the people there, or what went on. I can't tell you any more about Mr. White, though there is more to say about him. Most of what I wrote about the process in an earlier version of the book was completely redacted and blacked out. The government wants to keep it that way.

Very few in the military ever get a shot at the experience. But without the selection process, elite special missions units wouldn't be as badass as they are, or as legendary. Every member knows that they're working with the best and brightest in their craft.

It has to be that way. If you can't trust that the man or woman next to you is operating at the same elite level, everyone is in big trouble. Even the cooks go through their own gauntlet. It's like having a bunch of Gordon Ramsays who can serve you dinner and pick someone off in a crowd with an assault rifle.

What I can say about what I went through without getting into trouble is this: it was one big mindfuck from start to finish. And it was my first true introduction to the world of black ops, what we refer to in our club as "the dark side."

Because I was intel, my selection experience was different than a typical "operator." How operators get picked and the physical hell they go through has been detailed in numerous books. They make most of the military look like Girl Scouts.

For me, imagine the hardest job interview you can think of— over many days. Now multiply that by ten. Intellectual, psychological, and—maybe most important—emotional stresses that are unrelenting. You have no idea what's going on, and the only thing you know—and which many people take—is that there's an exit if you need it.

Most civilians would give up after the first few hours, the unknown too hard for most to cope. That uncertainty of what I was getting into was what fueled me. There were a gazillion tests right away. Tests for my character, intelligence, and capacity to mentally deal with the high-stress world to come.

They needed to know I could handle being put in situations by myself, with little or no information, and figure things out, no questions asked.

From the moment I arrived at the classified facility, I was watched and assessed by a handful of different people. I passed others sometimes in the hallways of different buildings. No one talked. No names were ever exchanged. We hardly even looked at one another, maybe just a split-second peek to get a glimpse at the competition.

At night I lay on my bed, the crickets screaming outside, and thought about what was next and where things could be headed. I never knew.

The absence of information made me feel at sea. There were times as I fought through the physical and mental tests and jousted with psychologists about my past and future that I felt like I wasn't good enough to be there.

Days of this ended when someone told me to drive to an un-marked building deep in the woods.

When I arrived, the one-story building couldn't have been bigger than a local fast-food joint. Two guards were waiting. They escorted me into a dimly lit hallway with only a few chairs pushed up against the wall. I walked in and was told to sit down and wait for further instructions.

One of the guards sat to the right of me while the other one waited outside. The white walls were chipping. As I sat there, I wondered if the lights were dim for a reason or if someone had just forgotten to replace the bulbs. The rusty metal chair felt like something given to prisoners in a holding cell.

I couldn't help but notice that the hallway led only to a single black door. And I could only make out the door because of a tiny sliver of light shining through a small crack at the bottom.

What was behind that door? Part of me wondered if I'd have to shoot someone who'd been tied up and covered in a hood. I nervously laughed at my own paranoia.

Hours passed, at least it felt like hours. I didn't have a watch or a phone to know the time. It was hot and my back was soaked with sweat. My mind played tricks on me. The hallway began to close, feel cramped. The guard next to me just stared silently at the opposite wall as the few lights flickered on and off.

Back then I was still wet behind the ears. I knew nothing, even with the years I had already spent in combat zones. What I know now was that this black door was everything: it was the potential of who I could become, it was the secretive group that few knew anything about.

Finally, the door I had come in through swung open and Mr. White appeared. I had not seen him since the day I arrived. He sat in the chair to my left and gestured to the end of the hall-way to the closed black door and told me to stand up and head that way. My heart was pounding. "When you get to that door, knock three times and wait until you are told to enter," he said. I looked at him as if to ask, What's in there? But he just gestured to the end of the hall until I started walking.

One thing that I would understand after this day was that this process had started before I'd even gotten the call from Mr. White and arrived at this secret place. The men assessing me already knew everything there was to know about me: all that I'd done had been recorded and put away in files. Part of my top-secret clearance meant verifying my past.

Everything I had learned up to that point, each combat zone, each piece of the intelligence puzzle that I had mastered in those earlier years, all of it was important. I finally understood why I had been put in the situations that led me here. Little did I know at the time, though, that I had so much more to learn, that I truly knew nothing. This was only the beginning.

When I got close to the single door at the end of the hall, walking blindly into it without knowing exactly what I was getting into, I stopped and turned around, hoping to get one last nod of approval from Mr. White before I knocked and went in.

But Mr. White was gone, and so was my past. I never saw or heard from him again.

What was behind the black door? Unfortunately, the government won't let me tell you anything about that, or what ultimately happened after I knocked and a loud voice urged me in.

But I can say this: since the moment that door opened and I walked in, nothing has ever been the same. I was Delta.

8

DAY ZERO

I showed up at the unit's U.S. base in early 2008.

As I passed multiple security checkpoints, showing my badge and trying to keep it together, I was flooded with a feeling of pride.

Am I really fucking here?

The unit was legendary in the U.S. military. Much of what it did wasn't even known to the outside world. It was off the books—and so were its people. Most only knew about the unit from what they saw in Chuck Norris movies. But that wasn't the half of it.

The organization had a lot of history and I learned it all. It was founded in 1977 after Special Forces operator Col. Charlie Beckwith spent some time with the British Special Air Service (SAS). Beckwith saw what the U.S. would come to know very well decades later: that terrorism would touch all of our lives at some point and there was a need for a specially equipped organization to take it on, no matter where it was in the world.

People mix up the different special forces operators and units all the time. It was an easy thing to do. But each one was unique. SEAL Teams specialized in water, though they did land missions, too, many times at night and within the borders of countries with which the United States was not officially at war. Army Rangers were the military's elite light infantry force. They went after large targets like enemy airfields and compounds with lightning speed. The Air Force also had the Pararescue, with guys who parachuted out of planes and helicopters on stealthy rescue missions.

Our group did all that, among other things, but the primary mission over the last decade was direct action (DA). When a terrorist cell needed to be taken out, a hostage needed to be rescued, or a terrorist group needed to be taken down, the unit was called in. The government had a tier system to designate different special forces elements across the services; we were considered the highest, Tier 1, the national mission force.

Every member was hand-selected, from the intelligence guys to the ground force operators, to the guys who serviced our customized weapons, even down to the doctors and dentists on our compound there to make sure we were ready to meet the demands of the mission.

Most of the operators—the guys who kicked down doors— came out of the Green Berets and the Rangers. They were already rock stars and highly skilled, but Delta turned that up a notch, turning them into supersoldiers. It was taking the world's best professionals, giving them the tools and technology they never had access to before, and then setting them free to do what they do best.

I would quickly learn that our core responsibility was very straightforward: hunting down the world's most dangerous terrorists. To that end, I'd be provided with all the assets and gear I needed to take out the enemy, including the most sophisticated unmanned aerial vehicles (UAVs) in the U.S. arsenal.

The base was its own mini-campus, with large buildings

housing personnel and equipment, medical bays, huge gyms with Olympic-sized swimming pools, multiple firing ranges, training grounds surrounding the main building that had mock-ups of Middle Eastern buildings found in war zones overseas. As I drove in I saw a bunch of guys in dune buggies and dirt bikes and armed to the teeth pull out in front of me and zoom off into a trail through the woods. This was a whole different world, sealed off from the rest of the Army.

As I unpacked that first night, my mind was all over the place. The intelligence side of our unit was a tiny group, just under twenty, so everyone knew each other. You were known by your reputation. That was all that mattered. You earned it like stripes on your sleeve. Up until then, I had been used to large intelligence units. But these guys prided themselves on their small teams. Even though they'd looked at hundreds of candidates, I was one of only two recruits brought into the intel unit that year. My initial selection was just the beginning. I had six months to prove myself to other members of the unit; otherwise I was out. I had been tested before, but this was the ultimate test. You were either varsity or not. In this game, there was no JV. I learned this fact fast.

On one of my first nights, I met the second recruit, Johnnie, who was on his fifth month of probation. It was late and we were all in the team room, which was part of the secure underground facility where I'd be working and training. He was a stocky guy, bald head with a trimmed mustache.

Early on, some of the senior guys were around and Johnnie joked with them. When they left, I asked him how it was going. I wanted to know what to expect.

His demeanor grew dark, as if a shadow had moved into the room, and he suddenly looked tired and beaten down. "I don't know, man," he said.

"What do you mean? You got a month left and then you're in."

"I can't do anything right in their eyes. They're riding me hard. Really fucking hard. You have no idea."

He sat down at a table and looked at his booted feet. We talked about the months he'd been there and it sounded rough. It got late. He said he was stressed and mentally broken and felt like no one liked him. "I don't think they're going to keep me around much longer."

I didn't know what to say other than "Don't worry, man. I'm sure it will all be fine."

He didn't argue, but he warned me about what was to come. "Forget everything that you accomplished before. That means shit. You're nothing now. You're zero."

I WAS ON A TEAM WITH THREE OTHER SENIOR INTEL ANALYSTS. BILL WAS THE TEAM leader. At forty he was the oldest in the group—a kind of Yoda. War had ravaged him and he was graying, something the team gave him shit about. Bill was a legend, though. He was part of some of the first and most devastating Predator strikes overseas. He was most famous for tracking down a well-known dictator and kept a photo of the capture on his desk. Just the two of them sitting next to each other in chairs shortly after capture. That photo was a stark reminder that a few men had the ability to change the course of a war. When I asked him about it, I was surprised by his modesty. "I wasn't responsible for that alone," he said. "People think I'm good, but it's really because I surround myself with great people."

This way of thinking and acting, I'd find out, was the unit's way.

"Nothing we accomplish here is done by just one person and nothing you do will be done alone," Bill said.

I liked him right away. He would become a mentor even

though he'd probably never admit it. I would lean on him heavily, especially when I was uneasy about making tough calls. He didn't always play by the rules when it came to targeting terrorist networks. He did whatever it took to take his targets out. Years later I would thank him for being such a big influence and going to bat for me even when I was wrong. "Stop stroking me," he said, "and get back to finding terrorists."

Jack was the number two. He seemed to know everything about the guys we hunted. If you asked him about any senior-level terrorists around the world, he'd recite their biographies and then tick off a list of ways to take them out.

Unlike Bill, there was no gray area for him: rules were black-and-white. Sometimes we'd find ourselves in tricky situations during a hunt, moral dilemmas that sometimes made me question what we were doing. Jack always knew what call to make.

He pushed me to the point of exhaustion early on, and then pushed me some more. Once he got on me because I was only working eighteen-hour days. "What the hell are you doing with so much free time!" he yelled. "Maximum four hours of sleep a day or we'll find someone else to do what you do."

At one point, Jack left the military for the private sector, but he nearly lost his mind. "Civilian life sucks," he said.

Mark was number three in our group. We called him "Angry One" because he hated pretty much everyone outside our inner circle, especially other U.S. intelligence agencies. Too many of them had burned him too many times. He wouldn't even get on the phone with the agency when they needed intel from him. "Fuck them," he'd say.

Mark was in his thirties, a big guy, solid as a concrete piling. Ironically, he always thought of himself as a nice guy, not realizing it didn't take much to set him off. Over the deployments, he was constantly firing our "augmentees"—the people whom various government agencies sent to support us around the globe. Any slight error and they were on the next military cargo plane smoking back to Washington, D.C.

Over the years, our team would become very close. In this job, you spent more time with one another than with your own family. We knew each other like brothers.

Most days before deployment were spent in one of the team rooms or in the main operations hub, which was sort of like the control center of a submarine, stacked with computer screens under a low ceiling. I got there at 5:30 A.M. and didn't leave before 7 P.M. Some nights I didn't leave at all.

"Every one of us has spent the night in this place at some point," Bill said to me early on. He wanted me to know that I wasn't the first person to do this and wouldn't be the last. It was exhausting, but something was different about this place than other jobs I had previously. I wanted to be there and knew I was following in the footsteps of the best. It wasn't a chore.

When I wasn't in the bunker, there was a lot of training. We practiced tactical driving and shooting pretty much every badass weapon under the sun—automatic rifles, pistols, shoulder-fired rockets. Even though the operators were the unit's boots on the ground, as members of the intel squadron within the unit, we still needed to know how to pull a trigger. My weapons of choice were a Glock 9mm and a Hechler & Koch (H&K) 416 long rifle.

The main job of our team was something that I'd been doing for years but was expected to take to another level: building target packages of terrorists, figuring which ones to go after, and finding them on the ground to capture or kill.

We had secret intelligence databases with entire structures of our enemies mapped out and massive line diagrams of the leading terrorist groups around the world, groups you've heard about on the news and others that you will never know.

Weekly, they'd interrogate me for hours, grilling me about terrorist packages I was assigned to put together. The idea was to get better at tracking and planning strikes on our enemies.

"You have to know these targets better than their own families," Jack said one day in the team room, the place we went for private conversations. Each of the intel teams had its own room. "You have to find that one chance, that one small window to capture or kill the enemy."

Stress was as constant as bad spring weather in those early months, but that was by design. You had to learn to deal with it because stress was the unit's natural state. One day Bill walked into the operations room, dropped down a ninety-page brick of papers, and said, "You have an hour to learn this and present it to the board."

These daily tests and endless hammering from superiors were designed to scare the new intel recruits into feeling like failures.

The legal document he gave me explained the authorization for use of military force (AUMF) and why we had the authority to conduct drone strikes against certain designated terrorists. He wanted me to quit, but I didn't. I burned through the document in record time, extracting the info I needed, and crushed the presentation. Bill left the room smiling at me, as if silently nodding his approval.

Training moved fast. It was like a treadmill running at 20. If you tripped or fell behind, there was an assumption that you'd never regain your footing. You'd be left.

After a murder board one day, I ran into Johnnie again. It must have been a particularly rough one. His face was white. He looked more beaten down than before. I tried to talk to him, give him a boost like he'd probably do for me.

"Hey, man," I said. He just kept walking, without a word.

A few days later, I heard that Johnnie had been cut. They told him to leave and he was gone before I could say goodbye.

THE "UNBLINKING EYE" WAS WHAT BILL CALLED DRONES.

He liked to say that drones were our most important tool, but to be a good targeter, you needed to learn how to observe, how to see what others don't see.

"UAVs are nothing without the right people behind them," he said during one of his teacherly moments, as we sat in the operation room staring at the feeds.

Bill and Jack came from a time, just a couple years before, when the group had access to only one drone in a given combat zone and everyone in the Army was fighting to use it. Now they had multiple UAVs in their pocket, Predators, Reapers, and others—many "unblinking eyes" that could rove the skies with their eyes wide open.

In those first few months, I watched hours and hours of drone footage: a strike on a vehicle traveling through the mountains someplace the U.S. government technically wasn't supposed to be, a Hellfire launch on a compound full of terrorists armed to the teeth in a war zone.

In our world, we didn't actually use the word *drone* much at all. That term came from the media. We called them UAVs, short for unmanned aerial vehicles. I also called them birds, like "put the bird up over the following location."

Our first birds had been unarmed and used for surveillance. They also made a lot of noise and crashed without warning after losing link to the ground control stations. The newest crop was completely silent and flew thousands of feet in the air. They varied in size. Predators were typically the length of a small commuter plane at twenty-seven feet, with the wingspan nearly double that.

Most landed like fighter jets on a landing strip and had hundreds of Air Force personnel maintaining them.

Drones brought us a completely new capacity for success on the battlefield. No other generation of warfighters before us had this kind of power. Hundreds of millions of dollars were spent yearly to make them better just for our teams, flying higher, faster, stealthier, with more firing precision. The overall intent was to be more exact at targeting while at the same time decreasing the chances of any harm to innocent civilians. Our teams were helping shape the future of drones every day by implementing technology that wouldn't be known in the public space for years.

Our drones could stalk targets for hours at a time, collect data, and of course kill. But we used them mostly for surveillance. Usually the camera sensor lives in a bubble pod along the belly of the bird and includes an electro-optical (daytime) camera, an infrared (nighttime) camera, a laser target marker, and laser target designator. In our jargon, this was the multispectral targeting system—all the components we needed to watch, hunt, and kill.

Early on, the cameras streamed back fuzzy images. The amount of data that needed to be transmitted from one side of the world to the other so that we could see the video clearly was initially too much to handle. The government spent tens of millions of dollars to increase the bandwidth for streaming data, adding secretive data relays that allowed the drone fleets to communicate to us from anywhere around the globe.

In the course of training, I learned how to manage the drones, the very specialized—and alien to most—language used over the radio and chat systems, and the various complicated processes involved in Pred strikes. The biggest surprise was the massive infrastructure around a drone. It wasn't just a couple of people flying these multimillion-dollar machines. I was in charge, but there were a lot of people in many different locations, watching the drone, launching it into the air, landing it, and helping to make sure that nothing went wrong along the way. I didn't pilot the drone or physically move the camera myself. There were Air Force teams sitting in trailers in Nevada or New Mexico that did that for us. The teams flew them from these trailers because it was easier to control the drone infrastructure from the United States instead of constantly creating new hubs in every new combat zone. But I was at the center of it all. I directed the drones where to go, who they followed, what they watched, and who they targeted.

The media sometimes referred to us as "hunter-killer teams." But I was learning that we were way more than that. We were part of one of the most efficient, sophisticated, and interconnected organizations in the world.

One video in those early days stuck with me. The target was a member of Al Qaeda in Iraq. Another intel analyst had tracked him down one night to a tiny mud hut in the desert.

As the Pred orbited the compound, an assault team came into view on the monitor and raided the house—a pretty typical operation. Except this time was different.

Within minutes of entering the house, the assault force started a fast retreat, every one of them sprinting in different directions from the building. And then, *boom:* thirty seconds later, the house exploded. They had been baited in.

"You see that!" Bill said, leaning into the monitor. "That analyst fucked up! He should have known that the target wasn't in the house."

Every day the assault force put their asses on the line based on our intelligence.

"You need to know everything about your target," he went on. "What if you called for a Hellfire and it got dropped on the wrong house?"

The criteria for a drone strike changed repeatedly over the

years. Mostly they were carried out when we couldn't get our guys on the ground or didn't want to risk their lives.

Bill gave me one bit of advice about all this: "Just be right. If you're wrong, you're fucked."

I KEPT HEARING RUMORS ABOUT MY DEPLOYMENT. MOST OF THE GROUP HAD BEEN sent to Iraq to head up teams since the war was at its height. I was sure I was going there and I was starting to get antsy.

While waiting my turn in the chute, I watched as others in our unit got to work. I looked up at the monitors in our dining facility one morning to watch our guys kill a senior Al Qaeda leader in a country U.S. forces didn't operate in. The media would later say that it had to be the CIA who did it, but they were wrong.

One week I was sent to Washington State for Survival, Evasion, Resistance, and Escape school (SERE). People called it Camp Slappy because of the interrogation training. I was tied up, blindfolded, and beaten up, just how you'd imagine it. The program was meant to prepare us in case of our capture by an enemy state—and train us to escape. I learned how to pick locks and get out of handcuffs.

There were about thirty of us, all from different special forces units. I learned a lot about myself at Camp Slappy. I saw grown men cry. And the trainers didn't take lightly to women, either. In their eyes, we were all the same. I remembered hearing girls screaming as they got slapped around.

The hardest part was that you didn't know what was going to happen next. It was like a house of horrors, where you stumble from one room to the next, each room offering its own unique pain.

One of the worst moments was the Box. We were individually locked in dark wooden containers for what seemed like days. Shoulder to shoulder, with no room to sit down. They blared rock music and sounds of babies crying. When one of us drifted off, water came raining down. It was freezing. One by one, they pulled us out and interrogated us for hours.

You never knew what was going to hit you from one moment to the next. I learned that I could withstand a lot more mentally and physically than I could have imagined and I sure as hell never wanted to get captured in enemy territory.

When I came back home from training, I got right back into the weeds of understanding the drones I would be using in the field.

During this time I was issued a pager. The pager had to be with me at all times because I was always on call. It buzzed at night, other times in the morning. It kept us on our feet.

The first time I got a page from our headquarters was after midnight. We used these coded communications—basically ones and zeroes—so that any foreign government watching us couldn't tell when our unit was activated on a mission. The translation of the code sent to me that night was basically: get your ass to the team room.

Hours later, I was suited up, with a bag of gear—computers, hard drives, guns, fake documents—on my back and put on a cargo plane with a crew of operators, zooming to an undisclosed location overseas where we'd set up and do a mock mission. I couldn't tell anyone where I was headed or what I was doing or how long I'd be gone.

I was being trained to essentially disappear, to conceal who I was. Being a part of a culture of secrecy could be both exhilarating and mundane at the same time. Exhilarating because I was doing something incredibly powerful and important and bigger than all of us, although most people would never know it, not even my mother.

Bill and the others said it wasn't always easy holding everything inside. You had to bottle war up, even when your instinct was to talk and sort things out. Any accomplishments could only be shared among the group. Pride wouldn't come from outside people telling me "good job." Success couldn't be celebrated in the ways a normal person would be able to celebrate. Awards were not big events. When somebody said "Jackpot" over the radio, that was the equivalent of a high-five. That was praise.

I had learned to give up the idea that I should be patted on the back or hugged every time I did good, which is what I had grown up in school learning. None of that mattered. I had an important job to do and American lives depended on me to do it well, whether they knew about our existence or not.

WE WERE JAMMED INTO A BUS RIDING TO AN AIRFIELD IN KENTUCKY.

"Is this the new guy?" one of the operators said. He had a thick New York accent, tall as a basketball player and ripped with a full beard. Other burly dudes with automatic weapons and optics laughed. I clearly looked like the new guy, still clean-shaven.

He grabbed my hand and introduced himself. Rocky was the commander of the assault squadron, an Army lieutenant colonel.

Six months had passed in a flash and it was near the end of 2008. Bill and the others had blessed this last phase in training: the operators. It was time to start working with the assault team, the guys who would travel with us on the ground and go after the targets we hunted.

Highly intelligent, Rocky seemed to know the intel side of the house very well, and he shared various insights and thoughts on the future outlook for certain terrorist groups.

Then his tone changed to deadly serious. "You know that you have an incredibly important job?"

"What do you mean, sir?" I asked.

"All of the men around you here"—Rocky pointed at all the operators kitted up around me—"they rely on you heavily."

The operators were the best in the business. They were the

badasses of special forces—muscled up, with tricked-out weapons, ready to go anywhere, anytime.

I nodded.

"We're going to risk our lives because of your decisions." He looked me in the eye. "You are choosing who lives or dies because you're the guy who finds the target. . . . You're the guy who's signing a target's death warrant."

I had never really thought of it that way until Rocky said it to me that afternoon. In my head I had always rationalized it as, "Well, I'm not the one pulling the trigger. It's someone else."

But the truth was that the operators would not be in the house of that terrorist unless I told them to go there.

"He's right," Jack said, leaning in closer. "You get that? You need to choose the bad guys you target wisely. Because they better be bad enough to make it worth them getting killed."

BEFORE MY DEPLOYMENT, I WENT HOME FOR ONE FINAL TRAINING EXERCISE. I HADN'T been back to Houston in four years and it felt strange arriving at the airport and driving into the city with my team.

We set up at a nonmilitary place in the city, a place that you'd never expect to find us in, and worked all day and night. If you'd passed us in the halls of a hotel or a fast-food joint, you'd never know we were conducting mock terrorist hunts in your city. We'd set up the full box in the suite of a hotel, managing drones, intelligence personnel, and operators from a single living room.

When the training settled down one afternoon, I called some old high school friends. I'd been wondering what they were up to because I hadn't seen any of them in years.

That night about twenty of us met at a restaurant a few blocks from my hotel and it was just like old times, the whole herd hanging out, guys and girls.

Everyone had grown up. Tim and Brad had settled into bank

jobs, just like they'd all talked about, Jenny was an accountant, and Greg and Steve were lawyers. A couple of the guys had just gotten engaged and had their fiancées along with them. They were starting to talk about having kids already, buying homes. The white picket fence stuff.

"What about you," Jenny wanted to know. "How's the Army?"

I simply said it was great, because I couldn't say anything else. I told them I was just passing through and then steered the conversation away, just as I had been taught.

A part of me thought they wouldn't really understand it if I told them what I really did anyway. I was working in another world. Where did I even begin?

As the hours passed and the beers went by, I realized I definitely missed old times. Since I left college, my life had become my job, and that night I missed the days when things were simpler.

We all said goodbye after midnight and went our separate ways. While they returned to their new homes, I headed back to the operations center in the hotel to continue work. It was another five hours before the sun rose.

I GOT MY ORDERS TO SHIP OUT NOT TOO LONG AFTER THE HOUSTON TRIP. SENIOR leadership had finally signed off on me running my own intelligence team overseas and we were headed to the northern Iraqi city of Mosul.

Word came later that the cargo plane was leaving in ten hours for Iraq, so I went home and packed the last of my things. I threw essential gear into a North Face backpack—civilian clothing, mostly cargo pants and button-down rugged shirts ideal for the desert environment, a seventeen-inch customized Alienware laptop, GPS handheld devices, and some additional technology lightweight enough to take on the long flight.

Days before, I had already sent off heavier things, like years of intelligence data on Drobo hard drives, my long rifle, and boxes of ammo. That would all be waiting on the other side.

It was 3 A.M. when I rolled into the office and climbed on the bus with my intel team, along with the assault operators. No fancy sendoff, no parade, no friends waving goodbye. This was how it would always be.

I didn't call my mother that night, but I thought about her and whether she would be proud. I didn't want to worry her and couldn't exactly explain where I was going. I didn't even think she knew I was heading overseas.

The bus slipped through the night and soon we were at the landing strip with the C-17 warming up. We didn't talk much, each of us in his own head. Wheels were up within the hour.

As the plane hit cruising altitude, the other guys passed out. They had been through this a few times already and were eager to get to where the action was. I tried to shut my eyes, but the excitement and nerves kept me up. I remembered Bill's advice: "Drones are nothing without the right people behind them. . . . Just be right."

Hours in, I decided to swallow the Ambien that the doctors on board had passed out. I drifted off to the sound of C-17 engines.

PART TWO

TARGET 3

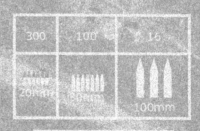

300	100	16
20mm	20mm	100mm

9

THE DRONE WAR BEGINS

My intel team and the operators suited up and headed for the Black Hawks and Little Birds on the runway. It was late afternoon, sun burning down, just north of Baghdad. As we walked down the long flight line, we passed a Predator drone, gleaming and sleek in the hangar. I did a double take as I walked past—it was the first one I'd seen in person—while the others around me kept moving as if they had seen hundreds before.

The summer air was burnt and whipping, same as it was when I'd left Iraq a year before, when I was living just outside Sadr City. Only now it was July 2009 and the U.S. troop surge had started to prove effective. It was important we capitalized on those gains and clearly the enemy was starting to lose, but many senior leaders remained. Fewer soldiers were getting killed and Baghdad was getting safer, or at least it felt that way. That forced the bad guys and killers underground, mostly to northern Mosul, which was where we were headed.

I had been deployed with the unit's "vehicle interdiction troop," which meant my job for the next four months was to stop the flow of bomb makers, suicide bombers, and terror leaders as they snuck across borders and between major cities. We were a stopgap to break the links that connected the enemy to each other across the various safe havens in major cities in northern Iraq. Our team was outfitted with its own fleet of 160th SOAR Black Hawks and Little Birds. The pilots were by far the best in the world. We needed to be as quick and mobile as the enemy and the fleet allowed us to travel anywhere we needed to go on a moment's notice.

We flew with the chopper doors flung open, 100 miles per hour, ready to jump into action. Sitting on the edge of the chopper, racing through the blue sky, legs dangling, and watching the open, mostly empty desert as an occasional village flashes past was a powerful feeling. It felt like we were explorers heading to stake our claim in a new territory.

When we landed, there was no time to waste. We had only four months to do as much destruction to the terrorist network in Mosul and the surrounding provinces as possible. I dropped my black duffel bag in one of the trailers hidden behind big cement blocks called T-barriers and headed straight to the Box.

Around the base, few knew what to make of our white trailers and the blacked-out choppers racing in and out night and day, all of it cordoned off from the rest of the U.S. soldiers. The trailers were windowless, equipped with satellite dishes on top, and locked at all hours. Our entire perimeter was covered by guards; they would not allow any other military personnel or locals inside. As far as the enemy was concerned, we were invisible. They had no idea we were there—and that's how it needed to be.

The Box was a double-wide trailer and had been outfitted

with one long plywood table standing across a cold cement floor, and a twelve-foot wall of flat-screen monitors. Images of a drone and the desert landscape streamed across them. *Here we go,* I thought. Inside I was nervous as hell, but on the outside I was weirdly calm. I had been preparing for this moment for a long time. I slugged a cup of black coffee that had been burning on a hot plate in the back—and got to work.

ONE QUESTION IS AT THE HEART OF EVERY TARGETER: WHERE DO YOU BEGIN THE hunt?

Finding terrorists who have spent their lives eluding U.S. forces is an art, not a science, and there were only a handful of targeters who could do it successfully night after night. We could find anyone if given the opportunity and resources—and our multimillion-dollar drones gave us the ability to do it with precision.

Every hour wasted debating would be another minute the target had an opportunity to adapt to our technology or plan his next attack on an unsuspecting populace. We needed to move at the speed of war because the enemy wasn't waiting.

A lot of misinformed people in the international intelligence community thought we had some Wizard of Oz in the sky magically locating guys we wanted to hunt down—with just a tap, tap, tap of a few buttons on our keyboards.

That's a joke.

Even within the U.S. intelligence community, most don't understand how it works or how an enemy leader is taken off the battlefield when they read about it in the news.

When an intelligence group from the United Arab Emirates special forces visited one of our teams at a U.S. military base as part of a routine partner nation exchange, they couldn't get over the fact that our targeting teams only contained a dozen or so personnel and that we could locate a guy based on a scrap of intelligence, and then pinpoint him for a kill in short order, hours in some cases, when it took them and others months, if they got their target at all.

"Where do you get the software to find these guys?" one of the men asked. "We'd like to buy it for our computers."

"Ha! What software?"

"You know, the analysis software that tells you guys which terrorists to strike and predicts exactly where they are in the world."

Typical Emirati. He thought he could buy whatever he wanted if he threw enough money on the table. Like others, he couldn't seem to grasp that it was only a few analysts doing the painstaking work manually behind the scenes—not some whiz-bang technology.

There was no magic formula to finding a terrorist. It was a combination of things, and every target was unique in its own way. We had several intelligence teams, which worked in different parts of the world, swooping in and out in the cover of night. Usually the deployments were four months at a time, depending on the mission, but it always felt longer because few of us slept much.

As targeters we had to be historians, reporters, and prophets at the same time. Not only did we need to understand a target so well that we could recite an enemy's life story, but we also were constantly providing up-to-date assessments to commanders and others high up in the U.S. government and ultimately predicting a target's next move.

Every one of our targets deserved what they had coming. With every one there was overwhelming evidence that he had actively engaged in planning, approving, or carrying out attacks against U.S. interests. Not a single one of them would think twice about killing an American—man, woman, or child—if given the opportunity.

You have to understand something about how terrorist networks are structured. Generally, an Al Qaeda or ISIS cell consists of several emirs: administrative, military, logistics, security, sharia (Islamic law), media, and the overall emir. I liked to target the admin emirs because they always have the most information about the cell and connections to every other part. The admin emirs are also a lot less fanatical, sort of boring, like accountants— unlike the military emirs, who would usually rather blow up in a ball of flames than be captured.

In our world, we had crafted and refined a specific methodology for this cycle of relentless pressure on our enemy.

The methodology was simple in concept, but difficult in execution.

I was always looking for that critical player in the networks, the one emir whose death could degrade the overall group the most.

Every terrorist had his vulnerability. These guys were human, after all. I had to get into the mindset of a terrorist operator, think like he did.

I usually started with the target's full name. Names are hidden gems in the Middle East—and usually overlooked by others. Men are named after their forefathers, so the second name would come from his father and the third from his grandfather, and then a part would also tell you where they were from.

One thing we had to be careful about were *kunyas*—fake names terrorists give themselves to hide from trackers like me and my team. Within jihadi circles, these men use *kunyas* when talking to each other to mask their true identities in the event that their associates are captured.

We diagrammed full names and families as a baseline for our

search. An analytic tool helped me see inner circles clearer, organize my findings, detect patterns, and manually draw quick diagrams and charts about his world, particularly who else I might
need to go after to get the target in question. Oftentimes we had to
track down two or three levels, such as a friend or family member
unaware of the illicit activities, just to get to the primary target.

All the names that came up were then run through advanced
software specifically for targeting, some of the best tools and tech
money can buy.

Then we go through their shit—their cars, homes, phones . . .
everything. And we look for pressure points (friends, family) at
the same time. There's no more useful leverage than family in
these parts of the world.

Then we start to build a pattern of life (POL) on the target—
places they visit, previous residences, even if they know that U.S.
forces are following them. Still, I needed to find a real "startpoint," a spot in the sky to start the drone.

Startpoints are numerous at the early stage of the hunt. We
collect additional ones outside of a target's family, looking at any
information we might glean from Internet sites, reports, and
databases. Locations could be anything, such as a distant relative's house, local stores, a mosque, historical sites tied to other
members of his immediate group, small villages we came across
that had similar tribal characteristics or that shared a common
background with him and his family.

Sometimes the key to finding our target could be the simplest
thing that others had overlooked. An office building he used to
work at years before he turned extremist, a café he was known
to frequent, the mosque where he prayed. I was also looking for
key things such as his education or distinguishing features like a
broken nose or a limp.

While this was going on, our resident signals intelligence
specialist who sat with my team would comb through signals in-

telligence related to a target—any communications, online propaganda videos, whatever he could dig up. Access like this made us unstoppable. For each target, we compiled PowerPoint slides that detailed everything about the target and their activities—the "baseball cards." Officially, the process was known as target "nomination." Those slides would then make their way up the chain of command.

With all that in place and a mission approved, we'd start the hunt. Following leads, connections, and relationships until we'd catch a break—an exchange between parties that was out of the ordinary, a trip into the middle of nowhere in a white bongo, multiple stops at markets without a single purchase, a visitor to a residence who suddenly appeared one day with no rhyme or reason.

We'd log such stops and the locations of any interactions into the maps, all while talking with the team and cross-referencing each stop with our database for any suspicious connections—other targets who might have used the locations before. We'd map not only their own history, but a given terror network's history, tagged by place, and cross-referenced with phone calls, text messages, and emails that related to any of it: the target's pattern of life starting to take shape.

Information was the key to our success—the large databases we built over the years included terabytes of terrorist dossiers, source reports, open-source information, interrogations, and detailed assessments of a village's allegiances to terror groups and religious sects.

Based on years of data contained in my maps, I could zoom over a house with the drone and tell you who lived there and if there had been an operation conducted before. Often terrorists liked to reuse other terrorists' houses (generally after their buddies had been captured or killed), as if America somehow forgot where any of these people lived.

All this happened in real time. Once we had eyes on the

right people who were a degree or two of separation away from the target, we'd almost inevitably get to our guy—provided we had done the right intel work, were patient enough, and didn't have some disruption in pursuit, like bad weather or a target lost in traffic.

And then? Ninety percent of the time we captured targets. The other times we shot them down with Hellfire. The criteria for kills varied. There were a lot of questions I would ask myself during the process, like, What would killing this person mean to the overall network or even to the local authorities? How would it help us? Would it make things worse? Did the target deserve to die?

OUR FIRST TARGET WAS AN ISI LEADER WE CALLED USAMAH. MY MIND HAD BEEN SET on going after him before we'd even arrived in the country. He was the admin emir for Salah ad Din province, which comprised a nine-thousand-square-mile swath of territory in the north— about the size of New Jersey. His responsibilities, coupled with the importance of this province to the overall strategic mission of ISI, meant that Usamah was a few removed from the top of the food chain and managed numerous files for the group's finances, he was the record keeper. He had a deep understanding of the men who made up the numerous terrorist cells operating throughout the north, as well as the finances and revenues of the group. He spent time with the commanders day in and day out; he had their routines down. We needed whatever he knew.

The taste of bad coffee still in my mouth, I called out instructions to Jake, the tactical controller, who sat next to me typing it all into the system's chat for the camera operator and Predator pilot back stateside. Four others worked alongside us: my deputy sifting real-time intelligence, a radio guy talking to other agencies looped in on the hunt, as well as three people doing signals intelligence, essentially eavesdropping on various electronic devices—email, cell phones, texts of our targets.

For days we used a rotating fleet of Predators and other aircraft to survey areas of interest—little villages and larger cities just outside Mosul. The team before us had done the same during its deployment and handed over to me all their knowledge from the previous months of targeting. Usamah was what we called "OPSEC (Operational Security) savvy"—meaning that he was very aware of his wanted status and knew he could be taken out at any moment. He did everything he could to minimize our ability to track him. But there was one thing I learned early on: the terrorists I tracked eventually slipped up. And that's when we got them.

Usamah was good: he didn't leave much of a signature on the ground and his experience eluding forces for so many years made him a worthy ghost for our team to hunt. We would get word of his presence through sources catching glimpses of him walking through a local market in Mosul one day; a rumor of him making an appearance at an ISI underground meeting in the southern corridor of the city the next. With each new discovery, dots placed on our maps started to take shape and tell a story; still, he disappeared too quickly at these sightings to develop any regular pattern of life.

It was probably a week before we got a break. After drilling into old intelligence files, we noticed that Usamah traveled each week from Mosul south to the city of Bayji to collect and distribute illicit funds to members of his tight-knit group within ISI.

The small city was vital to his extortion racket, which involved millions of dollars being siphoned out of the Bayji oil refinery.

There was a dusty road that stretched about 110 miles between Mosul and Bayji—I determined that Usamah would be most vulnerable on the road because it took him out of his comfort zone in Mosul, where ISI leadership had created a safe haven by lining the pockets of security forces and intimidating the local population. The only people who could keep ISI in check at the time in this area were U.S. forces; the Iraqi security forces just couldn't be trusted.

We had figured out that Usamah traveled to Bayji once a week on the same day and time in the morning, but we still didn't know where in the city he was going or who he was meeting.

We delved further into old files on Usamah's associates and family members. In Bayji, we soon discovered three homes where some old associates potentially lived. It wasn't much, but it was enough for a hunt.

"Z IN ONE," I SAID OVER THE RADIO.

The drone camera panned in on the dusty landscape through the electro-optical day-TV lens and zeroed in on the city of Bayji. We'd gotten word that Usamah had come.

I had played out this moment for months, dreamed of being a part of something like this, of taking the enemy down.

Where was he?

"Z in two," I said. A row of mud and stone houses came into sharp view, the camera got closer, and there was house number one: gray concrete, two stories, owned by Usamah's cousin at one point, according to the intel I uncovered in old files.

This was our first startpoint. The plan was to hop quickly with the drone to each of the three potential houses to look for something out of place.

There was no front yard, only a small, jagged fence separating it from the empty, dusty street. The drone orbited, allowing us to see every angle of the place, even through the window openings.

There was no one there.

"Move on," I said.

"Roger that."

We didn't have much time, knowing Usamah would only remain in Bayji for about three hours before returning to Mosul. Knowing how paranoid he was, we would be lucky if we found anything at all.

The second house was a small apartment complex in the downtown market center. Usamah's first wife's home. But it was too crowded to see much as the drone orbited. Laundry was hanging out most of the windows, so it was near impossible to get a good view inside. Traffic was jammed up and hundreds of people moved through the street.

"Dry hole," I said.

There was no way we'd find Usamah there. This wasn't promising.

I fought back the gnawing feeling that we might be screwed and made the call to head to the third house.

"Raise altitude," I called out. A suspected ISI associate owned the third house—a quiet spot outside the city. This had its dangers: if we kept the drone too low, someone might hear it.

The house was similar in size to the first one, except it was surrounded by ten-foot-high concrete walls that ran around a dirt yard. Perched on the northwestern corner was a satellite dish and I could see a dog slowly meandering around the small steps leading to the driveway.

Zooming in further, we could see a white station wagon parked not too far from the front door, its tracks still pressed in the dirt. It had rained heavily only days before, turning the dirt into thick mud.

We continued to take snapshots of the home, focusing in on windows, entrances, and hidden areas for us to reference later if necessary.

"Switch to infrared," I said.

As the drone camera changed from day TV to infrared, the images became sharper, white against black like an X-ray. This was typical and used to see different views of the target from the drone sensor even though it was still daylight. It also helped me get a better view of what we were staring at when heavy sandstorms blew through.

There wasn't any movement at the house, from what we could tell. But I was more interested in the station wagon. If Usamah was just visiting for his weekly finance run, this could be his car.

I could tell the vehicle's engine was hot because it was black, pulsating slowly against the white body. It was likely still turned on. When the drone orbited around, we could see someone was inside.

This was our best lead yet, though it still wasn't much. None of our files indicated what kind of car he drove.

"What do you want to do?" Jake asked.

"If the vehicle moves, follow it."

I began to pore over the old files on Usamah again, thinking maybe I'd missed a key piece of intelligence, anything.

A concentrated silence, except for the server fans and the occasional keyboard tapping, descended and lasted until the phone rang.

It was an analyst from another one of our drone teams sitting just outside of Tikrit.

"I know that station wagon," he said.

He'd been watching my team's drone feed from his location, in between chasing other targets.

"Three months back we got pictures of that car," he went on. "The event in Bayji was a large ISI meeting of top leaders in the area." I perked up.

"We found out later that Usamah was driving it," he said. But it had been too late. By the time they'd confirmed it, the car was gone.

I wanted to see the evidence myself. "Can you send me those photos?" I asked.

They came by email and I noticed the time stamp on the photo: just three months before. And the white four-door station wagon in our current drone view was the same one in the old picture.

I looked back up at the screen. This was Usamah. *We got you.*

Just then the white station wagon started to move. "Going dynamic."

"Follow it," I said.

The drone broke orbit around the house to maneuver into a follow pattern at 15,000 feet up, a ghost in the sky.

We watched the car leave the neighborhood and begin to make its way to the main road. There the driver turned left, heading back north toward Mosul, exactly where I thought he'd go after completing his errands for the week.

He'd be on this road for two hours. So the clock to get him had started. That was all the time we had to nail him before he reached Mosul, where he'd be difficult, if not impossible, to track in the narrow streets and crowds.

I called in Max, the commander who ran the assault team. Seconds later he was alongside me, staring at the screens.

A newbie to the unit like me, Max was looking to make a name for himself among the other legendary officers who came before him. I called him Superman because he was good-looking like Clark Kent, and tall. He was from the South, married, mid-thirties, always a dip packed into his lip, and stood out because he was clean-shaven. Like he took a knife edge to his face every morning.

"Did you get a look at the driver?" he asked, pointing at the station wagon on the screen.

"No, but my gut tells me it's Usamah. All the signs are pointing to that."

That was my assessment, but he had to make the ultimate decision about what to do.

"Let's go," he said—and the rush began. He radioed his team of operators. Time to get kitted up—guns, optics, vests, radios. He paged the Black Hawk and Little Bird pilots.

But just before leaving the Box, he picked up the phone and called the overall commander back at headquarters. What the hell? He didn't need any authorization, but he must have wanted a second opinion.

The overall commander had been around forever and was known to be a hard-ass. But he was smart and exacting. He didn't like what he heard.

"That intel guy is new," he said, referring to me. "He hasn't been tested yet. It's too risky to go on his gut."

Max hung up and I thought about what my mentor Bill had said months before: "You can say and do whatever you want, but you had better be right."

I felt like I had to take a stand.

"Max, that's Usamah in that vehicle right there," I said. "The signs are there. No one's had a lead on this guy for months. You're going to fucking lose him."

I went over the intel again, the connections we'd made, the photos of the car at the meeting months before. What did that other commander even know? He was at a separate site, not closely following what we were doing.

"We're running out of time," I said, as we watched the station wagon speeding toward Mosul.

Whatever I said worked. Max called the commander back and told him that we'd just received additional intelligence from another source that Usamah was confirmed inside the vehicle. It was a lie, he disobeyed a direct order, and it meant that the weight of what was about to happen was all on me.

"We're going!" Max yelled out to the team.

The operators were armed to the teeth—mostly H&K automatic assault rifles, with night scopes and silencers. Two kinds of grenades in their bags—the more concussive thermobaric grenades, designed to confuse more than kill, and the M67s, the ones you usually see in the movies, which just explode.

There were many ways a raid could begin, all dependent on the commander's decision and the situation on the ground. Usually you were either "landing on X," where the Black Hawk pilot dropped the team down almost right on top of the target site and a kind of shock and awe ensued, with the soldiers crashing in, or you were "landing on the Y," where the chopper dropped down far enough away so the operators could sneak up on the target. Tonight, we would awe them.

As Max rushed to get out the door, I told him we needed Usamah alive for interrogation. "Try not to kill him if you don't have to."

He nodded. "We'll let the target make that ultimate decision."

Seconds later the helos went screaming off into the sky, the operators in full camo, hanging off the sides.

WE COULD SEE IN VIVID COLOR THAT THE DRIVER OF THE VEHICLE HAD ROLLED DOWN his window and was now dangling his arm out as he drove at 50 to 60 miles per hour.

Within minutes the helos were landing near an Iraqi security checkpoint, a few miles north from the oncoming car. The checkpoint was basically a hut on the side of the main road with three Iraqi guards who were randomly inspecting cars entering Mosul.

As the helos raced away from view, the team headed for the hut on foot. A handheld monitor allowed them to see what the drone was seeing. We were also connected by radio so we could hear everything on the ground. In the hut, they told the Iraqi security forces to stay put—the forces must have been pretty surprised when they showed up—and they waited for Usamah.

I always got nervous during the quiet moments that seemed to stretch on forever before a strike. Max and his team had put a lot of faith in me. I had told them that Usamah wouldn't likely put up a fight, given that he was an admin emir and probably didn't even carry a weapon. But what if I was wrong? What if he wasn't Usamah? What if the driver was a foreign fighter who just wanted to kill Americans and we had given him an opportunity?

I didn't want civilian or a team member's blood on my hands. I worried about being wrong. We were trained to be right, and second-guessing questions always swirled in my head—a kind of tape subconsciously and quickly replaying every key piece of information I had previously gathered on the target, looking for missing pieces.

As the station wagon approached the remote checkpoint, my heart started banging. My throat felt dry. The operators were now within the drone's field of view, waiting to pounce—waiting, waiting, waiting.

They jumped out of the hut, more than a dozen of them, guns drawn and blocking the road.

The car slammed to a complete stop as the team surrounded it. At first the driver wouldn't get out. He must have been in shock. A few dozen guys coming out of nowhere, armed to the teeth, just waiting for him to choose the ending to his story. Seconds stretched on. *What the hell is he doing?*

One of the operators inched closer to the driver's-side window, gun trigger ready. The others followed, a circle closing in like a noose.

Where are his hands? Does he have a bomb?

Suddenly the door popped open, the driver's hands went up, and the operators, with lightning quickness, collapsed in.

The radio came alive seconds after: "Jackpot."

My shoulders felt like I had been carrying a concrete block for miles. Chills ran down my spine. I hurt all over.

I looked around at the rest of the intel team. I took a deep breath. For a split second, I expected that there might be a celebration. High-fives, even. Claps on the back and people saying great job.

But there was nothing. They had all been through this before. Just another day at the office.

I LEARNED A FEW LESSONS THAT DAY. I REALIZED THAT WE FEW HAD THE POWER TO shape the course of the war, and that for the first time, I had an opportunity to make a direct difference. My actions could change the world; this was the purpose I had been longing for. But the decision to go after Usamah had been agonizing. Bill and Jack at their sites, though, seemed to do this work effortlessly. I wasn't sure what it would take to get to that level.

A couple of people from the assault team stayed behind to drive Usamah's station wagon from the checkpoint back to the Box. We needed it for forensics. As the helicopters transported most of the team and our new detainee back, I had the drone pull security overhead for the guys returning in the station wagon.

Victor, one of the guys, decided to ride on the hood of the car—stretched out on his back like he was lying on the beach.

He was one of the wild ones—stocky and bearded. He must have known I was watching because when I zoomed in with the Pred, he was giving me a big thumbs-up as the vehicle sped along at least 50 miles per hour down the road, kicking up a cloud of dust.

Cowboys. He seemed to be saying, "You're good with us, kid."

It was a big step in gaining their trust. Trust I needed for what was to come.

10

THE HUNTERS

"What up, Intel?" Victor said, swooping into the Box one afternoon a few days later. "You got someone for us to take down today?"

That thumbs-up he gave me from the hood of the car following the Usamah mission was already a distant memory. He was ready for another target. Like a kid with attention deficit disorder. "You sleeping, Intel?" he said, walking up to our monitors. "What do you got for us?"

Victor wasn't the only one. All the operators were antsy, always angling to jump on a chopper and head out for a target. They came into the Box every day, wondering what was up, when they could go out, if we had someone on deck. Who was after Usamah?

I told him nothing yet. But he stood there for a few minutes watching our monitors—hefty bear of a guy, salt and pepper hair. You could tell just by looking at him that he'd been places, seen a lot of people die. He had a nose that looked like it had been broken a dozen times. He'd been shot at least twice and had scars to show for it.

"How about him, can we strike this one?" he said. I had one of our drone cameras on a guy on the ground wearing a white dishdasha and smoking a cigarette next to a beat-up blue car.

We'd been following him for a couple of days. "He's small fish," I said. "Not important enough."

"What the fuck are we waiting for?"

It was easy to get sucked into the operators' mindset, especially because I wanted them to like me. With them it was always go, go, go. The adrenaline rush from the danger surrounding these missions fed their addiction for constant action. They craved the feeling of blowing down the door to a roomful of insurgents, the exhilaration of firefights; it kept them sane. Civilians tend to think that soldiers would rather not be at war if they could help it. Maybe that was true for the conventional military, but most special operators wanted to be out there. They trained their whole lives. It was what they were bred for. The more time I spent with them, the more I realized that most would have chosen to die fighting for America any day of the week over playing it safe and living a normal life back home.

I was starting to feel a bit of that now. I was out for blood, too, for my fellow soldiers back in the 82nd who suffered regular strikes from the enemy and had their hands tied to do anything about it, for my family and friends back home, for America. I wanted to kill as many of them as possible.

My game was a slow burn with the big fish. I was meant to solve mysteries and see the larger connections, while the operators were about action. Sometimes I threw targets their way on nights when they were getting antsy. I always had options out there to feed the beast. There were tens of thousands of fighters running around the countryside.

But for the larger targets, sometimes I had to stalk them for months before it made sense to strike or go in. If we just captured a bunch of the low-level terrorists, it wouldn't matter to the broader terror network. Those small-time killers didn't talk much. They'd been in and out of jails and interrogation black sites. They knew the game already. But if we followed them, we could infiltrate their world—the connectors and the connections, the meetings and drop-off sites.

It was always a balancing act, of course: when to go and when to stay. Every situation was different. I had to know if one target could lead to more senior-level figures or if he was a one-stop shop with little interaction with the people higher up the network chain.

This was the distinction that operators like Victor didn't see and didn't really care much about. If you asked them who they'd captured or killed, they'd probably know only a few names, the big ones, if that. To them every animal was the same, just another terrorist waiting to be on the receiving end of a bullet.

"He's not a big enough fish," I said.

"He looks like a shark to me."

"He's more like a minnow," I said, pushing back. "But he could lead us to the shark."

I SPENT MOST OF MY DAYS JUST WATCHING—WATCHING ROADS, SCANNING NEIGH-borhoods and borders, zooming in on mud houses, cataloging any suspicious activity, building patterns of life—how one bad guy goes to one café every day until the one day he brings a package to a white building in a market; how another target goes to bed every night for months at 9 P.M. until the one night he heads out for a midnight meeting in the desert; and another who takes the same route to work every day but one day goes in the opposite direction to a house owned by a target we killed two years before.

We watched everything. Like a darker *Truman Show*.

We looked for anomalies, and pieced together pathways to people that led to the eventual strikes. These were the problems of detectives, where seeing a small, seemingly random piece of information—like someone stopping in the desert to look up at the sky—was often the difference between life and death, and solving them required extraordinary patience for the ultimate payoff—in one hunt we conducted more than twenty separate operations before finally getting a lead to our target.

The Box became my world. The double-wide trailer was mostly dark, except for the glowing computers and video screens. The six of us on the team sat at a long, knotty plywood table that had been built to fit the length of the room. Computers were scattered about, open, with chats always blinking with a stream of messages and mapping software that turned complicated landscapes of the nearby desert and mountains into 3-D. In front of us, a double row of screens lined the wall, streaming back images from the drones we had up.

Even with the air-conditioning and the table fans going on high, the air smelled of burned coffee and sweat from people who didn't shower enough. There often wasn't enough time in the day. You got used to it.

I was the youngest J2—intelligence chief—in my organization by a few years. That meant I had to work hard to get respect and prove myself. Surrounding me I had a young team from different backgrounds—mostly in their late twenties, early thirties. All of them were tech wizards, partly nerdish though a little hipster, too, in a *War Games* kind of way. Everyone spoke in techie slang: "Z in" (zoom in), "IR" (go infrared), "RTB" (return to base), "SP" (give me a starting point), "Put up a Roz" ("restricted operations zone"). We could hold a full conversation right in front of you in our language and it would sound like a bunch of garble.

Uniforms weren't worn much in the Box. It was mostly cargo pants and T-shirts, headphones dangling around their necks when they weren't in use. One guy always wore an NYPD ball hat, another the Yankees.

They were the new generation of warfighters, equipped with the newest technology. It's like they were born with chips in their heads. They'd logged more time behind computer screens than at shooting ranges. So had I.

Laura was the only female on the team. She was big-boned, with long brown hair and a loud voice. She was probably one of the smartest signal intel analysts around and she talked a mile a minute when she had something on her mind. Oscar, our radio guy, hardly said a word to anyone. The mute. Jake was probably the only one younger than I was. He was Air Force from birth basically—joined after high school. He wore polo shirts and had a beard that never quite grew in, like a teenager's, and we were always giving him shit for one thing or another.

Day and night, hours on end, for months, we hardly left the Box. There were too many targets to go after. I spent hours analyzing their patterns of life, as the drones did their work around the clock. To keep going, I cranked up the music on my headphones—Linkin Park or Green Day in one ear and the mission and my team going on in the other.

The operators were the opposite. They had a lot more downtime, waiting for us to find the next target. When they weren't out in the field or at a shooting range, they hung around the trailers killing time, bullshitting, smoking cigarettes, lounging on shitty couches, doing whatever it took to fight off the boredom. Mostly that meant Guitar Hero on Xbox or drinking that stretched late into the night and morning.

Max was their commander and spent most of his time in the Box with me or on a Little Bird or Black Hawk headed for a bad guy.

WE WORKED TWO OR THREE MISSIONS AT A TIME, DOZENS A MONTH. THERE WAS always a drone up, sometimes three or four at a time, depending on who we were following. We could be conducting a mission against one target while at the same time refining the location of another with a separate drone in another part of the city. This new way of warfare came with the mental burden of never being able to shut down; having so much information at my fingertips meant I had to put that information to use. My mind never stopped thinking about which target to set my sights on next.

When I needed a break, I walked out to the helipad and looked at the sky. At night it was pitch-black and so quiet that you could hear a bullet casing drop. I needed that peace after a day of computer monitors and radios.

Thick cement blocks called T-barriers surrounded us. On one side was a U.S. military outpost and on the other was the wide-open expanse of desert—miles and miles of desert brown.

One night Victor came out to the helipad. "You're like a ghost, Intel," he said.

I looked at him. He pointed at my arms, which were paler than I ever remembered.

"White as fuck," he said. "You've been in that room too many days."

We'd just come off three straight days of hunting. I hadn't slept in probably two days.

"You gotta eat more than cereal and ice cream," he said, then he walked away.

I spent another few minutes there before turning to my trailer. In the darkness, I could hear some of the operators playing poker and pounding shots.

Our sleeping trailers were the size of shipping containers, stacked in rows, back to back. Each one had a single bed stuffed inside and a flat TV on the wall, with hundreds of cable channels. Most nights, I tried to hit the sack around 2 or 3 A.M., and then fell asleep to the sound of the TV. Habits helped out here, I found.

That night, I lay down and flipped on Stephen Colbert's show, as I always did. I needed to laugh. When it was over, I turned on our drone feed streaming from the Box. It was piped into all of our bedrooms from the ops center and was burning circles in the sky. I liked to see what was going on, even though most nights at this hour, like tonight, it was just a sea of unmoving darkness. Our targets slept, like everyone else.

I slept three hours before heading back to the Box when the sun came up to follow the leads I had thought through in my head the night before, Rip It can in hand. There was rarely a time I wasn't thinking or strategizing about our next target. The lack of sleep and the twenty-hour days were hard the first few weeks. But I got used to it.

WHILE WE WORKED ON OTHER MISSIONS, WE WAITED FOR WORD TO COME BACK from the interrogators who were pressing Usamah for intel at a secret black site. All of our detainees went to a tactical holding facility just for us, and we got to question them before anyone else in the military or government.

Usamah was one piece in the larger picture of the new Islamic State.

At the time, Al Qaeda in Iraq (AQI) was going through a change. It had begun to grow into a new group called the Islamic State of Iraq, or ISI, which would later become ISIS when it moved into Syria. Few knew much about ISI yet, but we'd been watching them closely. We knew more about the transition of the group than even some of their own fighters did.

ISI started with the death of AQI leader Abu Musab al-Zarqawi, AMZ, in June 2006. My predecessors at the unit had played a significant role in killing him. The very next day, the AQI leadership council came together at a secret location in Anbar province to choose a replacement—an Egyptian named Abu Ayyub al-Masri. We code-named him Objective Manhattan.

While this was going on, Osama bin Laden and his number two in Pakistan, Ayman al-Zawahiri, were looking to completely revamp Al Qaeda in Iraq. Zawahiri and other senior Al Qaeda leadership believed AQI was losing support from fellow Muslims in Iraq for being too brutal and un-Islamic for all the killings in earlier years. They wanted a religious authority who could provide the religious context for their savagery and rally fellow Muslims around the AQI banner again.

Zawahiri chose a longtime friend he'd met during jihadi-led training camps years before in Afghanistan. His name was Abu Umar al-Baghdadi (AuAB), who was considered the first leader of ISIS. We called him Objective Brooklyn. That day, Zawahiri ordered AQI to change its name to the Islamic State of Iraq.

To my team and the others who came before and after us, there was no difference between AQI and ISI. Sometimes we'd get intel from a source who'd refer to one guy we were going after as AQI and then a completely separate source would refer to that same guy as ISI.

The day Manhattan and Brooklyn became leaders was the day that they topped our kill list. But they quickly went deep underground because they knew our teams were after them. This was a different leadership strategy from Zarqawi, who preferred to fight alongside other fighters in large-scale operations.

Manhattan and Brooklyn had learned a lot about drones and our targeting from Zarqawi before he was killed. Zarqawi seemed to know just about everything about our drones since he'd been constantly hunted. He'd passed the wisdom along to others.

Knowing the extent of our capabilities now, Manhattan and Brooklyn chose to remain in the shadows, hidden from even their own fighters. We believed the two leaders were always together and rarely met their lieutenants in person.

With every mission across the country, we scoured for them. When we captured people, we pressed for details. Most said very little about the two men during interrogations. Probably because they were mostly kept in the dark.

That was the same with Usamah. He told the interrogators he didn't know anything about Manhattan and Brooklyn.

But he did know about someone else: Abu Nasir, the ISI emir of the entire Salah ad Din province. I called him Scarface.

This was a major breakthrough. Usamah told us about a weekly trip Scarface made from Mosul to Bayji to meet with his underlings and collect money. But tracking him down was suddenly urgent: Scarface was planning a new attack very soon against a U.S. military base.

Usamah didn't know which base or any specific details regarding the timing of the attack. He just knew it would happen soon and that Scarface would likely deploy another foreign suicide bomber recently smuggled into Iraq from some other jihadi battlefield.

When I learned about what Usamah had said in our custody that night, I stood up and walked outside into the desert air, past the other trailers to mine, where I climbed into my narrow bed. I tried to sleep but I couldn't now; no time for that. It was only hours before the next mission would begin.

And I had a feeling.

We were getting some daylight on Manhattan and Brooklyn.

11

MY FIRST KILL

Scarface had been on our kill list for a long time. He was a hard-line extremist—as extreme as they came. There were stories that he'd raised his hand multiple times to drive bombs into American bases, insistent on killing himself in the process, but his bosses had instructed him each time to send others. He was too valuable to the overall insurgency. Thousands of fighters were at his bidding and he was probably the fifth or sixth most important boss in the overall terror network. I focused our team's attention on him, our new ghost.

Salah ad Din and Ninewah provinces had the most authority in the country (ISI placed its top guys in command of these regions, based on the higher concentration of fighters). Scarface wasn't your typical leader, though. Unlike some, he didn't seem to care about the money. Everything was about his Islamic cause and killing anyone who didn't agree with ISI. This was the most dangerous kind of terrorist. Nothing could motivate him to stop the carnage. He'd rather die than be captured.

Across Iraq, Scarface had become a kind of king grim reaper.

He was responsible for coordinating suicide attacks in the northern half of the country, including American bases, and ran rackets that brought in millions of dollars: contraband trafficking, kidnapping, beheadings, extortion, you name it. Zain, Iraq's largest telephone company, paid his group hundreds of thousands of dollars just so that he wouldn't blow up their telephone towers.

One of his biggest moneymakers was stolen oil trafficked from the Bayji refinery. His guys hijacked the oil as it headed north in large oil tankers into Syria, then resold it to the highest bidder, with the profits distributed among enemy fighters or reinvested into war (guns, explosives, suicide bombers). We assessed that their extortion rackets were pulling in about a million bucks a month, with a cut of that being funneled up to the top two leaders—Manhattan and Brooklyn. Money, men, and materials, we called it.

Scarface had a particularly important view into the current state of the insurgency, something we wanted a look at because it could open up a window into the group.

We'd been collecting intel on Scarface even before we got Usamah, and his name had started popping up regularly in my team's analysis. We'd get bits of information from one captured guy and then fuse it with information from another. We were filling intelligence gaps along the way as we built out the members of his inner circle. But he wasn't easy to track. He was constantly switching out phones and sometimes used a cutout—a go-between person for communicating his orders. He was basically only a rumor—until Usamah started talking.

"OUR PRIORITY IS SCARFACE," I ANNOUNCED AT OUR BATTLEFIELD MEETING THAT night. "We have strong reason to believe he's coming to Bayji to collect oil payments, and likely will try to fill the significant gap in their network now that Usamah is out of the picture."

We met every night around eight o'clock on video teleconference, the five intel chiefs and the overall commander. Because most of our missions were late at night, this was a strategy session.

These weren't the typical military planning sessions, either, where there were lots of bullshitting and staff officers presenting information that had no use for the larger audience. It was all business.

The screens in the Box were split between the five chiefs and a PowerPoint on Scarface detailing everything we knew about him and the planned attack.

Bill was there with his team. So was Jack.

I flashed a photo of Scarface on the screen. He was heavyset, with long, bushy hair and thick mustache, like a Middle Eastern version of Tony Soprano.

"You guys may remember Scarface from last year," Bill said, "when he conducted that big suicide bombing at a local food market in the north. Hundreds dead."

I made my case to the overall commander. "Sir, we've conducted some heavy analysis on his previous pattern of life and also believe he has some relatives living in the area. These guys are creatures of habit. If Scarface is heading to the city, there is a solid chance he may stop at one of these locations."

I added some maps of Bayji to the screen and a nearby compound located along the outskirts of town where we'd heard some chatter of a possible meet-up.

"In the morning we're going to push our birds to the area around the oil refinery," I said. "That'll be our startpoint and we'll go from there."

It was game on. "Happy hunting," the commander said, signing off.

I HARDLY SLEPT THAT NIGHT AND WAS ROLLING BACK OUT OF MY BED BEFORE DAY-light. The intel that Scarface was likely in the midst of carrying out another major attack turned the mission into a ticking time bomb.

Soon we had the Predator swooping over the compound I had pinpointed, the camera staring down, searching for any possible movement. The place was made of concrete and its size—three stories, with a wide open courtyard of dust and protected by tall stone walls—suggested wealth and connections to the city.

Out front there were two white 4-door Toyota trucks, one with orange stripes. But more suspicious were the three to four large oil trailers parked on the east side of the compound. Most of them looked clean, like they'd recently been washed and detached from trucks. A few others were completely covered in dust, like they had been sitting there for months.

We zoomed in, then panned out, then zoomed back in, looking at every possible angle, staring hard at the shadows along the courtyard walls. Everything was quiet, just a few truck tracks in the sand coming and going from the main gate that separated it from the highway.

While we waited, I logged the location of the compound into the map on my desktop—GPS coordinates with a snapshot of the place. Nothing in our database suggested that we'd done a mission here before.

The early stages of hunting hung largely on instincts and what you knew about the people and the enemy network. As we watched the screens, we were constantly filtering out what was, what wasn't, and what could be—looking for any kind of aberration. What was out of place?

We never assumed too much—assumptions were dangerous and got people killed.

"What was that?"

As the camera operator was zoomed in on a little nook in the courtyard, I noticed some movement. When we got the camera panned back out to see the full compound, the truck with the orange stripes was leaving. We'd missed the guy who got in.

"Stay on the compound or follow?" Jake asked.

We watched the truck pull out through the gate and then onto the highway toward the main part of Bayji. All kinds of questions raced through my head. It would be a gamble to go with the truck, because Scarface could still be in the house. And what if he left when we didn't have eyes on the place? But the thing was, the truck was our only real lead at this point. And we didn't know how many people were in the house. What if it was empty?

Just then, I emailed the photo of the compound to the lead interrogator, who had been questioning Usamah for days. "Can you ask him about this place?" I wrote, wanting urgently to find out if Usamah had ever been to this location before with Scarface.

The answer came back in minutes. He didn't recognize it. Which wasn't unusual, considering most of the population in the Middle East was not used to looking at photos of houses from the eagle's-eye view of a drone.

We needed to know where the truck was going.

I had seconds to decide whom to follow. Hesitation led to missed opportunities, and you rarely got a second chance with targets. "Stay with the truck," I said.

"Roger that," the pilot crew chatted back, sending the drone to follow at 12,000 feet.

As the truck made its way along the highway and eventually into the city center of Bayji, traffic started to pick up, raising the possibility that the truck would get lost. Cities were the worst place to watch with a drone. Too many people. Too many places to disappear.

We got lucky. In about ten minutes, the truck stopped in front of a long line of stores with colorful awnings and someone climbed out of the driver's side. It was a man wearing a white dishdasha and sandals. No beard, clean-shaven. He moved quickly, suggesting to me that he was young.

"Which shop is he walking into?" I said. But no one saw because the drone was circling around, losing that angle in the heavily populated strip mall.

At that instant, everyone in the Box stood up and looked at the screens for clues as to where he went within the local market. We had another six minutes in the current orbit before it came back around to the angle we needed for a better look. Each minute felt longer and longer. The energy in the room was tense, we knew what was at stake if it was him.

Four minutes now . . .

This could be our only chance.

"Jake, you see him?"

"Not yet."

Two minutes . . .

The camera slowly turned in the orbit, waiting.

The problem was that the younger male who had exited the vehicle could be anywhere now. His trail had gone cold in a matter of seconds. Markets in the Middle East are like bees' nests that have been kicked—people everywhere, crushed together, with the stall-lined paths winding this way and that like a honeycombed maze. *Did we lose him?*

Ten seconds before the exact point came back in view . . .

Jake looked up at me in disappointment. "We've lost him."

"Do you want to scan the storefronts to see if we can reacquire the driver or stay on the vehicle?"

"Stay on the vehicle," I said.

I was betting that the driver would return to the truck at some point. "Switch to infrared," I said.

The camera operator changed the camera sensor to infrared, and as the drone orbited around to another angle, we noticed something that had been obscured. There was another person still in the truck on the passenger side. Who the hell was that? A few minutes later, the young male returned from the store and the truck started up and began to head back in the same direction it came from.

A sigh of relief passed over the entire team. We had been given a second chance.

The truck pulled back into the original compound and we watched the driver quickly step out. Out of the front door, three children and a woman ran up to the men.

"Zoom to the passenger side," I said.

The camera operator zoomed in as close as possible without distorting the picture as the passenger opened the door and got out: a man with a very distinct, fat belly and huge hair. He wore a desert-colored dishdasha and sandals.

My pulse picked up a notch. *It's him,* I thought. *It has to be.* His body type fit the physical descriptions of Scarface; the compound was associated with him; oil tanks were littered throughout, indicating that whoever the owner was, he must have been connected to the oil industry nearby.

We'd been waiting months for this moment, just to get a glimpse of him.

Individually, none of these things were conclusive or enough to launch an operation. But collectively, they were enough of a reason to believe that this was our guy.

Scarface.

We got you.

"CONFIRM FOR ME SLANT COUNT OF WHO'S IN THE HOUSE," I SAID TO JAKE.

"Two/one/three,"—two men, one woman, three children.

It was impossible to know for sure if there were more inside. It was a big house and we couldn't see everything.

Often operations were put on hold because women and children were present and we couldn't fully ensure they wouldn't be injured. There was a specific procedure that the drone sensor operators had for diverting a Hellfire at the last second: "shifting cold." If civilians came into view on our monitors, the sensor operator had a location on the ground to shift the laser, which would divert the Hellfire to a safe area with no civilians.

It was always a tough call not to hit a target, because the target would live another day to plan or conduct attacks. And there was always a chance that we might never see the target again. But the cold-shift call still had to be made if the situation demanded it.

I never personally witnessed any military commanders make a call to strike knowing that women or children would be harmed. Innocent civilians did get hurt and killed. This was a war we were fighting, after all. And these were men who didn't think twice about unleashing violence on innocents. Of course, sometimes the drone feed didn't catch everything before the assault team went out. It happened.

One time, a team of operators cut off a fleeing truck and the target started firing at them. As far as the team knew from the drone, the target and the other passengers in the truck were all fighters. The slant count had called for three men, no women or children. From a chopper, an assault team fired back in force, taking out everyone in the truck in a matter of seconds. When they landed, the team learned that things weren't as they had seemed on the drone feed: they had accidentally just killed a woman and a child, along with the main target.

A mistake like this was horribly tragic, and took a devastating mental toll on the team, who was ultimately responsible. Incidents like these weren't passed over lightly as simple errors, either. Unwarranted deaths haunted the operators at night. Deaths like these haunted me.

IN THE BOX, WE BEGAN DISCUSSING WHAT TO DO NEXT. WE SPOKE IN FAST, CLIPPED conversations, sentences sometimes not finished because we knew each other like brothers.

"Have we been here before?"

"Check the logs."

"Roger."

"Photos?"

"Wait."

"I need callouts of all the entry and exit points."

"Is NSA picking up anything on their phones?"

"Nothing."

"How much longer is the Pred on station?"

"Strike?"

We could take him out now and immediately put an end to his work. But then we also gave up the chance to gather more information about the larger ISI network, while others in his group could just as easily carry out the same attack on a U.S. base.

The thing that made a strike against Scarface an especially difficult decision was that capturing him didn't necessarily have an upside. He was a hard-liner and the odds were that he knew our systems well enough to withstand interrogations before he gave us anything actionable. Plus, once word got out that we'd grabbed him, his people would burn everything and go deeper underground.

There was one other option: keep tracking him with the drone, sucking up more information about him and his people, especially since he was so close to the top of the network. There were only so many high-level leaders like Scarface. If we followed him for even one more week, he could take us to terrorist safe houses, weapon caches, and more associates, helping us to further map out the world of Manhattan and Brooklyn. Our drone would be there watching when he turned off all the lights in his house and went to sleep. The drone would be there as the sun rose, capturing and recording every single move. All we had to do was just sit back and watch—a movie unfolding in an array of highly defined pixels right in front of us.

I made the call. "Let's stick with him," I said.

But that's not how it went down.

A RANGER TEAM OPERATING IN THE SAME AREA HAPPENED TO BE WATCHING OUR live drone feed. We had a vast interconnected network across the battlefield, and it was necessary to collaborate. That they were watching was no secret. They didn't hear our conversations or know many of the details about our operations. Usually they just monitored our feeds for situational awareness and in case one of their aircraft needed to cross into our drone's airspace.

Most times this interconnectedness worked.

Our special ops group didn't often hold specific territory. We went wherever we wanted—unlike the Rangers, who were responsible for specific swaths of terrain.

Just to eliminate any problems, Max, the assault commander, had gotten the Ranger commander on the line to tell him that we'd located Scarface in their operating area and that they should stand down.

"We're good to go," Max had said to me. "They're aligned with us."

On our monitors, the entire compound was now in view. Everyone had gone inside. The sun was out and there were no heavy winds or clouds on the horizon. Beautiful drone-flying weather. We were all set for a typical follow and began to wait it out.

I wondered if we should bring in another asset just in case the one drone wasn't enough. *Do we need a backup plan?*

Another ten minutes went by, just waiting, the drone circling the compound as I skimmed through old files we had on Nasir, looking for anything.

Then Jake saw something flash out of the corner of the screen.

"Multiple vehicles are approaching the compound from the main road," he called out.

"What?"

"They're coming fast."

"Shit, those vehicles look large. Zoom in to see what kind of vehicles they are."

The camera operator took us in.

What the fuck is this? Those are American Strikers. What's going on?

Strikers were very distinct: eight big wheels, a rocket launcher, a manned turret. They were almost as large as tanks and built to carry troops into combat zones. Now there were four of them barreling toward the compound, speeding like they were going to conquer the territory, huge dust clouds rising in their wakes. One crashed right through the gate, while the other three followed behind and lined up in formation parallel to the house.

Who the hell were these guys?

In the Box, we stared in disbelief as the scene played out. Suddenly I had no control. It was scary. Not a situation anyone wants to be in. We watched as the Strikers' rear door ramps dropped open and soldiers in full camouflaged combat gear jumped out, automatic weapons leveled at the compound and pressed up against the vehicles for cover.

Army Rangers.

The Predator camera operator confirmed: "U.S. forces in the picture."

"Son of a . . ." someone yelled next to me.

"We just confirmed that they weren't going to be there, right?"

"Right?"

Everyone was looking around the room in agreement.

One of the soldiers had a loudspeaker pressed to his face and we could tell that he was yelling into it, probably calling for Scarface to come out.

Knowing him, he was not going to step out with his hands up.

Meanwhile, Max was on the phone with the Ranger commander again. He was pissed, spitting into the mouthpiece.

"What the fuck, I thought we were on the same page with this? Why are your guys at the fucking compound?"

After a brief, heated discussion, Max hung up. The Ranger commander blamed the whole thing on a breakdown of their comms system; he was unable to call his guys off before they showed up at the house.

"That's such bullshit," I said. "I don't believe it." The comms systems don't just go down. It was clearly a case of the Rangers wanting to take credit for a big target. We were on their turf and they didn't want anyone showing them up, even if we'd found the guy.

There was no time for bitching.

"All right, guys, it is what it is, but we need to support them now. Switch the Predator to squirter control."

Squirters were people who scurried or "squirted" out the sides of a building or car or escaped an explosion.

The Predator now had a completely new mission to perform: force protection of U.S. troops in the picture. We'd look for any threats to the Rangers and make sure no one escaped out the back.

But the compound was still quiet. For a solid five minutes or so no one came out, despite the megaphone.

Finally, a woman hesitantly walked out of the front door. She had three children by her side and her hands were full of something. The younger male walked out behind her. At the front of the house, the group came to a full stop.

Typically, people were asked to stop moving in a situation like this to ensure they didn't have any bombs or weapons.

The woman and children started to walk very slowly and carefully toward the soldiers and were then guided to places behind the Strikers. After a pause, one male followed, leaving one inside.

We all put our headsets on and switched to the Rangers' radio frequency.

One guy was in the middle of explaining what they found out.

"The woman told us that the male in the house asked to have all the guns brought to him. He hugged them goodbye, gave them his phone and money, and told them to leave immediately. She said the man told her that he was not coming out."

That's when the shots came.

I could see the muzzle of an AK-47 sticking out of a high window, spraying the ground in front of the house, like he had just blown through a line of coke. The Rangers returned a blizzard of fire.

In our camera, we could see hundreds of bullets like little flashes of light, streaking the air, pummeling the house.

The barrage of bullets kept coming.

But the guy wouldn't die. The muzzle of his AK-47 still stuck out sporadically through different windows in the house, spraying rounds everywhere.

Then, out of nowhere, the Striker launched a rocket, demolishing the top corner of the house and opening a huge hole in the roof.

"Switch to infrared," I said.

Now the drone camera operator zoomed into the corner to see if we could get a glimpse inside the house.

Within minutes another rocket hit the same top corner of the house, opening an even larger hole and damaging the complete exterior. That's when we saw a body curled on the ground: lifeless and contorted in a way that a body should not be.

The Rangers eventually stopped firing and a quiet settled over the scene. It seemed like hours had passed because of the chaos. After a long waiting period, the Rangers moved into the house.

Was this Scarface? Or someone else? I worried that there were others in the building. But my biggest concern was that Scarface was wearing a suicide vest and was trying to draw them in.

The drone continued to maintain a solid orbit around the compound, the camera still looking for other signs of life or squirters. It took a good five minutes for the all-clear but we finally heard it come over the radio.

"We have confirmed jackpot, one enemy KIA."

In the Box, we were conflicted. We were of course happy that Scarface wouldn't live to see through his attack on American forces. His death would be a blow to the network. All that was good. But a part of me couldn't help but wish we'd followed him for a few days or weeks longer. Manhattan and Brooklyn were still lurking out there.

Staring at the feed, I couldn't take my eyes off the lifeless body. I'd found Scarface and brought the Rangers here. Intentionally or not, it was my first kill.

12

FINDING A GROOVE

"You need to sleep," Max said to me one morning when he came strolling into the Box. "You look like shit."

The guys had started calling me Casper because I'd become pale all over and was losing weight. My clothes hung off of me. I had lost nearly thirty pounds. The shirts ballooned, dwarfing my stature. I had to cinch my belt to the tightest hole to keep my pants up. It was October 2009 and by then I had logged thousands of hours of flight time in four months. Some days felt like I was living inside the screen, my eyes the unblinking drone camera, flying endlessly over deserts and cities.

"You need to eat more than that damn cereal, Casper," Max said, pointing at the mess of emptied-out Frosted Flakes bowls in front of me. A stack of empty Rip Its sat at my elbow.

"Later," I said. "I'll eat and sleep later."

I just couldn't take my eyes off the screens anymore. I got

more and more sucked into the hunt, failing to grab regular meals at the mess hall, breaking for a piss only every four hours, stinking of body odor because I hadn't showered in a week. As the weeks passed, the hunt had long started to feed me like a drug. One mission fueling the next. I sudied intelligence files, watched the drone camera scan, scrutinizing nearly every single pixel of the streaming images burning on the screen.

Day after day, night after night, we took the war to the enemy. At the same time, my body was fighting a war within itself, coping with the mental stress of it all and starting to show on the outside the health toll it was exacting, despite my trying to hide it from others. I didn't want any of the team perceiving weakness on my part—physical or otherwise. They needed to trust me, and to have confidence every time I sent them out. But the reality was that I was wasting away at an unhealthy rate.

There was no sense of time in the Box. It was always dark, with the monitors lit up on the wall, our laptops flashing with messages from other Boxes around the globe, and Washington, D.C., and updates on new targets. Our birds could stay airborne eighteen to twenty hours at a time so we tried to keep up with that, the technology driving us almost as much as knowing our targets were still out there plotting against us.

The footage was at times mind-bendingly boring. Image after image of shitty trucks, empty rooftops, dusty compounds, and snaking desert roads. But I couldn't look away, for fear of missing something.

I fought to keep my eyes open and hated giving in to sleep. Every hour wasted was another hour the enemy had to plan, another hour it had to kill. There were hundreds of them out there and I had become addicted to finding them.

When I wasn't watching drone feeds, I looked over home-made terrorist videos and bloodstained documents recovered from our nightly raids. The things I saw were sickening, things no one should see in their lifetime. Our targets videotaping themselves slashing the throats of other Muslims like goats, or holding severed heads up in front of the camera. Burning children alive, raping women in their own homes.

I saw the worst of humanity during those days. But I kept watching because some videos provided clues to help fill intel gaps in our larger puzzle. The barbarism my enemy displayed during these scenes only emboldened me more. My mission became more important than ever.

When I slogged back to my trailer in the middle of the night or in the hazy early morning hours, I began to have problems sleeping, even though I was tired to the bone. I couldn't switch off my brain.

After one long day, I lay there on my stiff single bed, a paper-like sheet over me, while my mind played through different strategies, as if part of it were still back in the Box. What had we missed that day and how we might have done it better? I spent that night dreaming I was a camera in the sky, scanning a city I'd never seen before.

With every target taken out, I gained more and more confidence. I refined my craft of puzzle making, one target after the other, got better at seeing things through the haze of repeated images, spotting the anomalies in the data, more adept at the endless circling and waiting involved in the lead-up to the perfect hit.

The job was breaking me down, but the stakes were too large—I couldn't give up.

SOMETIMES BACK HOME, PEOPLE WOULD ASK ME, "HAVE YOU EVER KILLED ANYONE?" Usually I responded with a version of a quote from one of my favorite movies, *True Lies*. In the scene where Schwarzenegger's character is asked about all the people he's killed, he answers, "Yeah, but they were all bad."

In my mind, I don't know that I can say I've actually killed anyone.

I imagined a lot of military guys got that question from civilians who don't know any better about what they are truly asking. I didn't keep track of the dead as the months passed. Didn't think about death in terms of numbers. That wasn't the point.

The point was to protect Americans and other innocent people who didn't wield the same power I had now. I don't want to disappoint people, but it's really not much more complicated than that. We were after terrible people. End of story.

I remembered a guy we'd been after for months. One day he drove a car into the middle of a busy market in the Shaab neighborhood of Baghdad. He had a small boy and a small girl in the backseat. The kids couldn't have been more than ten years old.

Local civilians in the market watched as he left the kids in the car and disappeared into the shops nearby. A few minutes later, the car exploded. More than fifty people in that open market died—including those two children.

The driver had rigged the entire vehicle to explode—and he'd used those children to make the parked car look harmless to security nearby. I wasn't surprised. These people, but for biological technicality, were not human.

And yes, we eventually tracked that guy down and killed him. That one didn't get a choice.

These atrocities were now becoming commonplace.

BUT WHILE I MAY HAVE BEEN ISSUING ORDERS AS TO WHO LIVED OR DIED, VERY often it meant someone else had to pull the trigger.

On a particular 2:30 A.M. assault, we sent the operators in— and it unfolded according to plan: the flicker of gunfire, followed by the assault team rushing the house, the man coming out with a gun, the man falling to the ground, and then Max, the commander, calling over the radio, "Jackpot." The operators shot the target dead.

Over the crackling radio, Max relayed that they were going to examine the site for any leads or material that could be used later. But they'd have to do it quickly, before the rest of the town woke up.

Another day at the office.

I always stayed up until the team returned home, so they'd know I wasn't going to sleep until they were safe. Plus, those few late-night hours alone in the Box gave me more time to analyze new targets for the next day.

The Box was as peaceful as it ever was at that time, hours past midnight now, most of the team asleep or on their way. It was the kind of calm that made every small sound louder in my head: the computer servers with all our intelligence whirring with activity, the occasional stutter of a radio comm from somewhere else, some machine beeping.

It wasn't until about 4 A.M. that the loud thumping of the Black Hawk blades broke the peace of the Box, shaking the makeshift building as it landed outside.

On their return, teams usually went straight to unloading their weapons and gear, and then to bed, before doing it all over again the very next night. Tonight, an operator named Eric came in to see me.

"Who did I just kill?" he asked, pushing open the door, drenched in blood.

He was the one who shot the target at point blank.

"Who did I just kill?" he asked again.

I didn't know how to respond at first. The question threw me off.

Eric was still kitted up in full body armor, radios hanging off his gear, an automatic assault rifle in his right hand pointed down and almost dragging the muzzle along the floor. He reeked of sweat and dust and something humid—blood, dark red and splattered across his vest, as if he had tried to wipe it off. It was still wet in places, soaked into parts of his camouflage and stained across the big American flag patch Velcro'd above his heart.

A veteran operator who had been doing this for years, Eric had a shaggy beard and bushy hair, and sort of looked like a caveman. He always wore a navy blue FDNY shirt under his gear, as if it was his good luck charm. He'd been shot more than any other person I knew. A teammate once Photoshopped an Army photo of Eric dressed up in his nice Class A uniform, superimposing about twenty Purple Hearts over the medals running down his chest to make light of this fact. Whether he was lucky or just simply the best at his craft, either way I knew there was no one else I'd want to save my ass in a firefight.

He took off his helmet, which was beat up and scratched, and placed it on my desk as he sat down in the wobbly chair next to me. He leaned over.

"Well, man?" he said in a calm voice.

I thought, *What do you mean?* The guy he'd taken out was one of the most prominent smugglers along the border, funneling men, money, and materials to feed the insurgency. How could he not remember that?

I started to go through this, getting a bit defensive, but then I stopped.

It hit me.

Eric wasn't really asking who he had just shot and killed. He knew that already from when I'd briefed all the operators on the mission. What he was really getting at was something different: was this guy worth it?

He was making a point that this had been a real life, and that he had taken it. In the Box I only saw his death from a distance. But right up next to me, with the wet stink of human blood on his vest, Eric was saying: this is what death looks like.

Eric had put the target down with two shots at close range be-fore the man even had the chance to pull the trigger on the AK-47 he was holding when the team rushed in.

"Don't worry, Eric. He was bad," I said.

That was all he wanted. That I knew. That I got this. That I didn't take any of this lightly. That this was my death as much as his.

We both had blood on our hands.

He looked at me, shook his head. "Good night." He didn't say another word.

As a reminder about the gravity of our actions, Eric would wear that bloodstained American flag across his vest for the rest of that deployment.

We would never discuss this again. In general, silence was the agreement that we all made when we signed up for this. We didn't talk about what happened, we didn't dissect it. We lived with it inside.

STILL, WE COULDN'T HAVE SURVIVED IF THE HUNTS DIDN'T ALSO PROVIDE THEIR own brand of perverse humor to give us all some distractions.

For us, the best was the utter paranoia we bred in the terror cells. We'd been following a particular target for hours on a hazy, hot-as-hell day as he weaved through the streets of Mosul traffic jams like he was trying to lose someone, then followed him out into the desert, where he eventually climbed out of his car. He walked a few feet away and then looked up. He did the same thing at the front of his car and then at the back, as if the different loca-tions might give him a better angle into the sky.

That happened a lot. Our targets drove to the desert to listen and look for us, or just stopped along an empty stretch of road. Over the months, I could see the paranoia growing in our enemy—the worry about the unblinking eye. By now drone surveillance was becoming commonplace, and it wasn't a secret anymore that the Iraqi skies were full of them. ISI started to issue guidance down the terrorist chain about how to counter drones. It was funny to hear the methods: tin foil on roofs, removing batteries from their own cars at night because we could somehow lock on to them. Another day a guy spent thirty minutes standing next to his car, head arched back, looking up into the clear, sunny blue sky as if it were some terrible TV show he couldn't take his eyes off.

But as they adapted, so did we; we flew our drones at different elevations to keep out of earshot and flew other standard military aircraft low, loud, and in separate parts of the city to trick them into thinking we were preoccupied with someone else.

You'd think the bad guys were always up to something shady, but the truth was different when you watched them all day long from a drone. On the surface, the people we hunted were trained to appear normal, and for the most part they were. You saw some funny things people would never tell anyone about—just think about all the stuff people do when they think nobody is looking.

A lot of people sleep on their rooftops during the summer because they don't have air-conditioning, so we saw a lot of sex. We saw men taking craps in their backyards at night and spraying their shit everywhere. One time we were watching a guy on a roof in downtown Baghdad who we thought was sneaking up on our ground team, but when we zoomed in, he was masturbating. Another time, we caught a guy having sex with a cow on a remote farm. We laughed about that one inside the Box for days.

I heard from a source we'd captured that the fear of our drones had begun to cause some of them to start trading in their hard-top bongo trucks for cars with sunroofs. The dumb-asses thought that they'd be able to see us when they were driving.

The network's leadership, meanwhile, sought refuge deeper

in the shadows as we pounded them from the skies. The more drones that we brought into our army, the worse it got for them, the less time the big guys could spend out in the open. More and more, they deployed couriers to ferry instructions between the group's various layers. Phones were constantly dumped, email mostly abandoned; Internet cafés started to lose regular business. One guy we captured had a duffel bag jammed with twenty-five different burner phones.

IRAQ WAS STILL A TERRIBLE HELL, BUT OUR DRONE WAR WAS SHOWING SOME SIGNS of change. We saw attacks against U.S. troops fall in September and October 2009. There were fewer IEDs on the roads, not as many suicide bombers exploding, less contraband traffic coming over the borders.

In total at this point, I ran forty missions in just under two months. Dozens of targets dead. Hundreds captured. Bill's, Jack's, and Mark's teams were moving just as fast. Our interconnected missions had blanketed the northern part of Iraq, making it difficult for the enemy to sleep at night or feel comfortable meeting in large groups anymore.

All of this was good, but we knew that it could slide the other way at any time. If we let up, things could go south fast.

We worried about the Iraqi government and their struggle to maintain power. That summer they passed a law requiring us to go to judges for warrants to carry out operations.

We all got a little freaked out. What did this mean?

It didn't make any sense. The work we did was highly classified. Few people were in on it—and for good reason. Giving out operational details to anyone outside our small circle risked leaks to the enemy.

We couldn't have that. We ignored the law, worked on our own terms to get the job done. The moment the law came to fruition, we slipped deeper into the shadows, right where our enemy was now digging in.

TO OPERATE IN THE SHADOWS THE WAY WE DID, IT'S CRUCIAL TO UNDERSTAND THE extent that we worked with and relied on some extraordinarily courageous local intelligence officers. Members of the team trained small groups of local citizens, men and women, in surveillance tactics and gave them gadgets to use for spying, like a camera in a box of cigarettes or a camera in a key chain. We codenamed this group the "Cobras." Many of them gathered intel for us for years in places we simply couldn't get to ourselves.

Since we couldn't just walk into the middle of a city without being noticed, we'd communicate with our Cobras in real time through the birds flying far overhead. Often they would direct our drone's eyes right on a target for strike. These locals worked with us because in one way or another the terrorists we hunted had turned their world upside down. The locals wanted better lives for their families, community, and country.

One day, we had a ground pursuit going for a target we needed a photo of for a visual confirmation. He'd been holed up for months in a housing complex where we had precious few opportunities for any kind of visual confirmation from the drone. So on a lucky day when he left his hideout, we sent in our Iraqi to follow him by car. But things got a little hairy.

There was too much separation between the cars, and then a traffic jam, which was a stroke of luck, because at least the target was fixed for a moment. Our guy was ten cars back, and all of a sudden he jumped out of his car and started moving in the direction of the target.

What's he doing?

The Iraqi just strolled through traffic, cursing and yelling at everything and everyone, pretending to be pissed off at traffic. He ranted for a good fifteen car lengths, doing this crazy act, and on the walk back to his car he snapped a picture of our target. Perfect photo.

"YOU HAVE A SECOND TO TALK?"

It was Bill on the phone. Something was up.

"Only a second," I said. "We're following a target through the city. He's dynamic. What's going on?"

I had the phone pressed to my ear, held between my shoulder and head as I kept my eyes glued to the drone feed as my target rushed through a crowded market in a white truck, making turns, stopping at lights. He had a truckload of bombs that could explode at any time. I couldn't lose focus.

"We got an emergency message in from the HQ back home," Bill said, referring to our home base in North Carolina.

I half-heard him the first time. "What happened?"

"We got an emergency message. Your family is trying to get a hold of you but they don't know where you are in the world."

His voice suddenly came into clear focus.

"What's going on?"

I hadn't spoken to my mother or anyone in my family since I'd arrived in Iraq more than two months before. This was when I realized for the first time that I had for the most part forgotten all about them. My family had been replaced by the team members around me and the drones had swallowed me up.

"It's your cousin," he said. "He died in a car accident. Sounds like it was really bad."

For a second I didn't say anything. I tried to take it in, grasp it. I grew up with AJ in Texas. The news suddenly snapped my mind back to my hometown and what I had left behind. He was twenty-two—three years younger than me. We used to be close, almost like brothers. I spent my summers at his house in Odessa because he had a big pool and a huge backyard that led out into the arid land stretching for miles nearby. I remember us trying to drown each other in his pool and camping out overnight in his backyard far away from the house. One night a massive storm came through and I woke suddenly to a lightning strike. I found him holding the tent corners down with all his strength, the wind swirling, heavy rain, and the crackle of thunder all around us. The tent felt like it was about to lift off, like we were going to be swept up by the same tornado as in *Twister*. When we got our courage up, we popped our heads out through the opening, counted down from three, and made a frantic dash to the house through the dark, slashing night. We were young, but it felt like we'd just escaped death.

I found out later in regard to his accident that he'd slammed his car into a railing on a bridge and died instantly. It should have been awful life-stopping news. But I just couldn't think about it as I sat in the Box. It was so far away and I was living in the mission in front of me.

"Okay, thanks for letting me know," I said to Bill. "I have to go now. I don't want to miss something significant with this target."

Bill tried to break through my fog and pull me out.

"Listen, I've been doing this a long time and I know what you are thinking," he said. "I have had a few close family members die over the years and I always chose the mission over seeing them. I wish I could take that back."

He stopped for a second and then said, "Hey, listen up. I wasn't thinking clearly at the time. None of this is worth more than your family. None of it. You should go home, go to the funeral. We'll set up a flight to get you back right away."

But I didn't want to go anywhere. "I can't, Bill. This is more important right now."

Bill finally gave up. The last thing he said before hanging up the phone was "You'll regret not going." And that was it.

The funeral would happen a few days later. Everyone in my

family would be there. When people asked where I was, my mother would tell them that she couldn't get a hold of me because I was somewhere overseas. I wouldn't call.

At the time, it seemed like the right decision. I couldn't see anything outside the drones and my personal mission. I was fighting the great war and saving lives. Years later I'd wonder if all the killing and the destruction we did was worth it. Why didn't I say goodbye?

But that was still years away.

The mission pushed all that out of the way for now. That night, we took out the bomber I had been pursuing. And then the phone rang again; another target popped up on my radar.

It was the agency now. No time to think.

THE AGENCY HAD A SOURCE WHO MIGHT KNOW THE LOCATION OF MANHATTAN AND Brooklyn, the top of the pyramid we were in the midst of dismantling.

"Come to us," they said. "You need to meet him."

I worked with the agency often. They were in weekly target meetings and we hunted together sometimes. They needed us because we controlled the drones in the war zones and had operators to go in and kick down doors.

Still, there was bad blood between us at times. Our team had a strong distaste for them because we'd been burned by their bureaucracy, gotten tips that didn't pan out. Their guys would take credit for our missions. We would get wind of reports they'd send back to their headquarters in Langley, Virginia, telling their superiors they were responsible for our latest kills. Some of our guys wouldn't even talk to them. Many hung up when they called. The feeling was mutual. Some of the senior analysts at the agency didn't like us because they thought we had too much power. But intelligence collection had changed drastically in the years after

9/11. The agency wasn't the only game in town anymore and they didn't like that.

When Bill heard about the tip, he warned me. "You should think about it before going anywhere." He had little faith in their sources, especially someone saying he could bring us to the top leaders. I understood that. But at the same time, I felt that no possible tip on Manhattan and Brooklyn could be ignored.

13

WILD GOOSE CHASES

The next morning I jumped on a helo with one of our operators and headed to a secret outpost in Baghdad. I packed lightly, just a computer, my sidearm, and some body armor.

We landed on a tiny airstrip in the north of Iraq where an agent picked us up in an armored car and shuttled us to their base. It was late morning, hot as usual. Sweat beaded on my forehead.

The outpost was one of Saddam Hussein's old palaces: sprawling and made from stone, with a pool and a bunch of smaller buildings sprinkled around the larger main house.

Usually places like this were guarded by traditional military men in military gear. This was heavily protected by men in civilian clothes.

Inside one of the guesthouses, the agent who'd called us waited with a translator and the source. I'd never met the agency officer before. All I remembered about him was that he had a mustache, was a fast talker, and was a big believer in his source, whom I called Silencer.

I DIDN'T KNOW MUCH ABOUT SILENCER, BUT THAT WAS COMMON. FOR SECURITY we're usually kept in the dark about the intelligence sources of others. We all used sources. Some were good; others were just doing it for the money. Silencer was definitely getting paid a lot. At the beginning of our meeting the agent had dropped a large stack of cash on the table in front of us just for him, tens of thousands of dollars at least.

I didn't like him right away. When we shook hands, he didn't look me in the eye. He was tall and his mustache was unevenly shaved, the left side shorter than the other. Later, I'd find out that he'd been responsible for the deaths of some U.S. soldiers. The FBI actually had a standing warrant out for his arrest, even as the agency protected him. He was an evil human being, for sure, but we had to deal with a lot of questionable kinds to save other lives. It was a messy business.

The room was filled with nice leather furniture, an oak table, polished hardwood floors—definitely a place that would make a visitor feel comfortable, compared to a traditional Iraqi room with hard, uninviting, dusty furniture that always looked like it had been dragged out of some bunker.

We sat down at the table, had Cokes and Iraqi shawarma, and talked casually about the country and local politics to loosen things up and make him feel comfortable before we turned to business.

"He can help us," the officer said finally, making a hand gesture in Silencer's direction.

"How's that?" I asked.

I was armed with enough information on the network to poke holes in anything that seemed far-fetched.

"Why do they trust you?" I wanted to know. We'd been hunting Manhattan and Brooklyn for years. They'd been ghosts. "How would you be able to get close to them without them being suspicious?"

Silencer said that he hadn't seen them but knew how to get to their location. He had worked with ISI and was friends with others in northern Iraq who knew the leaders' whereabouts. "They trust me like family," he said. "I will have no problems getting to them."

He didn't know all the guys in the network in the area he talked about, but we wanted to believe that he was a credible source. Mainly we trusted the agency to be right about him.

By the end of our conversation, we decided to go with him and worked out a plan. Silencer said that he would go up north to meet a guy who would take him to people close to the leaders. He said they would blindfold him, make changes to what he was wearing, and move him around to different safe houses so that he wouldn't know where he was for days. It was like entering a maze, he said. Then they would take him to a secret location for the meeting.

"If you follow me for two or three days," he said, "you will find your Jackpot."

THE WORRY IN THESE SITUATIONS WAS THAT THE SOURCE COULD VANISH: EITHER the network discovered him to be a rat and killed him or he got cold feet and decided to become a ghost on his own.

Later, when he was with the two men, he'd pull a series of strings connected to sophisticated tracking devices our technical guys had sewn into a special book he was holding. One string would send us a signal that the meeting was taking place. And the second was for when he left them. That was also when our team would know to strike.

The one thing I didn't tell him that night was that we'd also be watching every move he made along the way from the sky—our birds would be on him, making sure he was doing what he said he was going to do. Our security.

Three hours later, I said good luck to Silencer and the team there, climbed back on the helo, and headed back to the Box. We were on.

BY 7 A.M. WE HAD THREE BIRDS UP IN THE SKY, BUT NO SIGN OF SILENCER ON THE ground.

"Where's your source at?" I said over the radio. "We're over-top the location now."

The streets of downtown Baghdad were already jammed with cars and people and bikes.

"Give him a few more minutes," the officer said. "He'll be there."

The night before, I'd gotten the commander to give us two more Predators along with ours for the mission. One came from Bill's group, the other from Jack's. We didn't want to take any chances on this case.

On the other side of the drone feed, a large audience had gathered to watch the show. The high commanders watched on their monitors from different parts of the country, same with people back in the United States. Bill's and Jack's teams were on the feed, too, in case we needed their operators. It was turning out to be like the Super Bowl.

"Is that him?"

A white Toyota Corolla suddenly approached the street we'd been watching and a man exited the vehicle to make a phone call.

"Gray slacks, yellow polo shirt, white Toyota Corolla," I said. "That's him."

When he got back in his car and began to drive, we had no idea where he'd go—just north. From then on, there would be no direct contact. Going forward would be like a game of chess. He'd move and then we had to countermove, calling around to multiple agencies to clear out the airspace for our drone army to follow.

"Looks like we're in business," I said.

Silencer traveled a few hours north of the city, like he said, before stopping at a low-slung concrete house outside of Tikrit with a big dusty backyard and lawn furniture scattered about like they were expecting a party.

He went inside but a few minutes later emerged with two other men. Instead of going anywhere, they plopped themselves down on three lawn chairs and began to smoke and drink, like they didn't have a care in the world. I saw one of them had his feet kicked out and crossed as if he couldn't be happier.

What the hell was going on? Hours passed and no strings were pulled. As far as we could tell, the house was totally normal. No security guards, no unusual activity inside or out. The streets around were calm. No movement on any of the rooftops.

The oddest thing was that Silencer still hadn't pulled the first string—the one meant just as a test. Maybe we should have started to worry at this point, but we waited. I chomped on some granola bars and then a bowl of Frosted Flakes. Then I paced around the Box. It started to annoy me to look at the monitors and see him lounging around with smokes and drinks. Who did he think he was? Something seemed off. I started getting messages on our secure chat line from Bill and Jack telling me this guy was full of it. But all the time the agency officer continued to reassure me that Silencer was good to go, that this was how he worked.

"Everyone needs to just calm down. I trained this guy myself. He knows what he's doing," he said.

It was three hours before Silencer finally left. One of the men tagged along with him and they drove to an ice cream stand not far away at the side of the road, where they began to talk to either a worker or the owner.

"Do we have any previous reporting from this location?" I asked Jake.

A quick search of our files was done.

"Looks like the spot was cited as a location for a date stand connected to Al Qaeda in Iraq."

This seemed potentially promising. At least there was some link.

"Do we know the name of the guy who owns it?"

"No name given."

I had the three drones stacked on top of each other, orbiting at different altitudes.

Silencer still hadn't pulled the first string.

On our screens, the three men sat around the stand for an hour or so until the ice cream stand closed down for the day. By then it was getting close to sunset and I was starting to lose my patience.

The men split up. Silencer got back into his Corolla, while the ice cream guy climbed into his car, along with the third man.

"The priority is still the source but I want to know where these other guys are going," I said, preparing to divide up the drones.

At first the cars stayed together. Through heavy traffic, they traveled for a couple of miles before stopping at another house, where they stayed for an hour. Pretty uneventful there, too.

The ice cream guy left first, along with the other guy. They all drove to another house, where they stayed for the night. The house was nicer than most, with a manicured yard, palm trees, and even a separate guesthouse out back. Chapter closed on them. Nothing to pursue.

But not Silencer. Not long after the lights went out, he left the house and climbed back into his car. Within minutes of pulling into traffic, something alarming happened. He yanked the second signal string in his book.

Was this for real?

We all looked at each other in the Box. The second string meant that he was in the presence of the two leaders.

I immediately got on the radio to confirm that the second beacon had indeed been activated. "Are you sure?" I said. It had. That's when the chaos began and everything got turned upside down.

Are the leaders in the house or did our source fuck up the signal? Should we launch an operation?

IN OUR FILES, THE HOUSE THAT SILENCER HAD JUST LEFT DIDN'T HAVE ANY TERRORism ties. It was in an upscale neighborhood of similarly trimmed gardens surrounded by garbage-free streets—an unusual thing for Iraq. There wasn't any visible security or signs on the block that something was being hidden—not a lot of cars outside the house, no one standing guard on the roof, no weapons that we could see.

High-level terrorists wouldn't be at a house like this in the middle of a city. These guys were always on the go and they'd want to conduct a meeting with Silencer swiftly and covertly. They knew that we had sources and that anyone outside their circle would be a danger to them. Something didn't add up.

We watched Silencer drive, making turns from one street to the next. If this was real, we were losing time.

"Jake," I said, "can the sensor operator rewind our tapes to see if anyone else got in the vehicle with him?" I wanted to make sure he was alone. The recorded drone video appeared on the screen and we played it back in slow motion. He was alone.

I started to get angry—was this guy fucking with us? He'd been running us around all day. We looked like fools in front of all the commanders watching.

"Do we know how many people were in the house?"

"Just the three who'd gone in."

Other teams began to call into the Box, wondering what was up.

"This guy's not real," said Bill. "He's fucking with us."

I looked back at my meeting notes regarding the chain of events Silencer said would happen once he left that morning—he was supposed to go immediately to his source, who would take him to the leaders. None of that had happened. All he'd been doing was drinking and smoking with friends, and then the pit stop for ice cream.

I had wanted to believe in Silencer. I had wanted to believe there was an easy way to find Manhattan and Brooklyn, that we could wrap up our deployment there with them in body bags. I had wanted to believe in this mission. I felt duped—and it had to end.

My pride wanted me to keep pursuing the lead, but my gut told me differently. Silencer had wasted our time, money, and precious resources.

I called the commander and said we were standing down the operators. The officer didn't argue about it. Having watched the video, they'd also come around to the fact that their source was crap. A few months later they'd fire him and issue an official burn notice as a result—to the disappointment of the officer who'd spent months recruiting him. Silencer won in the end, though; he had come away with hundreds of thousands of U.S. dollars through years of providing the agency with false leads and fabricated intelligence. Our only redemption was now the FBI could take their gloves off, because the agency wasn't protecting him anymore.

"WE'RE WORRIED ABOUT YOU," MAX SAID ONE NIGHT AFTER COMING IN FROM CAP-turing a target across the border. "Seriously, man, you're going to disappear if you lose any more weight. You need to rest."

It was late. I shrugged him off as usual. I went back to my room later and took a look at myself in the mirror. *Oh shit.*

My skin hadn't seen the sun in weeks, because I'd been staring at TV screens nonstop for months on end. My teeth were yellow. So were the whites of my eyes, the bags underneath starting to look permanent. I looked like a dying version of my old self.

I walked over to the shower and pulled out a scale. I was down nearly forty pounds now. No wonder my cargo pants didn't fit anymore. Everything was loose on me.

The stress and pressure of finding targets had taken its toll. I'd been going for four months, but it felt like years. Long hours filled with energy drinks, candy bars, and nothing else. It had gotten harder and harder to wake up after a few hours of sleep. I was running on empty.

If it weren't for the fact that we were leaving in a few days, the beating my body took would have only continued to worsen. My physical and mental state was less important to me than not running out of time to pursue my targets.

"Whatever it takes," I told myself out loud while taking one last glimpse in the mirror before heading back to the Box.

Luckily, my first deployment wound down after that, just a few more days, with a few more missions, and it was over.

It was November 2009—the end of our assignment. There was no sendoff. Our replacement team arrived on helicopters and, once we'd gotten them up to speed on the missions we had in the works, those same choppers ferried us out.

As I got on the plane home with Bill, Mark, and the rest of the team, my body was shot. It wouldn't have let me continue much longer. I needed rest.

We arrived back in the States on a C-17 cargo plane in the middle of the night. Other military units returned to a celebration— marching bands, families with signs waving, announcements of their return in the local papers. Not us.

The landing strip in Virginia was empty and dark, except for the workers servicing the plane.

When I stepped off the ramp of the cargo plane with my gear, the desolation of the moment overcame me for a minute. We had accomplished a lot in a short amount of time. Missions accomplished that would have taken conventional forces months, if not years, to carry out, if they could have handled them at all. Except there was no one there to share the successes with other than ourselves. It was the way our unit liked it, and I had to learn to get used to it. For us, it was like any other day.

That night I drove to my condominium in North Carolina, squinting to keep awake behind the wheel, before finally falling into my bed. I don't remember taking off my clothes. I don't remember talking to my girlfriend Sarah at the time; we hadn't spoken in months. My new life left very little time to talk with her and I couldn't tell her anything about it. My life outside the office had begun to divide itself further, but I couldn't think about it for now. I closed my eyes and pretty much slept for three days straight.

14

HOME?

In North Carolina, I lived on the thirteenth hole of a community golf course, miles outside the main town. The secluded complex was surrounded by woods. I had to drive ten or fifteen minutes just to get to the nearest grocery store or restaurant. But HQ was close. Through some winding back roads, past farms and fields, was a secret entrance. It was located there to help prevent our being seen—and in case we were being followed.

The first few days I woke up strung-out, like coming off an amphetamine bender. My head hurt as I plodded around the condo. I was thirsty and my stomach felt hollowed out. One of the first things I ate was a big American burger, everything on it. My girlfriend Sarah watched me devour it.

"A little hungry?" she said, trying to edge into a conversation.

"Starving," I said, looking up for a second and then going back to it.

We tried to talk that night. Anything resembling normalcy was no longer easy. There was so much death and destruction behind me, inside me, really. How do you have a conversation after seeing what I'd seen, doing what I'd done? The transition was harder than coming home from a war zone in the past. Don't get me wrong, it wasn't as if I had experienced some horrors and a PTSD-like event. I was behind a desk most of the time and didn't see nearly the action the operators did. They were the real heroes. It was more the fact that my life had changed virtually overnight, the sensory overload of being brought into a world that I never knew existed and then having to perform almost around the clock. My mental capacity had been jolted, almost like waking up and discovering you had been taken to another planet, and nothing you knew before existed anymore.

I couldn't talk to anyone at home about anything. Everything I did was top secret. I'm not sure I wanted to talk about it anyway, fearing that people outside of it wouldn't understand. It made any kind of interaction difficult. Normal sentences became censored, my mind reciting the lines in my head multiple times before they were spoken aloud. It forced me to become quieter and more introverted. I simply shut down when I wasn't in the office.

But still I just couldn't get the war out of my head—the cameras looking down at our targets, following them wherever they went, watching other people's families and lives unfold right in front of me. I was killing the worst terrorists in the world one day and the next day sitting at a cozy restaurant, chomping a burger with cheese and bacon and watching people around me talking and laughing, without a care in the world. Could normal life be this surreal? It was like I had been living inside a nonstop action movie and all of a sudden someone hit the stop button, ejecting me out of it. Now I didn't recognize the place I had landed.

When we got home from dinner that night, Sarah pressed me some more. "What happened over there?"

It was late, but I wasn't tired. We sat on the couch in the living room. I tried to look at her and she followed my gaze until I couldn't look anymore and turned away.

"Your eyes, they don't look the same," she said.

"My eyes?"

"They're like stones. They just sit there."

The silence that rose up between us was unbearable. It made the night shrill. The crickets were out in the woods and golf course, whining and chirping louder than the whirl and beep of our computers in the Box after missions.

I wanted to tell her about all of it, but I knew better.

I shifted the conversation away from me to her that night and the rest of the nights going forward. I wasn't a very good listener and didn't hear a lot of it and I'm sure she knew. I had trouble looking her in the eyes.

When you're a soldier on deployment, you forget what life back home is like. The people you leave behind also forget about you while you're gone. You change and they change. And you stick out like a sore thumb when you come home.

Some soldiers see combat as a break from their families, their wives, the monotony of the day-to-day grind that is normal life. I liked that you didn't have to deal with all the bullshit of life back home that takes up so much time, like random text messages, always being on your phone, driving in traffic just to get groceries.

None of that was required overseas. Our teams were virtually self-sufficient because of the amazing infrastructure built to support all our operations.

I wanted to look at the war and home as two separate lives, like a split screen. But sometimes creating that separation was impossible.

That first week back was the hardest. The tension grew between Sarah and me. But it was impossible to avoid. We were together, sleeping in the same room, eating breakfast and dinner at the same table—but I might as well have been on Mars.

"Are you even here?" she asked me another night.

"Come on, Sarah."

"You come on. You need to talk to me. We need to talk."

"We're talking," I said.

"Has someone kidnapped you?" She was joking, but she really wasn't.

MOST OF MY FAMILY AND OLD FRIENDS HAD NO IDEA WHAT I DID, EVEN THOSE WHO were close to me. People had their own lives to think about, jobs and families. The war on terror had gotten old after nearly a decade and in that time terrorist attacks around the world had become commonplace. America was becoming desensitized to the horrors of terrorism. In turn, the media cared less about reporting on military operations and the rising death tolls. At the beginning of the global war on terror you saw an attack that killed ten people reported on the front page of CNN. Now highly coordinated suicide bombings that killed fifty or more were lucky to make the bottom ticker. Everyone else had moved on, except for those of us who continued to live it, like my team.

I wanted to get back in the action because that was all I knew now, back to where I could be surrounded by people who got what I was going through, what I'd seen, without having to explain. The same went for the rest of my team. Until we got back, we were all in a holding pattern, waiting for our war lives to start up again. We were hungry but didn't know what would make the hunger go away.

Days passed and the waiting turned to boredom. I flipped on the TV, but there was never anything I felt like watching. My mind kept wandering to the targets I had left behind. Evil people who were still out there. Manhattan and Brooklyn. Sometimes I walked outside the condo with a three-iron and drove balls off the thirteenth hole late into the night. One after the other. I wasn't very skilled, but it felt good to strike the balls and watch them sail off into the darkness.

I also took long drives. I had a Corvette and liked to speed down the long stretches outside of town just to feel something. But I grew agitated with traffic and the new speed bumps they had installed in our neighborhood. I wasn't normally hot-tempered but the war had changed that. Sitting at a standstill on the highway got me anxious at times, even a little paranoid.

"Come on, let's go!" I shouted at a silver Camry stopped in front of me one afternoon on my way to the mall. I looked in my rearview and up at the sky, as if there might be someone watching me. The watcher becomes the watched. The sky was blue like Iraq. I had to remind myself I was in North Carolina.

One afternoon I got into an argument with a woman from Time Warner about installing my Internet. It wasn't working at home and I started freaking out about it. "Sir, I can help you," she said. "No you can't." I hung up.

I was used to the efficiency of the Box. Out there I had every resource and support personnel I needed to get the job done. If I needed highly encrypted Internet in the middle of a barren desert, it was done—and these guys couldn't even install my Internet correctly in the suburbs?

I SAW MY MOTHER AROUND THIS TIME. IT HAD BEEN OVER A YEAR SINCE I HAD SEEN her last. She came up for a visit and we went out for dinner at an Italian restaurant chain. I was happy to see her because it had been so long. But everything felt stifled. When we sat down and she asked what I had been doing overseas, there was nothing I could say.

"Not much," I said, chewing a piece of bread.

"Something must have happened."

I couldn't say, but at the same time I didn't want to lie.

Before drones, I had told her a little more about my assignments. There wasn't anything particularly secret about them. She knew exactly where I was overseas most of the time. I never told her anymore about where or what and it was probably better that she was in the dark. Maybe she wouldn't have agreed with my choices, some of the things I was in charge of doing.

"Just another deployment," I said.

The dinner dragged on like this. It was hard not being able to tell my mom anything. I wanted to tell her that I was making her proud, explain that we were doing things to save lives and protect Americans like her. Because I'm sure she imagined the worst, that the military had corrupted me or that maybe I had seen so many bad things I would need some sort of medical help later in life. It probably didn't help that PTSD was becoming a common term for soldiers returning from battle. None of that was the actual case. The secrets hurt sometimes.

When our food came to the table, I didn't look up much, but I could tell she was watching me stab my rigatoni, as if she might be able to understand something from it, as if she might pick up a signal that I was okay.

"Why are you being so short?" she asked finally. "It's like you don't care to talk to me."

Once we'd shared a world together in that small house in Katy, Texas, and now she had her world and I had mine and the two were hard to bring together. She didn't bring up my cousin who had died. And I was grateful for that.

I asked her to tell me about her new job and she relented and didn't ask any more questions about the war. She spent the rest of the night talking about her move from Texas to North Carolina and her work as a business analyst. She seemed happy about that.

She did press me about my weight as we got up to leave. "You're so skinny," she said as we stood by our cars. "You need to eat more." I told her that I would.

AFTER THE FIRST WEEK BACK, I HEADED IN TO THE UNIT'S HEADQUARTERS, AS IF IT were an itch I needed to scratch. It was a fifteen-minute drive and the first thing I did was flip open my laptop and connect to the live drone feeds. I watched the birds look down over a stretch of desert in northern Iraq. I switched to another feed and watched a white van weave through traffic. Another camera was zoomed in on a mud hut out in Yemen as a target went about his day.

Bill and Jack were there, too. They were as addicted to it as I was. I found being in the office more comfortable than being at the condo. We spent days going over old missions, watching our drone videos, looking at what decisions were made and how things might have been better, like a team combing through old game tapes.

We also dug into old intelligence files for things we might have missed the first time around. We talked strategy for next time because each of us wanted in his own way to have another go at the guys we didn't get.

Scarface came up one afternoon in the underground office, files flung out around us, the fluorescent lights buzzing overhead. "Man, I wish we'd followed him longer," I said.

"We could have used him to map the network," Bill came back.

"The main thing is to spend more time following these guys around," Jack said.

That was the main mistake I had made over there—not following targets around long enough for them to lead us even higher up the terrorist chain. I had let the operators with more experience convince me that we should strike, to satisfy their own craving for action.

Bill liked to tell the story of the famous hunt for the Al Qaeda in Iraq leader Abu Musab al-Zarqawi. They'd watched Zarqawi's spiritual advisor for a full month, just going about his business, doing nothing notable. It had been tempting to take him out, watching him twenty-four hours a day for weeks. Everyone was antsy and every day he and his team had argued with the operators about why it was important to stay put. They waited until that one day. "He packed up his family into a vehicle and traveled hours outside of the city," Bill explained. "He drove straight to Zarqawi's location. And we got them all."

"Patience," he added. "That's when you get the big fish."

DURING THE MONTHS I WAS HOME, WE CARRIED PAGERS AND WERE ALWAYS ON call. The unit kept a tight leash in the event there was a global incident that needed our response.

Pagers, outdated though they might seem, kept the enemy from tracking us. Cell phones were more easily hacked. At night I kept my pager on my bedside table, waiting for the call to go back to Iraq. My black duffel bag of gear was ready to go. Sometimes it went off in the middle of the night and I raced to the office in my car, running red lights, my blood flowing again. They were just drills mostly, but I loved it and you never knew when it would be real.

I kept up to speed on the teams that replaced us and monitored the reports of their operations as they came in—I needed to know what we'd be climbing back into when we returned.

There were rumors, of course, about when we'd be going. It would likely be Iraq again. But no one would confirm it. Probably because we never really knew for sure until it happened. Things were constantly changing.

Sources were telling us that the network was hurting for new recruits, people to keep the cells going, as we killed guys off. Some of the cells had begun to show significant gaps in leadership: one was missing a military emir (we killed Scarface); another was missing an administrative leader (we captured Usamah); and another cell only had a logistics emir left.

The new leaders also seemed to be getting younger and younger, as experienced ISI guys continued to fall with every additional strike by our teams.

We never forgot Manhattan and Brooklyn. We watched for clues but somehow they managed to stay out of sight. From what we could tell, they were getting better at hiding, using more couriers, adding more layers above them, sinking deeper into the desert.

The days were also jammed with a lot of training—and that helped distract me. One week there were war games in a warehouse that had been retrofitted to look like a city block in Iraq, with dozens of actors playing insurgents. Later I was in Poland sharing counterterrorism tactics with the GROM special forces. Then I was back in North Carolina again, jumping out of airplanes.

Then there were the suits. I hated the suits.

It wasn't unusual for us to go to D.C. to debrief the other intelligence agencies—FBI, DIA, NSA, and NGA—so they could learn from our experiences. We called these guys nine-to-five. A bunch of suits: the "Beltway Bandits." They were always curious about how we were able to find targets so fast. They liked to pick our brains and talk about the bad guys they were following in their cable traffic while we were busy in the field taking them down.

There had been a time before 9/11 when we didn't mix or work well together at all, when everyone guarded their information. That only hurt the overall goal of saving American lives in the long run. Our efforts at closer collaboration and strengthening relationships enabled us to turn the war around.

But that doesn't mean that they didn't ask stupid questions. They did.

"Whatever happened to terrorist leader X?"

"Well, our group killed him a few years ago."

"Oh, guess I'll take him off my chart."

Or another guy had no idea the military controlled more drones in the sky than his own organization did. He thought they were only being used in Pakistan. At the same time, however, these meetings were important for us because maybe there was an analyst who didn't know he could reach out to me and how he could call with time-sensitive information. Who knew when they might turn up something or someone we'd been hunting for months. Sometimes it was that one missing piece of information that brought down an entire empire.

The girls there always seemed to perk up when we arrived. They were from Defense Intelligence Agency, which was a kind of connective tissue between all the military branches. There was something that got these girls hooked when they worked with us or the SEALs. I think they got a taste of what it was like to get out from behind their desks—we called it "touching the magic." The upside for us was that the girls from DIA were always good-looking.

We met the suits three weeks in a row and things went smoothly until week four, when the meetings started to wear on me. That's when Jack called. It was February 2010.

"I need you immediately," he said. "We're going back down-range."

Heading back to Iraq.

"You ready?"

I was ready weeks ago.

15

THE BOYS ARE BACK IN TOWN

"What's the plan?" Jason asked as the Black Hawk raced us to our headquarters in the center of Baghdad. It was February 2010. We were both eager to get started again.

"I got the list," I said. "That's the plan."

Jason was the new assault commander—super smart, a West Pointer and Ranger before becoming a unit member. He replaced Max, who had been assigned to another part of the world.

The kill list was the list the Beltway Bandits had sent me just before leaving North Carolina. Twenty of the most wanted men across Iraq. The worst of the worst, the cockroaches who survived the Surge.

The people on this list made up the ISI network's core leadership. Even though I'd already done a tour in the Box, I was still the young guy. I was a lot more battle-ready, but I still had no idea what to expect. That's what I loved about drone warfare.

In camo, Jason was G.I. Joe: tall and ropey, with short blond hair. He was well-known among the guys for winning a few military fitness competitions and was looking to prove himself on the battlefield. At some point he'd actually been an extra in a movie about surfers in Hawaii and the guys liked to crack jokes about him being Mr. Hollywood.

Most team commanders let us do our intel thing and worried only about the operators. Jason was different. He wanted to understand exactly how we gathered our intelligence and made the decisions about who to go after and kill.

We landed in our own blocked-off area on the base, grabbed our bags, and headed for the Box to meet the team we were replacing. High fencing surrounded us, the city just outside. Our base was inside a couple of old Iraqi government buildings in the international Green Zone. Everything had been rebuilt with plywood—walls, chairs, desks, beds. I had a plywood bunk bed to myself that smelled of undried paint. Not much better than the last place I lived, but who was I kidding? I wouldn't spend much time in bed anyway. We had a name for this place: the Plywood Palace.

"The A team's here," I said, walking in. Nothing like a good joke to get things started. It was around 1 A.M. Marty, the intel lead, gave an eye roll. He was stiff and had been around for a while. "Things have been nonstop," he said, getting down to business. He was ready to head home.

The Box was just a few steps off the chopper landing, through multiple doors with cipher locks. It was double the size of the one at my last deployment months ago. The wood desks were tiered upward like a movie theater and the front wall was hung with a dozen sixty-inch TVs tuned into our birds flying in different parts of the country. The smell of it was familiar: bodies, sweat, and old coffee. Home sweet home. But this one was flashier and felt more like the center of the universe. It also came equipped with three drones.

The first thing I did was pop open my laptop and flip it on. This was the brain of the operation now. We didn't even really need the Box these days. I could set up a top-secret encrypted Internet network anywhere in the world with connections through satellites. I could control a fleet of drones from a hotel suite if necessary.

I grabbed a Rip It out of the fridge at the back and Marty and I talked late into the night. He laid out everything they'd done: kills, captures, who was still out there.

One thing about the Baghdad box was that it was the place all the top hunters wanted to hunt. The city had always been a key stomping ground for bad guys. Even with the heavy security checkpoints, Marty and his team had started seeing a rise in enemy leaders popping up across the city. They'd knocked off some of the network and the Surge was clearly working. Fewer American troops were getting killed each month and the country was settling down. President Obama was talking about armed forces leaving next year. But the network's commanders were still in the wind and he confirmed the rumors we'd been hearing back home. "The network is getting a lot smarter," he said. "They're adapting to us."

I asked about the two leaders, Manhattan and Brooklyn.

"Nothing."

After that, Marty and his team were out the door, gear bags on the choppers and heading home. "Good luck," he said.

When we officially took over, I remembered thinking, *Fuck, where do I start?*

The world felt like it had suddenly fallen smack onto my back, and it was more than a bit unsettling. I truly believed that there was no other group capable of doing what we did. The larger military didn't have a chance getting these guys. It was up to us, it was up to me.

My team was around ten now. Kate was my new Jake, the tactical controller, who sat next to me, passing along my instructions through chat to the camera operator and Predator pilots. She was Air Force, young, thin, and pale like she didn't get sun, with very long brown hair that she kept tied up in a ponytail. She was unassuming otherwise. She came to get the job done, she did it expertly, and she didn't waste her breath on anything.

The FBI, DIA, NSA, and NGA had all sent people. I had been hooked up with superstars from nearly every agency—a testament to how close we worked together after 9/11. It was good to have others experienced in our craft on the team because we didn't have time to bring them up to speed.

One of the superstars was the map genius, Brian. Straight out of college, he'd joined the NGA and worked his way up the chain to land here. It was like he was born with maps in his head. He could get me things that others couldn't—the 3-D layout of a building in Baghdad, all kinds of military terrain maps. He could literally move top-secret satellites in order to give us crystal-clear images from space of neighborhoods from every imaginable angle. Like all of us, he was young and eager, and he was always in my ear, saying things like, "You seeing this, dawg?" "Check it out, bro." He talked like kids on the street.

Mark, my teammate and superior from back home, was also there. Being so close to Baghdad, we'd frequently meet up with various U.S. generals and senior Iraqi government officials, like Prime Minister Maliki, who wanted to be briefed regularly about our missions. Mark took on those high-level meetings and spent most of his time keeping the seniors out of my business. I ran the day-to-day targeting.

I was tired from the ride in but spent the next day sucking down Rip Its and getting up to speed. I made one run to the chow hall in a building next door. Same cereal in the plastic bowls—plenty of Frosted Flakes to eat.

We knew the top twenty guys we needed to go after but most of our leads had been run down by the group before us. They had killed or captured all of the smaller fish over the last four months, but these were the leads we could have used to find the big guys. The reality was that the other team simply hadn't left us much to go on.

I worried that the mission was going to be a disaster. I had the birds coming on station soon and the operators would be banging at the doors to get out. I suddenly needed a mission like a junkie needed a fix.

That's when we got our first tip about the bomber.

THE BOMBER WAS A MASTER OF ROADSIDE KILLINGS, A KIND OF ASSASSIN OF THE highways. If you needed someone to die in a car, if you wanted to knock out a U.S. military convoy, he was the guy ISI called.

Intel came in that the bomber was shacked up at a falling-down concrete house not too far from the Green Zone. At first, I wasn't sure if we should bother. Typically we'd leave a low-level guy like him to the regular military forces or the locals. We got flooded with intel reports on these lower-level fighters and most times we didn't pay much attention. That would just turn our job into Whac-A-Mole. But this guy was different.

Deep in one of the files, I found a report connecting him to a commander named Manaf al-Rawi. Rawi was big-time. He was the leader of ISI for the entire city—the Baghdad Wali, the commander of the district commanders. We even had a name for him, Objective Dark Horse. Dark Horse was one of the few who likely spoke to Brooklyn and Manhattan. It was a long shot, but maybe picking up this low-level fighter could lead us up the chain.

It didn't take long to figure out where the bomber was hiding out and Jason made the call to grab him that night. He was bunked down at a house in the Mansour district, an area of the city known for terrorist hideouts. Jason and the operators did what they did best. They crashed the place, grabbed him, and got out without a problem.

It was early morning when they got him back to the Box—the bomber almost immediately cracked. He claimed that he hadn't seen Dark Horse in years. But then he gave us something else—a real gift. "You know the Baghdad Sniper? I can tell you where he is."

THE BAGHDAD SNIPER WAS INFAMOUS. PEOPLE CONSIDERED HIM ONE OF THE MOST ruthless killers in the war, with hundreds of deaths on his hands. Locals across the country called him "Juba the Sniper." A higher power must have decided it was his turn, because now he had found himself on my radar. It was time to end his terror. *We're coming for you,* I thought.

No one really knew who he was. Some believed that he was a marketing and recruiting tool for Al Qaeda and ISI. He filmed some of his brutal kills and posted them online, set to jihadi soundtracks. I forced myself to watch them over and over again for clues, anything that might tell us about his network. It was hard to stomach, but I kept them on: him stalking a U.S. soldier on patrol before gunning him down and watching him slowly die. Another of him murdering an Iraqi soldier at a local checkpoint by putting a bullet right between his eyes. It was sickening and each viewing only worsened my hatred for him.

Some even wondered if Juba was one man or many—a media creation. The enemy's production skills had become as good as Hollywood's. The foot soldier we captured, however, claimed that Juba was in fact just one man. He said he knew that because he'd helped hide him from the authorities, shuttling him from one safe house to another. And tonight, the man said, Juba was at an abandoned house in the city. But he wouldn't be there for long. "He sleeps with his sniper rifle at his side," he warned.

THE PROBLEM WAS THAT I DIDN'T FULLY TRUST THE PRISONER YET. I HAD LEARNED that lesson once already with the agency's source, Silencer. "Let's get a Pred up over his hideout," I said.

The drone was our way to vet intelligence when we were dealing with shady guys.

In minutes, we had eyes circling the target.

"Pretty quiet," I said. Dim streets of row houses.

"Not many people," Jason came back.

It was a small one-story home, surrounded by a crush of crumbling and leaning one- and two-story places. I didn't see any guards or lookouts on the roof or the street. There didn't even seem to be any movement inside the house. It was completely dark, like much of the neighborhood.

"I don't like it," I said. "It could be a trap."

During my training, we spent days looking at videos about situations where things went wrong. In one video, we watched an assault team just barely escape a house packed top to bottom with explosives.

I turned to Jason. "Maybe we should watch it for another day with the Pred before the guys go out." Jason radioed for the others to be ready.

"Let's watch the house for a bit more to see if anything happens," he said. "And then we go."

By 12 P.M., nothing much had changed. Little traffic passed the house. The one thing that nagged at me was that we still couldn't confirm whether anyone was inside—a factor that had caused us to cancel or postpone earlier missions. You never knew what you were walking into—a bomb or an innocent.

These missions were all about precision and knowing the situation on the ground. But in the end, none of that mattered. This target was important enough to take a chance. Juba had a lot of blood on his hands.

Just before midnight, we gave the green light and the operators headed out. They took the bomber with them to ID Juba, altering his appearance completely. We fattened him with pillows stuffed under his shirt, and gave him a scarf to cover his hair and eyes, just in case locals took notice.

I WATCHED AS THE GUYS MADE THEIR WAY THROUGH THE DARK STREETS, NIGHT-vision goggles snapped to their helmets. I could see the outlines of their bodies, about a dozen of them moving silently to the target house, just shadows.

Some of the operators with us this time around were legends in the covert world. One was part of a team responsible for the death of Zarqawi. Another had been on the mission that ended with the capture of Saddam Hussein—the first one to put eyes on the dictator when the team found Saddam hiding in the spider hole. He liked to tell me the story about how he punched him square in the face and said, "Greetings from President Bush."

I moved the camera to the house and a few minutes of silence passed. There was a moment, right before the raid began, when I watched the house through the drone camera as it spun in circles like an astronaut spinning in space. The camera was fixated on the center of the flat roof, not looking at anything else around it, to make sure no one popped out right before the operators arrived. And then slowly, out of the darkness, the silhouettes of the men began to appear out of the corners of the drone camera, creeping closer and closer, setting their positions. My heart jumped. It was always the same. In those split seconds of stress, of not knowing the future, between total calm and total chaos—the sustained boom of grenades exploding and the violence of swift action—everything suddenly woke the fuck up.

Soon the guys were outside the house, where they waited for a count. Still no movement that I could see from above. It was a spooky thing to see a densely populated part of Baghdad look so completely deserted.

I could hear the operators on the radio, their chatter heating up. "Zulu Three, Zulu Three, setting position, over."

And then the raid began. It happened in seconds. The door came down, grenades exploded, and the men rushed in. What they found was anticlimactic. No bombs. No booby trap. Instead, a man lying on a barren concrete living room floor in a sleeping bag.

The entire house had been completely emptied out. The only possession he had was a customized Russian Dragunov SVD Military Sniper Rifle. It was right next to him, as if he laid it down when he was finished for the day and planned to grab it when he woke and went back to work at his killing.

The detainee was spot-on.

Juba looked skinny, disheveled. This was definitely a man who had been on the run for a long time. The operators interrogated him heavily on the spot and then we whisked him away to a secret prison, where we spent days interrogating him some more. Another team typically took over the interrogation process. Their job was to extract as much information as possible from them within forty-eight hours, before the network reset. Almost immediately, he caved. He took credit for more than one hundred kills over the last few years—both U.S. soldiers and Iraqi security forces. His memory of them was as if he'd stored each one away like a snapshot in the back of his mind for later. He went through every single assassination with the interrogator in explicit detail, outlining where he was positioned, how many shots he fired, where the body fell, and how he got away.

When we turned him over to the Iraqi police force ten days later, they checked out all the details, talked to the families of those killed, and found out that he was accurate about all that he'd claimed.

The Sniper had terrorized a lot of people over the years. Now there was closure for the city and the families of the deceased. A few months later, they'd hang him.

It was good to be back.

16

THE SAUDI

"You have to see this," one of my intelligence analysts called out one morning. I hadn't slept much that night and had just slogged over from my trailer.

"I think I have something here," she said. Megan had been digging into the files for hours already, hunting leads.

She showed me a picture on her screen of a man who was tall and thin with bushy black hair.

"You want me to guess?"

"It's the Saudi."

Our missions had started to pick up after Juba the Sniper. We began to kick loose intelligence, accumulating more leads, and soon it felt like I hadn't been away. I was back to my old routine of Rip Its and riding out multiple days on adrenaline and no sleep. Two to three drones up in the sky at all times.

A big part of why the missions started moving was Megan and two other girls, Jane and Lisa. They'd come from the DIA, and their job was to find things the rest of the team missed: gaps in our intelligence, stray photographs of guys who'd gone missing, bits of overlooked chatter, details lost in reports. We called them the Pink Mafia.

But it wasn't only because they were young and easy on the eyes. They were also extremely fierce. They were brilliant, with strong personalities and just as hell-bent on taking out ISI as all of us. They were in their late twenties or early thirties and never flinched at any of the horror that streamed across our monitors in vivid closeness day and night.

It was likely just by chance, but there was a joke at the time that the DIA's recruiting questions followed a particular order: Smart? Check. Hot? Check. Hired. There was a SEAL team that requested the same DIA girls every time they needed someone.

Given that I was younger, I sensed it was hard for the Pink Mafia to take orders from me at first. I didn't know them and they didn't know me. They never said anything, but I got the feeling from their body language that they were like, Who the hell is this? But it didn't change the way they worked. Here everyone had to earn respect. And they kept me on my toes.

Jane was an athletic girl with some Asian roots, short and thin, always in running shoes and a T-shirt. Her particular attention to detail was encouraging. With her, we knew it wasn't likely we would miss something about our targets' backgrounds. She had these eureka moments when we were at a loss for a key detail about a target. Out of nowhere she'd pop up and yell, "Found it!" If a guy was using a fake identity, she'd figure out who was behind the mask. One time she had nothing more to go on than the fact that our target was overweight and last seen wearing a black dishdasha. Somehow she found him in our historical records.

Lisa was the biggest talker of the group. Her voice was fast and loud like a chain saw and she was constantly up in my grill, pumping me on new people to chase. She wasn't always right, but she always thought she was and didn't back down even when she was wrong. She was from Jersey, so sometimes her mouth pissed people off. When the operators returned to base without killing a target we told them to take out, she was the one who got the most fired up. "They should have killed that piece of shit," she'd complain. It was kind of like being polite to your boss (the operators), but then talking shit about them when they left the room. She was the queen of that.

There was tension with the Pink Mafia in the Box. It was always there, like the coffee-drenched humidity. Some of it was emotional, but some of it was sexual, too. Not that anyone was getting any. It was just that there were so few women in the combat zone. And because of that the operators always found a reason to hang around when they didn't have a mission.

"Trying to understand the intel," they'd say.

Megan ended up on the drone team after leaving a career as a lawyer to fast-climb the ranks at DIA. She spoke Arabic, had long and dark curly hair, was skinny as a telephone wire, and became obsessed more than most with her targets.

Now it was the Saudi. She flipped through his files on the big monitors. The Saudi was close to the top of the ISI food chain as the military commander in Baghdad. Guys we'd captured over the years had helped us piece together his inner workings. He ran hundreds of soldiers, helped organize the large-scale bombings, and managed in detail the illicit trafficking of arms and bombs through the city's maze of security checkpoints.

For a long time, we'd been trying to figure out where he was, if he was even in Baghdad or somewhere else. From what we could tell, he hid behind layers of messengers, front companies, and dumped phones. He also had very close ties to Dark Horse, his boss.

"He's been living as a doctor," Megan said, laying things out.

Being a doctor was how he hid and at the same time blended in with every other normal citizen. He owned a pharmacy and had a family. He drove a black Suburban. This was exactly what made some of these targets very hard to find. They looked like everyone else and neighbors didn't even know what they really did. They probably saw the Saudi as someone who went to work every day and came home to his family. Nothing unusual. Boring for a city at war.

We got to work fast after that, mapped out a few startpoints, and then called the drones into action, directing them first to the pharmacy.

The parking lot was crammed full of mostly white cars like Toyota Corollas and bongos, but one vehicle stuck out like a sore thumb, a dark and dirt-covered Suburban.

"Is that it?" I asked Megan.

She quickly flipped through her files on her computer. "Same one."

"Z in one," I told the drone operator, wanting to keep the camera closed in right on top of the Suburban.

There was no one in it.

AROUND THE PHARMACY WAS THE SPRAWL OF BAGHDAD. THERE WERE BUILDINGS, twenty-story apartment complexes, traffic jams, and people all over the place, which was a lot more crowded than the cities I hunted in during my first deployment.

All the activity required our targeting to be even more precise. In the desert, we could lose a car or a person for a few seconds with the drone and then pick them up shortly after because of the speed or direction we knew they were traveling. Here one wrong jerk of the camera by the sensor operator or a malfunction of the telemetry equipment and the target would be lost forever in the maze of streets and shops.

There was one benefit to working in the city. Unlike anywhere else, we could fly the birds a lot lower. Because people were so accustomed to the sounds of aircraft coming and going from Baghdad International Airport, they didn't think twice about a drone overhead. We used this heavily to our advantage.

We could fly the birds at a low 4,000 feet in the city, compared to around 12,000 feet in the desert. Everything was clearer, colors richer. It made our work easier. I could almost make out a guy's face in the street and distinctly see that, say, his shirt was yellow with a pocket or that he was holding a pack of cigarettes.

We orbited the pharmacy's parking lot for hours and hours, just watching the parked truck until a man finally showed up and got in.

"That our guy?" I said to Megan.

"Got to be."

He wore khaki pants and a tucked-in brown polo shirt. Athletic build. Same as the photos we had.

"Looks like he's alone," I said.

We watched as the Suburban pulled out into traffic and drove for a few miles before it came to a house and pulled into a driveway.

"Where we at?"

"Adamiyah."

It was a nice, middle-class part of the city, dominated by Sunnis, which meant that it could have sympathies for ISI.

"Do we have anything on the house?"

It was two floors, with a balcony on the second floor overlooking the main street.

"Nothing," said Megan. "But there was a mission about a block away that an earlier team conducted in 2007." That one ended in the killing of one of the network's military heads.

"Let's get closer," I said.

We saw him disappear under the awning, then head up a stairwell toward the back of the house and from there onto the balcony. He walked along the balcony to the end of it on the right and used his keys to unlock a door. We sat there and watched for hours, taking notes about the house and the neighbors around it.

Three days straight we stuck to him—I remember thinking about Bill telling me to be more patient when we had the bigger fish in our sights. Make sure first that this was the Saudi.

I asked Brian to take some new satellite snapshots of the neighborhood. We needed to know routes in and out of the house and the surrounding streets for the assault team if we decided to go in. Were there larger roofs for a chopper to land on? Security checkpoints nearby? There was an eight-foot wall in back of the house that would need good measurements for a ladder.

Bill called one night to remind me that his guys had carried out a raid in the neighborhood a few years back. "It was bad," he said. "The guys got hit."

As the assault team had driven to the target house then, heavily armed men loyal to ISI had popped up on multiple rooftops and started shooting down into the vehicles. It was a huge ambush. Some of the crew had sustained heavy injuries. "Just watch out for that," he said.

Days passed and the Box started to feel more like the reality show *Big Brother*—only the guy had no idea he was being filmed. At first his days didn't appear to be unusual at all. He didn't leave the house except to go to the pharmacy and back. We followed him in both directions and loitered above the pharmacy and the house all day long.

There was one odd thing about the house. He kept the lights on all night every night, as if he was expecting someone or hoping to keep someone away.

The kids were key to the picture. They were young, probably under five years old, from what we could see. That confirmed our intel. The Saudi's kids were the same age.

During the daytime, we watched them play with toys in the

front yard, chasing each other, running in circles while a woman in a veil looked on. They seemed like any kids you'd see in a suburban neighborhood in the United States. Which made me wonder if they even knew who their father really was. Probably not.

But with the children there, I knew one thing—a drone strike was out of the question.

INSIDE A WAR ZONE LIKE IRAQ, WE COULD LAUNCH A HELLFIRE WITH THE APPROVAL of our higher headquarters commander. I'd submit a justification for why we were targeting a guy, and once the target was in the Pred's crosshair and cleared for hot—to shoot—the pilots and sensor operator would fire away.

When Barack Obama came into office in 2009, the rules about killing began to change. Inside a war zone, there was a lot more time spent looking at the potential blast radius of a Hellfire and who exactly was on the ground, that is, the collateral-damage estimates, the precise point of impact, and who unintentionally could get hurt. When the Iraq War started in 2003, the threshold for collateral damage was huge. Because we were taking over a country, there was little regard for outside casualties. You could have twenty or thirty bystanders near a big enemy target and military commanders would still order a strike. As the years went on, an intolerance for collateral-damage grew. If even one or two innocents were in the line of fire, we called the strike off. The change was brought about in part by the fact that there were a lot more drones going online in 2010 and people understood there needed to be more oversight. It was also because tactical mistakes in our world had strategic consequences, as killing even one innocent would play out on the world stage.

Much of the change in the world of drone fighting, however, happened outside officially designated combat areas, where more targets were popping up. Obama seemed to feel personally compelled to approve each strike because he knew the strategic consequences that came with mistakenly killing women and children.

The president started asking his staff to implement specific criteria before each strike outside a war zone. While it constrained targeting a lot, it was necessary to ensure that only the guys posing an imminent threat were taken out.

These strikes began with guys like me at the tactical level, determining whether a target was worth going after.

Since Iraq was still officially considered a war zone, things were a lot easier for us; we already had the authority we needed to do the job.

If it was outside the officially designated war zones, those same slides would then make their way up the chain of command—and through a lot of lawyers looking for reasons to reject the request along the way.

These decisions were never made lightly.

First it went to the overall commander in the region. That might be the general in charge of all U.S. troops in the Middle East, who then passed it along to the Joint Chiefs of Staff at the Pentagon. There much discussion happened with suits in the intelligence agencies, Army reps lobbying to get buy-in.

At that point, there were always snags. One side didn't agree or another side wanted to add in more information about the target's worthiness for a strike. Out of that scrum, it finally went to the secretary of defense, who would then take the file to the president. Obama made the ultimate decision.

From our place at the bottom, we could see that the president made it a priority to understand everything about the targets on the list—something that Bush had delegated to others. We could tell that he took personal responsibility in ensuring he understood the targets.

Sometimes it took days to get a nomination approved, other times months, and still other times years. It depended on who tried to block it, or if, say, the target was an American citizen, along with many other factors.

We ended up calling this huge bureaucratic process death by PowerPoint. Drone strikes outside of war zones were literally being decided at the executive level based on the efficacy of our PowerPoint presentations, how well we essentially "sold" the idea that a guy was evil enough to obliterate.

Once the president approved the targets that our teams had presented up the chain, each target was added to the kill or capture list. We called this the authorization for use of military force, or AUMF. The AUMF was signed into law by President Bush after 9/11, allowing the military to go after Al Qaeda and its affiliates around the world. The strike authority was then passed to the overall commander.

In the end, even after the president's approval, the commander had to bless the strike. But before he did, there were final considerations: Was the target at the location? Were there any women and children? Was capture impossible?

That a guy was impossible to capture was one of the most common arguments for a strike. I never bought the argument. We could capture someone just about anywhere in the world. Killing was optional.

AS WE WATCHED THE SAUDI GO ABOUT HIS BUSINESS ONE MORNING, HE SUDDENLY switched up his routine. We were following him as he drove to work one day when he made a right turn instead of the usual left. What was he doing?

He drove a few miles until he stopped at a crowded open market two or three blocks wide. He parked his vehicle along the street, packed with twenty or so other cars, and then proceeded to walk quickly through the maze of corridors into the shops.

"You getting this?" I said to Megan.

"I see it. Something's up with him."

He kept looking back for some reason.

"Who's he looking for?"

Eventually he made his way to an area that was secluded, covered in part by awnings. Soon after, another man in a white dishdasha approached him and they talked for a few minutes.

That's when I noticed that the Saudi had something in his hand—a small package or envelope. He handed it to the other guy and within seconds the meeting was over. They then departed in opposite directions.

I kept the first drone on our target as he headed back to his truck, while the other drone followed the new guy. The new guy picked up the pace, as if he knew someone was following. I could see him look side to side as he speed-walked through the crowds. At one point, he looked up.

But it was hard to follow him. There were people everywhere, going in all directions. Then the man broke into a run, like he was suddenly on a mission to get out of there, zigzagging around people in the marketplace.

Soon we lost him. We spent a few minutes zooming in and out on people in the market who fit the man's description, but he wasn't anywhere. He was gone.

It was time to grab the Saudi. We couldn't wait any longer.

IT WAS AROUND 1 A.M. WHEN I BRIEFED THE ASSAULT TEAM ON THE HOUSE: ITS entry and exit points, which way certain doors opened, the four people inside, the lights on the second floor that were never turned off, the flat roof for potential squirters, and the absence of any weapons. They needed to bring a ten-foot ladder to get over the wall in the back. "The Saudi is in his room now," I said, pointing out where his room was on the monitor.

The team listened very carefully. It was a moment when I saw how far I had come since the last deployment. I could anticipate their questions about what they could expect to find there.

I handed them Brian's maps of the neighborhood, the walls they might have to scale, interrogation questions for the Saudi, and photos of his associates.

"See you guys soon," I said.

Excitement and a little anxiety took over soon after, as I watched the operators sneaking down the street of the house late into the night, weapons at the ready.

Radio noise erupted and fell off.

"Zulu Three," Jason called over the radio. That was me. "Can you sparkle?"

"Roger, Echo One."

From the drone, we beamed an infrared laser on the Saudi's house. It was like a giant flashlight—a sparkle—but only visible to people wearing night vision.

Just as that happened, we got a surprise. I noticed the shadow of someone on a neighboring roof. My heart jumped a beat as I remembered Bill's team getting ambushed. "Z in on that," I said urgently, worried that the team was just about to take enemy fire.

I was about to radio in to them when the roof guy came into clear view. Too clear, actually. The guy was completely naked—and masturbating furiously.

"Oh man, dawg," Brian said.

"Awww!" Kate cried out.

Megan made a sick face.

"Only a threat to himself," I said, directing the camera operator to return to the target's house.

THE ASSAULT CREW PAUSED A HALF BLOCK OUT AND THEN KEPT MOVING. I COULDN'T stop thinking about that one dangerous question: what was going on inside the house that we couldn't see?

There was no way to know until they crashed through the door. I didn't have any idea how the Saudi would respond, either. Since he had been so smart at hiding all this time, it was difficult to predict what he'd do.

The drone's infrared sensor had been switched to black hot. On the monitors, I watched a bright flash as the operators breached the door with a charge and then raced inside.

At first it seemed like things were going as planned. Then I noticed the guys pulling security outside suddenly moving fast to the back of the house. *Something's not right.*

"Squirter!" yelled Kate, pointing at the roof.

"I got him."

Our guy had climbed out to the roof somehow and was now running from one side to the other, looking over the sides of the house, as if to see if someone was below. Then, in one quick movement, he leaped to the neighbor's roof and began to flee.

We could see him perfectly in the infrared camera, even though it was pitch-black. Our team huddled in front of the monitors. We sparkled him with the drone's infrared beam as he moved so the guys could track him. He hopped from one roof to the next, making his way down the block like an alley cat, before finally arriving at one gap he couldn't jump.

But that didn't stop him. He threw his body over the side of the house, hung there for a second, a swinging bit of pixelated blackness in the camera, and then dropped—two full stories to a stairwell. He crumbled to the ground.

When he stood up, two of our guys who had given chase were right there. The rest happened in a matter of seconds.

The Saudi lunged, reached for a rifle, got one of them, but was then shot twice point-blank by the other in the chest. I watched the Saudi fall backward and go completely still on the stairwell.

The call came over the radio then. It was over. He was dead.

The last thing to do was comb the house and the pharmacy for whatever intelligence he had lying around. We took documents, photographs, and computers. But there wasn't much. He was very careful.

When it was over, Megan responded like all of us that night: professional and indifferent that the Saudi had met his demise.

"Good riddance," she said, as we zoomed in on his lifeless body still lying bleeding on the stairs.

Although the loss, of not being able to extract the intel we hoped the Saudi had to fill in more clues on Manhattan and Brooklyn's whereabouts, stood in the back of all our minds, there was little time left for reflection. We moved on to the next target.

17

THE KIDNAPPING

The photo of the kidnapped woman wouldn't leave me alone.

I lay on my lumpy single bed after forty-eight hours of juggling multiple missions and all I wanted was to sleep. My pillow was flat and hard like a big slice of Melba toast. I kept trying to toss some shape into it and close my eyes. But she was still there.

I flipped on my light and sat up. The air-conditioning was on the fritz again, making rumbling sounds. I grabbed the photo off my side table and looked at it. The edges bent over, little wrinkles in the face.

The woman was in her late twenties, with long black hair and light skin. She had these piercing blue eyes and looked Lebanese.

A few nights before, a colleague had walked into the Box with her photo and handed it to me.

"An Iraqi general came to us about her," he said. She was the wife of a prominent Iraqi doctor. An ISI cell had grabbed her off the street a few weeks before and a man had begun to call the doctor's phone daily, demanding ransom payment for her return.

They said they were raping her and would continue to do it until he paid them millions of Iraqi dinar. But the doctor didn't have that kind of money. He pleaded for the Iraqi general's help in getting his wife back, and the general came straight to us.

Sadly, this wasn't an unusual situation in Iraq. ISI had employed kidnapping cells for years to target Iraqi government officials, women, and children—anyone with elevated status and money. They used the money to finance their activities. And most of the time it didn't even matter if the ransom was paid. They killed their captives anyway.

"He could really use our help if you have the time," the colleague said.

He handed me the phone number of the guy who'd been calling the doctor with the threats. It was the only clue they had to go on. This was yet another instance of a terrorist group that claimed to fight for their fellow Muslims but instead did harm to them—an everyday occurrence, it was clear from where I sat.

It was mid-deployment, sometime in the summer. We had dozens of other targets that still needed to be taken out. Guys who had killed a lot more people and were plotting against Americans back home even. I remembered thinking, *Why should I help this man I don't even know, especially when we have bigger fish to find?*

"I wish we could," I said.

People were always asking us for our help. We had started making a name for ourselves as a force who could find ghosts, guys no one else could find, and pinpoint their location in a short amount of time. So it wasn't uncommon for other military units to ask us to track down targets they had lost.

But we had our own priorities. We knew the network better than anyone—we were living and breathing it every day. And even though we officially answered to headquarters, they rarely forced missions on us because they knew the importance of staying out of our way.

"Can't you just throw up a drone?" an FBI agent asked us one day over a video meeting about the search for some target he wanted tracked down. The suit was being beamed in from a comfortable conference room in Virginia.

The question was ridiculous. *Why don't you try putting a fucking drone up and see where it gets you?*

"Drones don't work alone," I said diplomatically.

The suits never got it. They thought a drone was like a remote control airplane—just hit a few buttons and it would go to work finding whomever we needed to find. What we did was very complicated and technical. We just made drones look easy to people on the outside.

We just couldn't help everyone. There were not enough of our teams to go around.

But something in me changed that morning as I stared at the Iraqi doctor's wife's photo again. I couldn't put it down. The organs inside my chest were all tightening as if something was telling me this time was different, a feeling that I hadn't experienced in years of chasing these assholes. It hurt my head. For the first time I began to sense that I had been slowly losing what made me essentially human: the ability to care about people, about the lives around me.

Long ago, I had come to terms with the fact that we were doing bad things to very bad people, because that's the reality of what it takes to deal with fanatics who care only about killing.

The thing was, in this world, emotions couldn't apply. Emotions clouded judgment when it came to the decisions we had to make. On our drone feeds, I had to stare at families as they went about their lives, women and children, who had no idea their worlds were about to be upended forever.

I had to look at the bigger picture of our strategy, which was larger than any one person. It was about trying to save hundreds, even thousands, of lives—not one or two here and there. Because this woman didn't have anything to do with our higher-level goal, she didn't fit into my calculus.

Death happened every day. And sometimes I had to do things to remind myself that these were real human lives.

I felt light-headed as these emotions swirled inside me. I remember suddenly thinking, *What if this was a member of my family? What if this was my mother or somebody close to me?*

My inner voice wrestled with itself: If you saved this woman, it would be one of the few times that we could see the tangible results of our actions. Isn't saving this one life the real reason you're here anyway? It wouldn't even take very long, and yet it would mean the world to her family.

That's when I got up. I threw on clothes and headed for the Box.

The rest of the team was already at work. We'd been following another high-level target for the last few days, but not much had changed. We had built a solid pattern of life on the guy—he was going back and forth between work and home. Nothing unusual. I was certain we'd know where to find him again in a day or two if we redirected our drones.

"We have a new mission," I said to Kate. I held up the photo. "We are going to find this woman."

WE SPENT A COUPLE OF HOURS DIGGING INTO THE PHONE NUMBER OF THE GUY WHO had been calling the doctor's mobile. It helped that our technology was probably the best in the world. We used a special tool to ping the mobile to give us a general location of where its signal was coming from. Soon we had our startpoint.

I don't know if we were lucky that we were dealing with relative amateurs or we were just that good, but in a matter of hours we were orbiting a house in a neighborhood slum in the southern part of the city, where I was sure the woman was being kept.

The neighborhood block was a jam of worn-down concrete houses in various stages of falling apart. Some were barely standing, tilting left and right into one another, and others had no roofs at all.

It was daytime, clear and sunny, the streets full of activity, with people walking around, kids playing, and guys doing nothing much at all but smoking. Everything was covered in dust from the dirt streets.

The target house was tiny, probably just a few rooms inside. The yard out front doubled as a parking lot, with a couple of cars and a van pulled up right to the door—a sign that someone was home.

We waited out the day and watched from above. A couple of men came and went. One was a smoker. But there was no sign of the woman.

Jason and I talked it over in the Box and came to the conclusion that if there was even a slight chance she was there, we needed to go before it was too late, since her captives might move her.

We decided to strike that night. Jason and his assault force came into the Box and talked out the hostage rescue. It wasn't a typical planning session. If the woman was inside, they needed to be extra careful. When they crashed a house, everything moved lightning fast. They only had a split second to decide if the person in their crosshairs was a friend or foe. It was easy for things to go wrong. If they didn't carry out the raid just right, the doctor's wife would die.

An hour later, we were spinning up and the operators were breaking down the door. They found three men from the kidnapping cell and dragged them out to the street. The woman was locked in the back bedroom. "Got her," the radio erupted.

The barbarians had handcuffed her to an air-conditioning unit and it was clear that the men had been assaulting her. Her face was bruised and her clothes were ripped up.

The men deserved to die.

Throughout that deployment, I kept the woman's photo with me in my notebook as a reminder: in a world of all this evil, we had the power to make a difference. Saving someone good was just as important as killing and capturing our enemy.

That woman won't ever know who I am, but it felt good knowing she was safe. Despite what people said about our team and the drones we operated, despite all the bad stuff people said, we were the good guys.

18

THE BOMBING

When I picked up the phone, I knew immediately that something was up. "You hearing about these bombings in the city?" the voice said.

It was an analyst upstairs at headquarters. HQ rarely called unless there was a major situation that needed fixing fast. "We're hearing that there were just multiple coordinated blasts," he said. "You have anything for us?"

We actually didn't have much yet. Before the call, intel had only started to dribble in from our local sources. "Coordinates of one of the attack sites just came in," I said. "Let me get back to you."

I leaned over to Kate. For the last few hours, we'd been circling another target's house. But the place was looking like a dry hole. "Don't shift the Pred's orbit yet," I said. "But zoom out."

We were a few miles out from the bombings, but we could maintain orbit and still get a sense of what was going on. The camera quickly zipped away from the house and looked into the distance. Within seconds we confirmed the call. Clouds of smoke were billowing up in the horizon.

"Okay, we need to go there. Center the Pred up over that location," I said.

In minutes we were over top of what looked like a bombed-out storefront. The images were in stark black and white on two of the monitors. Smoke was still pouring out and crumpled cars littered the streets like they'd been picked up, crushed, and then thrown. Crowds surrounded it and we could see Iraqi firefighters and police climbing around the rubble.

We kept the Pred there as we sifted through the heavy chatter of intel coming in by email and phone. One report claimed multiple buildings had been completely destroyed; another report stated at least twenty-five dead, dozens more wounded. Some first responders were scared to go provide medical support at the site out of fear of a second attack, so accounts were disparate.

Most of the reports were from sources on the ground, local agents, or our Iraqi friends in the military. In a situation like this, the expanded Box in Baghdad became frenzied, like a trading floor, with people yelling back and forth as new information came in.

As the hours passed, the picture on the ground shook out. The bombers had rented out nine apartments in heavily populated markets across the city, packed them for weeks with hundreds of pounds of fertilizer bags rigged up to create bombs, and then used cell phones to detonate them all at once.

It was grim. More than eighty local Iraqi citizens had been killed, more than one hundred injured—it was one of the most lethal bombings in years. The images were devastating.

The markets were in neighborhoods dominated by Shias, meaning that there was likely only one group who could have been responsible: ISI. This attack had been professionally coordinated and meticulously planned out. Al Jazeera's news channel displayed multiple buildings burning across other parts of the city. No one had claimed responsibility yet, but one man clearly stood out to me: Dark Horse. Staring down at the smoldering death pits from the Pred's monitors, I wondered if he was sending a message—that the network was still capable of doing something at this scale, even with the heavy losses. That he wasn't hiding anymore.

The attack was a jolt to all of us, coming amid a series of calm months. Calm was relative in Iraq, of course, since it was a condition that would still be considered chaos in America. The bombings got leadership nervous that Iraq was starting to fall apart, and politically, they couldn't have that.

That night we got another call from HQ. The military higher-ups and suits at the State Department had been meeting with Iraqi politicians and generals all day. The Iraqis needed help on the attack. They didn't know where to even begin hunting the perpetrators and there was some fear that this was just the beginning. "We need you on this," HQ said.

The first thing I did was walk over to the refrigerator in the back of the Box. I grabbed a Rip It and stood there for a moment, taking a breather and feeling the carbonated caffeine start to do its work in my head. The area around the refrigerator was muddy with boot marks. I started to think about all the dead that day, the bloody photos, how many lives gone. The unlucky Iraqis who were present that day for the attack, they were powerless to do much about it. I hated that. I craved retribution.

I got to work right away. It was going to be a long night.

"HEY, YOU KNOW THE CHAPLAIN IS ALWAYS HERE?" SAID JASON SOMETIME AFTER midnight. He was sitting next to me, watching the live screens of the war-beaten city below.

There was always a military chaplain assigned to our team in case people needed help or just some consoling. A lot of the operators held their demons inside. Usually you wouldn't hear about them until a long night of drinking, when some of the stories of things they had seen and done would suddenly come vividly back to life. The stories I've heard would surprise most.

"I always ask the other operators to go, but no one goes," he said.

"All that Xbox," I said.

"It's usually me and the chaplain. It's surprising," he said.

"I don't even know where to find the guy," I said.

We laughed.

In addition to being Mr. Hollywood, Jason had this other side. He was a devout Christian even in the Box, but he wasn't a Bible thumper or anything. He was just religious and went to church regularly when he was back home.

I didn't have much time for religion and I didn't even think much about it other than how the enemy perverted their god and used him to make killing sound righteous, as if it were the only way to go to heaven.

Still, I wondered about Jason. He was a stone-cold killer by night and then heavy on his faith when he was alone and back home. I always wondered how he separated himself from the killings and justified them internally. Did he believe he was doing God's work? I never asked. It wasn't my business.

There was a long silence after that, where we both just sat there and watched the TV glow. Finally he said, "You should join me one day, if there is anything you need to talk about."

Looking back on it later, Jason was probably the only one who really saw the emotions going on inside me or sensed their absence. What the sleeplessness was all about. The growing hatred for the enemy. How the chase had totally consumed me. Maybe he thought God could help, because God helped him.

I always maintained my own faith. My mother raised me

Christian. But I was never big on attending services in those days of deployment. It seemed somewhat of a distraction from the mission. There were always other things pulling me away. Or maybe it was because I would have learned something from the chaplain about myself that I didn't want to hear, that my heart was becoming too cold to feel, my bloody hunts turning me into a ruthless version of myself that others around me no longer recognized.

I told him that I'd think about it. "Thanks, man," I said. "Maybe one day." But I knew inside that I wouldn't go. Because going meant less time hunting.

A LOT OF OUR ENEMIES HAD HUGE BOUNTIES ON THEIR HEADS—PAID FOR BY THE U.S. government. One hundred thousand dollars for one guy, $50,000 for another, a few million for others. Brooklyn and Manhattan were each worth $5 million. Dark Horse was in the six-figure range.

The State Department put out posters for them, just like the Wild West. I spent a lot of time looking at these online as they came across our screens. Some were sent internally; others were made more public. It also served as a source of pride for the terrorists, who were more than happy to see their names on the posters across the city. They were the same guys we were chasing. Wouldn't it be nice if we got a cut of that money?

The rewards would go up and down over the years depending on different things, like whether or not someone was still killing or was in hiding. I never understood who was responsible for maintaining the lists or how it worked. From what I could tell, it wasn't anyone in our larger organization.

The big money ransoms got me thinking more than once about how much money I actually made. In comparison to those rewards, what I made was practically peanuts. One late night, after a long mission, I sat in the Box and did some back-of-the-napkin math. The twenty-hour days. The 140-hour weeks. What that kind of work and pressure did to my body and my mind. I had been having trouble sleeping again.

I scribbled some quick numbers down on a notepad. My pay equated to about $6.50 per hour—below the poverty level. I laughed at that. I had a lead role in America's answer to its terrorism problem, at the tip of the spear, and doing this work for less than you can make working at McDonald's.

The math was just for kicks, to kill time when sleep didn't come. It really didn't matter to me because I loved what I was doing. Money obviously didn't drive me. It didn't drive any of us. The mission did. It had taken over my life and at that point I would have done it for free, despite the toll it had taken on my mind and body.

We were different from the agency guys. The people doing similar work on the other side of the fence, who got hefty bonuses when they found someone. Their jobs made me think of paid assassins. My friends who worked there got paid thousands of dollars every time they killed someone higher on their lists with a drone. I always found that to be contradictory to the purpose of why we existed: to go after the right targets for the overall mission, not the ones that brought the best bonuses.

THE INFORMATION COMING OUT OF THE BLAST SITES WAS LIMITED AT FIRST. LITTLE was left after the explosions and I started to worry that we might never get a lead.

With a suicide bomber, we could at least examine body parts, and IEDs left trace residue—tiny hints about what happened and where to start a hunt. But these blasts had burned hot and it seemed that the flames had turned almost everything in the buildings to dust.

The guy behind the attack appeared to know exactly what he was doing. When our Iraqi colleagues interviewed the real estate agents about who'd rented the apartments to the bombers, they were clueless. The renters used fake names and paid cash for the properties six months up front. No trace.

We worried that we'd have to forget it and move on—until we turned up a mistake. The call came into us late on the second night from our friends in the U.S. embassy. A bomb in one of the nine houses hadn't actually detonated. Somehow the cell phone didn't initiate the bomb and the site was mostly contained, with the stacked bags of fertilizer still intact. The Iraqi bomb squad had also pulled out the cell phone.

"Call them now and get that phone," I said. "Make sure they don't mess with it." Hours later, it was ours and the technicians were picking it apart. This was our first lead.

IT WAS A BRAND-NEW BLACK FLIP PHONE. NO STORED NUMBERS. BUT THERE WERE four missed calls that had been made to it that coincided with the timing of the other bombs that went off. These missed calls were likely the ones meant to detonate the bomb. We had the trigger-man's number.

A cell phone number wasn't much to go off for most people, but it was gold to the experts around me, who began to run the numbers through their laptops. We could do a lot with them, much more than most people realized. But our tools and how we used them could never be revealed to the public.

It appeared that the triggerman used his phone often, not just to detonate bombs. We couldn't figure out who owned the phone, but the techs managed to trace the calls around the time of the bombing and map out a network of the triggerman's associates. One thing stuck out. Most had links to the Wali of Baghdad—Dark Horse.

Still, we didn't have an address for anyone. None of the phones seemed to be on.

Days of grueling intelligence hunting passed. While I carried out a few missions against other targets, the techs kept working on the blasts. One night I took a break from it all and went back to my bunk, lying there in my sweat-stinking clothes for a long time before I drifted off. My pager startled me around midnight and I ran back to the Box.

"What's up?" I asked Kate.

"We got a location for the suspected triggerman," she said, pointing to the house our drone was now orbiting. The phone had been switched on and whoever had it was in there right now.

THE TRIGGERMAN'S PLACE WAS A NARROW BUILDING ALONG A QUIET STREET OF wood row houses. Few streetlights were on and most of the neighbors looked like they were already asleep, their houses dark.

Our target's place looked wide awake on the monitors. Lights on and activity. "We got movers," I said to the team.

"Have we seen this house before?" I asked Brian, as he flipped through historical satellite photos.

"Yeah, another team killed the previous owner on a mission in 2006."

"Send me whatever they got from that mission."

"Stand by."

The info popped up on my screen, but not much had been recovered, just some dead-guy photos from the scene. The guy looked like he was part of Zarqawi's old gang.

The black silhouette of what looked like a man emerged from the front door and was greeted by two others who appeared out of nowhere.

The sensor operator zoomed in. "Three MAMs," he said, referring to military-aged men. "One looks like he might have a weapon."

"Smoker there, too," said Brian.

The black glow of a cigarette expanded in high definition on our monitors. Maybe a cigarette break. A few minutes later, the cigarette was tossed to the ground and the three men returned inside.

By now, the group of Navy SEALs that worked with us on occasion had all piled into the Box. My assault crew was out on another strike so the Seals were with us tonight. And they were antsy to get out.

There was a deep rivalry between us and the SEALs—it was mostly guys competing for who was the bigger badass. But our groups had grown a lot tighter since the war on terror began. We worked closer, sharing tactics and often personnel.

The truth was everyone secretly wanted the chance internally to say they were responsible for a successful mission or to be the first called on an important raid. The goal to take out enemies was the same, but everyone wanted trophies.

The SEALs slugged coffee and munched protein bars. They started firing questions off at me. Who's in the house? What's outside? What are we missing?

Brian pulled out the route maps and put them up on the screens. It was pretty straightforward. I gave them a rundown, as they geared up and loaded weapons. Since it wasn't far to the house, they'd take the Hummers.

Usually we didn't chase a cell phone until we knew who was using it. We knew that Dark Horse's group was sophisticated and I worried that we were getting pulled into a trap—that they turned it on knowing we would come and that the cell phone was connected to a bag of fertilizer rigged to explode. Going now was definitely a risk because we didn't know what lay ahead. But we had no choice. Time was against us.

OUR BIRD PULLED PATROL AROUND THE HOUSE, IN CASE ANYTHING CHANGED OR went wrong before the SEALs arrived. We scoured every nook and cranny of the shadows, every corner high and low, anything that seemed out of place. Nothing. The smokers never came back out. But the place was still awake. Something was up in there.

"Zulu Three, checkpoint one, TOT thirty Mikes."

"Roger that."

It was about thirty minutes before the Hummers rumbled into our drone's view. They were about a block from the target and thirty SEALs jumped out. There was little talk after that. Silence was necessary. Everyone knew what to do.

Instead of charging through the door and moving in fast, they sent in a dog. I watched it stop immediately, signaling explosives on the other side. The team leader got on a bullhorn and told the people to come out. Nothing happened for a while after that. The house was motionless, as if the guys inside were trying to figure out what to do.

We kept our eyes on the roof. On the surrounding streets, neighbors had started to spill out. The scene had the potential to get ugly.

Suddenly in the black and white of the infrared, we noticed three men on the flat roof of the house. "Z in on them," I said.

All three had pistols and were huddled up, as if trying to make a choice between fighting it out or surrendering.

Seeing more than two dozen burly SEALs with assault rifles pointed straight up at them like one big arsenal ready to blow them to the moon made the decision an easy one.

Only a few seconds more and the SEALs would have lit the

entire house and rooftop up, violently ending any chance the targets had at survival.

I was personally hoping they chose death. I wanted them not to return alive. If these guys were even remotely responsible for the bombings, they deserved their instant execution on that very rooftop.

What was it going to be?

Finally, their hands went up, their guns thrown down in the process. They chose to live for the time being, though again I was disappointed in their choice. It was over.

When the operators swept the house later, they found hundreds of pipe bombs, fertilizer, guns, and mortar rounds. The men had been using the house to construct various smaller explosives. They confessed that the pipe bombs were going to be used during the upcoming Iraqi elections, distributed at different polling sites to create havoc during the new democratic election process.

We brought them back to the Box and it didn't take long before they admitted their roles in the previous nine bombings. None of them, however, mentioned Dark Horse. Maybe they were scared shitless of him or maybe they just had no idea. In the end, it didn't matter.

A few days later, Dark Horse made his own mistake.

19

DARK HORSE

"Are you fucking kidding me?"

Mark and I were at our desks in the Box, scanning reports, watching the drone feeds on a mission in progress when the intel about Dark Horse came in.

"This doesn't seem right," I said.

"What do you mean?"

"The intercept I just got says he's been captured at a checkpoint."

"It's probably a rumor again," Mark said.

It was March 2010. Mark and I shrugged the report off at first. We had known for years that Dark Horse had a twin brother and intelligence services and even other terrorist leaders within his same network regularly mixed the two of them up. But we happened to have the less barbaric brother in custody, so this time we figured it was simply bad intel.

Yet soon after, our resident source handler, Tom, came rushing in with the same news. "It's true," he said. "They got him!"

A zap of electricity hit me. Captures never happened this way. Checkpoints were usually for the minnows, not the sharks. At this point Dark Horse was one of the most wanted men in the country. Photos of him had been posted nearly everywhere in Baghdad by Iraqi forces looking for information on his whereabouts. It wasn't like him. He must have gotten sloppy. Being on the run for nearly eight years did that to a man. But perhaps it had just been us, our doggedness. We had spent so much time and resources on smoking him out.

Dark Horse had not only been captured, but captured alive. We were the only U.S. military group that seemed to know they had him; even the rest of the coalition forces spread throughout the country had not picked up on it yet. I should have been happy about that—he could give us so much intel—but there was one potential wrinkle. He was now in the hands of an Iraqi death squad who had grabbed him up at a random checkpoint when he presented a fake ID.

The squad was an ultrasecretive, extraterritorial strike force controlled by Iraqi prime minister Nouri al-Maliki and tasked with hunting Al Qaeda and ISI figures. Many saw them as Maliki's personal hit squad, designed to target political rivals with force. None of their captors stayed alive for long . . . hence the hit squad.

I had no idea if we would even be able to get to Dark Horse. Was he even still alive? The Iraqis could easily tell us to fuck off and kill him.

We needed to move fast. I braced for fierce pushback as we kitted up, jumped in our up-armored vehicles, and headed into the city for a visit with the Iraqi general behind the squad.

It was me, Mark, Jason, and the source handler Tom. Tom was CIA trained and played a key role with many of the targets we took down. He had an office just behind the Box and his job was to recruit sources on the ground and squeeze them for information. As a full-fledged case officer, he was as good as they get.

The general's office was on the other side of the city in a government building. We'd called ahead to let him know we were coming and that we wanted to talk about Dark Horse; that way we didn't have to beat around the bush. One of his staffers met us at the front and led us inside to a room of dark brown couches and a big oak table. Steaming tea was served.

When the general came in, he acted like he knew nothing at all. He sat down at the head of the table in a brown leather chair with gold trim. It seemed higher up than all of us, like a judge in a courtroom. His military uniform was like a Christmas tree, it had so many medals.

"I don't know what you're talking about, we don't have him," he said, sitting back in his chair with a wide smile that suggested he knew exactly what we were talking about.

Tom wasn't having that, though, and laid it all out. "Listen, General," he said, leaning across the table. "The men in this room are the best in the business. You should trust we know what we are doing."

The tension was high. The general was definitely more curious about us than ever now. He was used to lying to the regular military units, but he had never come across guys like us. He looked at us like he was feeling us out, making silent calculations about what to do. I got the feeling he was playing with us. Tom did most of the talking, but I spoke up when the general wanted to know if we understood who Dark Horse was. "What do you know about him?" he asked.

"We've been tracking him for years," I said, ticking off a bunch of his close associates that we'd either killed or captured recently. I told him Dark Horse was likely one of a few left who had contact with Manhattan and Brooklyn. "He could be the key to the extinction of the entire ISI network."

The general just nodded, not giving up much. That went on for more than an hour. At one point he waved his hand, calling in for more tea.

Finally, Tom had enough. "We know you have him," he said. "We want to meet him. And we can help you in return." We offered up years of intelligence on Dark Horse and promised access to drones on missions we worked on together going forward.

A few seconds of silence passed. I remembered the general scratching his chin and staring at all of us as if he were about to make a big poker bet. He turned to his aide, who had been standing silently behind him the whole time, and talked quietly to him in Arabic.

When he turned back to us, the feeling in the room changed, the tension suddenly gone. "Okay," he said, smiling, as if he were the one who had won and we were now all friends. "You will go see him today."

NO ONE IN THE U.S. GOVERNMENT HAD EVER SEEN DARK HORSE IN PERSON, BUT later that afternoon I was on my way to meet him.

The prison was about thirty minutes away from the general's office, hidden at the edge of an old, unused Iraqi airport and inside a run-down set of buildings that looked like military barracks. Our government didn't even know the place existed.

An Iraqi officer who worked for the general met us at the gate and walked us in. It was just me, our interpreter, and Tom. The others had stayed behind at the Box.

The place was heavily guarded by Iraqi military personnel, but you couldn't tell until you walked into the compound. Guards appeared out of nowhere as we walked into the main courtyard, some of them coming in to look out windows in the one-story building rising above us. It felt like an old western where the out-of-town cowboys walk into a bar and the piano player stops, with everyone turning around looking.

A few guards stepped out of doorways as we passed, lighting up cigarettes, smoking and gesturing toward us as they talked among themselves. It was clear that Americans were never brought here. The prison was their version of a black site, where they hid detainees. The people who were brought here were meant to disappear.

We walked inside, down a long, dimly lit hallway. The Iraqi officer didn't say anything and our feet were loud on the concrete floors. Doors were closed as we passed, as if most things were off-limits and they didn't want us to know the war crimes that lay behind them. We came to a stop and the Iraqi officer turned around and spoke to our interpreter.

I couldn't keep still, all these anxious thoughts flooding my mind. Finally, the officer made a sign with his hand and we crossed another courtyard and walked into another building. The place was a maze of concrete floors and walls. It was darker and damper and dirtier, and I felt in my gut like we were stepping into the worst kind of haunted house.

The lights began to flicker along the way, the open air-conditioning in the hallway dripping water onto the ground. Peeled white paint was everywhere. Handprints of dried blood on the walls from who knows what. The floors were covered in dirt and muddy boot prints from people coming and going. Behind one door I could hear a man screaming in pain. He was clearly being beaten. The air was hot and stale and smelled like death. The screaming echoed around the halls until it was just our boots again.

We walked down one hallway, past doors that were shut up with more prisoners. It seemed like they had dozens of people locked up. The officer finally stopped and opened a door. He nodded, as if to say, This is it.

When we entered, the room was surprisingly nice, considering the hell we had just walked through to get there. The room was large and windowless with a glass wall unit full of old weapons, medals, and photos on one side. Deep leather couches ran the full length of the room. Behind a large dark wood desk was another Iraqi officer, who gestured for us to sit down.

I pulled out a key chain with a secret pinhole camera built into it and laid it on the table next to me. Through our interpreter we talked back and forth with the officer at the desk. He was in charge of the site and there was something oddly cold about him. I didn't think too much about it then, though, because I was anxious to meet Dark Horse. I still didn't believe he was actually there, that the general was telling the truth—and that I was about to meet him.

The Iraqi government officials we worked with over the years were notorious liars. When you listened to some of them talk, you would think the entire war had already been won by them, that we could all go home. For the last decade of the war, I couldn't recall one single instance where the Iraqis had ever captured or killed a senior-level terrorist figure without the direct help of U.S. forces. So the fact that they had captured Dark Horse on their own was still a bit shocking to me. I didn't believe it. All I kept thinking was, *I'm about to meet a guy we've been chasing for years.* The five or ten minutes of waiting condensed, as my mind flipped through all those years of hunting, the horror this guy had inflicted on the world, the families he'd destroyed, the U.S. soldiers he'd killed, and how the hell he'd managed to elude capture for so long.

When Dark Horse finally walked in, I clicked the key chain and the camera began to record.

I expected him to enter the room in handcuffs and an orange

prison suit with armed guards, like any prisoner in the United States. After all, this guy had murdered thousands of innocent civilians over the years. But it wasn't like that at all. Dark Horse didn't have any guards walking with him and he wore street clothes—a black and white Adidas tracksuit and an untucked long sleeve shirt underneath. It was strange. No handcuffs. He seemed to move as if he didn't have a care in the world.

I made a quick glance over at Tom sitting next to me, as if to silently ask him if he was seeing what I was seeing. His reaction was the same as mine. *You got to be fucking kidding me.*

At first, I had my hand on my Glock sidearm, thinking Dark Horse might lunge at me. He'd spent his life trying to kill Americans and wouldn't think twice about trying to kill us. He was clearly surprised to see Americans, too. He did a double take as he walked past us, stopped for a second, and then glanced over at the Iraqi officer behind the desk as if to seek direction on what to do. The officer gestured to him as if to say, Go ahead and relax. "Hello," he finally said with a smile and sat down in a couch across from us.

He had black eyes, black hair, and his eyebrows were thick and overgrown across his forehead. A thick mustache curled downward slightly at the ends but was just short of a handlebar. His hair was messed up, as if he'd been sleeping. He didn't look at us at first, just stared off at the wall or down at his knees.

I watched him for a few minutes, trying to catch his eyes as they darted like cars around the room, but he eluded me. He had a nervous tic of running one finger across his mustache.

"What is your name?" I asked him.

He wouldn't answer me right away. He looked back at the colonel behind the desk, seeking approval to speak. He didn't quite understand what was going on. The colonel and he went back and forth in Arabic before he finally answered.

"I am Manaf al-Rawi."

We spent three hours there that first day and he didn't say much. We didn't tell him our names and he didn't ask for them. We came back the next day and the next and he mostly fed us things we already knew, things that he knew we already knew. He was messing with us.

It wasn't until a few days later that he began to open up and talk about Manhattan and Brooklyn.

Who knows why he started talking a bit more. Maybe he thought it was a way out. Maybe he heard the screams from the other prisoners dragged through the halls. Maybe he wanted to prolong his own inevitable death.

"The last time I saw them in person was 2006," he said. He told us he only communicated with Manhattan and Brooklyn by letters via a courier system.

Dark Horse eventually provided a basic understanding of the courier network, which, although lacking in any significant detail, became very important later. His notes to Manhattan and Brooklyn were passed along through a series of people, who made their way north. Days or weeks later a response would come back through the same system. The couriers were also switched out regularly to confuse security services from picking up a trace.

For a minute, I thought we had them. "Is that where Manhattan and Brooklyn are? Up north?"

He smiled, blocking us again. "I don't know anything more."

He didn't budge on that. Perhaps he thought he'd given us enough about the leaders and we'd be satisfied and that he could now wait us out. But the Iraqis hovered. They had their own ways of questioning and we preferred not to know about them. There would be a time and place for enhanced interrogations. From what I'd witnessed, that kind of pressure had directly led to the capture or killing of numerous high-level targets.

Not long after, he had a surprise. "Do you really want to know something?" It was followed by that smile again. This was one of the only times he looked directly at me. He said he'd put into motion four separate operations before he'd been caught. "Believe it or not," he said. He crossed his legs and sat back on the couch, like he was in Club Med. He was clearly ready to die for his cause.

Suddenly talkative, he happily detailed the operations. His hands made large gestures as if to signal a big explosion, as our interpreter quickly translated the Arabic for us. He smiled as he talked about the destruction he had put into play, like a serial killer laying out his master plan. I could tell he was enamored with himself, as if he weren't even in prison, like he still had full control over his sprawling network.

He said a plane was going to crash into an Iraqi government building; Iraqis turning out to vote would be killed by hundreds of small pipe bombs laid out in the city during the upcoming parliamentary elections; and four different foreign embassies in Baghdad would be attacked.

This was as specific as he'd get; he left out any information that would have allowed us to stop the attacks, and he refused to help anymore. He was bragging, letting us know the man we were dealing with and that there was nothing we could do.

Other teams scrambled to decrypt what he said, but soon it was too late. Three of the four attacks ended up occurring, including a multipronged suicide car bombing at the Egyptian, Iranian, and Syrian embassies as well as the German ambassador's residence. Hundreds of people were hurt.

"You see," he said when we saw him after the attack. "I wasn't lying." Then he didn't tell us anything else for a long time.

FOR THE NEXT FEW WEEKS, I CONTINUED TO HUNT DOWN OTHER TARGETS WHILE TOM and other members of our team returned daily to visit Dark Horse.

We picked up a guy whose fingerprints were on an exploded car bomb; another who was about to begin flight training in the

United States; two more who had been distributing ISI propaganda videos showcasing their horrific attacks on U.S. forces. Another night we killed a leader within the network's military cell called the "special groups." Then one of the cell's finance heads. We were running through the key fighters fast. Collectively we had already picked off eight of the top twenty targets in the country from the list we started with.

When our interrogators started talking to them after capture, most played dumb. "What are you talking about? I don't know any bad people," one said. Another said, "You have the wrong guy." This was typical, but I did run into one at the time who seemed to be refreshingly honest. He was a midlevel player in ISI, more of a soldier than a planner. "Sir," he said, straight-faced, "I don't know anyone who isn't Al Qaeda." Then he told us all he knew and led us to a few more.

There was a stretch where we did two or three new missions each night—and everything began to click.

This was the first time that I felt in total control, that we could find anyone we wanted, even starting with the most insignificant morsel of information. That control made me feel like our team couldn't be stopped. I loved every minute of it. It was just a matter of time before we uncovered that one crucial lead that would take us straight to the top.

In my head, I mapped out how we were going to work our way to Manhattan and Brooklyn. We were unraveling the Baghdad network, one target after another, night after night. Even though ISI had tried to shroud their organizational leadership in secrecy, I could tell you exactly who filled what leadership positions, even when others in the organization remained in the dark. My craft became more and more refined, because there was never a moment when I wasn't thinking about the intel coming in and how to fill the missing gaps. I had been so connected to how their network functioned that I could have taken leadership over one of the ISI terrorist cells and never skipped a beat. And when our team killed or captured the new guys, we knew who their replacements would be—before they were even officially replaced.

Every new piece of intelligence, every interrogation, every photo, every tip from our sources on the ground brought the cell into greater focus. Then they went up on my computer charts, like one big family tree diagram.

I'd spent so much time with the drones now that I knew the technology to a T, how to use each capability to our advantage. I regularly had two or three birds stacked on top of each other as I played chess with the enemy, following one target and then peeling one off to follow another.

I reacted faster. I made calculations without second thoughts. Tactical patience had seeped into me. All the missions had given me experience and knowledge. I could quickly determine if a guy we were staring at was an innocent civilian or the actual enemy hiding in the crowd. My team worked efficiently, knowing what each was going to do before doing it. We spoke in half sentences or a couple of words sometimes.

Running missions felt like second nature now. I could spit out everything about these targets, their life stories and in which areas they were likely hiding. Before, we were spies in the sky. Now it felt like we were living with our enemies, getting into their heads as they moved through their days. In a lot of cases, it felt as if I knew more about my targets than their own families did.

Our successes were briefed to the highest levels of leadership. Our higher-ups told us that some of the captures made it into the president's daily brief. The requests for help on other targets only made things more frenzied. The CIA wanted us to hit a guy in the south. The FBI wanted us to look into someone moving IEDs with connections stretching back to people in the United States.

At one point, I was sleeping three hours a night, the drone

feed on my TV a kind of never-ending night-light keeping the dark away. It was the same story with my unit's other teammates at their locations in the north and west. We all gelled together and fed off one another. We talked at night over video teleconferences and shared leads.

"They're on the run," Jack said one night. "We're hearing more and more guys packing up their operations and moving into Syria."

"They're actually killing off members of their own cells because they're so paranoid of rats," said Andy.

"A few less targets for us to worry about," I said with a laugh.

"We also just got a report that the leaders were telling their guys not to wear wristwatches into meetings anymore," Jack went on.

"What?"

"They think we have those bugged, too."

"No more Swatches," I said. "We're in their heads."

"Let's keep up the pressure," said the overall commander. "We're in their homes and they know they can't live there anymore."

ONE NIGHT JACK CALLED FROM HIS SITE UP NORTH AND TOLD ME TO TAKE A LOOK AT his drone feed. "Hey, man, flip one of your screens to my channel."

I called out to get it on one of our big screens.

"Check it out," Jack said. "That's the military emir of Mosul right there. He's on the run." He laughed, almost as if to say . . . this guy is about to meet his maker.

"Hell yeah," I responded.

The target was hopping from roof to roof, with Iraqi security forces giving chase. Jack's operators had brought in the Iraqis on this mission, and the target had escaped before they had a chance to grab him in his house.

The Iraqis worked with us on a lot of missions. Worked with us—well, that was a bit of an overstatement. The Iraqis had to be a part of our operations more and more in Baghdad because a new government law required us to have at least one Iraqi on every U.S. mission—a kind of marketing campaign to put an "Iraqi face" on strikes, even when the Iraqis didn't do much at all. We didn't allow them into the Box, but they went out with the operators. Later, news stories would come out saying that the Iraqis were responsible for killing so-and-so. That was usually an exaggeration. It was our guys and we just dragged some of the Iraqi forces along for the ride. Which was the case now.

Jack said, "Look, he's about to run out of rope!"

The roof hopper was still being pursued and managing to evade the Iraqi forces, who looked like they were losing wind.

Every so often the target turned around and shot his gun, which slowed the Iraqis even more. The hopper might have gotten away if it weren't for his own miscalculation. Eventually he arrived at a roof that was too low to get to another roof and too high to jump to the ground. So he crouched down behind a wall in one corner, as if to hide.

The drone camera parked right over top of him. I put my headset on to listen in on the comms. Because they could see the same live drone feed from their location out in the field, the assault team on the ground was communicating over the radio his exact hiding location to the Iraqi security forces, who couldn't tell where he was exactly. Now they slowly made their way to him.

When the hopper noticed, he started firing his gun, popping up and down from his corner. The Iraqis then started lobbing grenades at him, one by one. I could see the grenades landing on the roof from the drone. The first one wounded him, but he was still alive. I could see him stumbling around, still trying to hide as he crouched in the corner. Another grenade came after, *boom,* followed by a big cloud of smoke. That one got him. We watched the hopper die slowly, his body bleeding while we orbited over top.

"Good, another shithead off the list," Jack said.

"Yeah," I said, "thanks for my daily dose of Kill TV," before signing off.

Meanwhile, Dark Horse wasn't talking—and we needed that to change fast.

"I got an idea," the case officer Tom said one night. "Remember the twin brother?"

After weeks of interrogation, we were tired of Dark Horse's bullshit and his repeated lies about the current state of Manhattan and Brooklyn, where his other ISI commanders were hiding, and where the next attack would take place. I worried that we were losing time in our hunt to find Manhattan and Brooklyn. We knew he kept lying about not knowing anything and that he was buying days for the network to adapt to his capture.

Tom decided it was time to bring his twin brother into the mix. He had been in custody for some time after the previous team captured him.

Tom visited the twin at another prison and kept going back for days before he caved. Gradually, Tom convinced him that it was his brother's actions over the years that had landed him in jail, and that Dark Horse was bringing shame on their family, which meant everything in this culture.

The twin, Ahmed al-Rawi, stirred with anger. Now all we needed was to engineer the moment when he came face-to-face with his brother, neither expecting to see the other in our custody.

We transported Dark Horse to the twin's prison and watched the two talk on a video screen. They hugged each other as though they hadn't seen each other in years, and might never again. They were already cracking, just in the initial encounter of seeing each other in this way, handcuffed, defeated mentally, and in orange jumpsuits. The initial loving embrace ended quickly as things sank in.

The twin's face turned to one of anger, as if disappointed in his brother and what he had done. All of his killing had finally caught up with him, Allah had brought him there for his sins, and the tension in the cell quickly boiled. He looked at Dark Horse as if he had been contemplating for months what he would say if he ever got the chance.

The long and the short of the twin's message to Dark Horse: the Americans know everything, they are in complete control, and the only thing Dark Horse is doing now is screwing his family. The twin encouraged him to cooperate, in the hopes that there might be a small chance to save what was left of his broken family.

Dark Horse began to cry. He put his hands up to his face and looked down at the ground. That's when we knew we had him beat. The twin was a real-life version of Dark Horse's conscience. Tom had broken him.

I've seen enough of this stuff to know that no matter how hard someone is, putting a guy in a box for a couple of months and introducing the sight of his family does something to him.

This was the turning point we'd been waiting on for years.

20
MANHATTAN AND BROOKLYN

I visited Dark Horse a few days later.

This time he was in an empty tiled room in our compound, behind the Box—a bit of change in scenery from the same ratty couch where we'd met before.

"Hello," he said. His voice was soft, barely audible. He looked smaller somehow, less confident. His clothes were looser on his body; he'd lost weight in his face. When I'd first met him, he was arrogant, still ruthless and loud like he was in control, even though he was in custody. Now he looked mostly at the cold floor, like he knew we owned him.

I brought out some photos of targets from a file and placed them on the floor. As I stood over him, he squatted down to look. Two Iraqi officers looked on from each side of the room. He seemed scared, like an alley cat in a corner. But of course, he had no idea what was going to happen next—I would have been scared, too.

We sat with him for hours and he began giving us information on everything and everyone that he knew about. There was no more bullshit this time. He even knew about attacks that were being planned to hit the World Cup in South Africa that year. We immediately passed the information to the CIA.

One target he mentioned was on our kill list: ISI's new military commander in the north. We sent the intel to Jack's team, who took him out that night.

Around the same time, Dark Horse gave us locations of weapons and explosives hidden across the city, and, most important, where his seven lieutenants were shacked up. These were the guys who carried out the bombings that he'd bragged about a few weeks before. That night, we sent out a team to take them down.

The birds went up to each of the locations and Jason got started on strike plans—they'd hit all seven locations simultaneously, with support from the Iraqi special forces elements. If we didn't do them all at once, the guys would figure out that their cells had been compromised and flee.

It was past midnight in early April. I remember having been up nearly seventy-two hours. I'd probably gone through a case of Frosted Flakes.

With the drones overhead, we began to scour each site for any sign of weapons, explosives, vehicles, slant counts, everything—all so that the various raid teams could be fully briefed before going in.

My head worked through the dangers as the operators headed out with our new Iraqi partners. Part of me wondered if Dark Horse was setting us up. You never completely know if a detainee is leading you to a trap. The other possibility was that he was sending us to innocents.

I watched now as each of our teams stormed into the seven

homes, blowing off the doors with charges, seeing the quick flashes of light in the infrared camera, and then the men being led out minutes later.

We captured a slew of ISI operatives that night, but one of them was particularly important—Dark Horse's uncle.

He was a senior courier in the Manhattan-Brooklyn chain and was due to make a special delivery the very next day.

Uncle was a mother lode and changed everything. This was when our takedown mission of the top two leaders of ISI began in earnest.

THE IRAQIS IMMEDIATELY GRABBED THE UNCLE AND BROUGHT HIM BACK TO ONE OF their holding cells and got to work shaking him down for information. A few members of our team went along.

He sat slumped in a chair in a barren concrete room. Uncle was fat and bald, with a scrappy beard, and wore the traditional white robe. He said his job was to deliver a letter in a yellow envelope to another man, who would then deliver it to someone else, all the way up, hopefully, to Abu Ayyub al-Masri and Abu Umar al-Baghdadi—Manhattan and Brooklyn.

Uncle had never interacted before with the other couriers in the chain, except for a man he passed a letter to each week. The courier chain had been set up in a way that allowed for extreme compartmentalization in the event that any one link was discovered.

If Uncle or any other courier in the chain didn't show up at a juncture, the courier network would evaporate. All messages would be destroyed and a whole new system would rise up in its place.

At first, Uncle was reluctant to work with us. But the threat of the Iraqis carting him off to some dank underground prison, where all bets were off, changed that.

We learned that the courier chain, which was swapped out every three months, brought information weekly and always in person to the "Sheikhs"—Manhattan and Brooklyn.

Uncle provided limited details about it, but enough to verify that a letter was about to go out. "They expect me tomorrow," he said.

He was expected to pass it off to the next courier in the chain by hiding it in a flowerpot. The letter was destined for Manhattan, but it was unclear how many other members in the courier chain would have to pass the message and the level of scrutiny it would receive before reaching the top.

As much as we wanted to look at the letter, we didn't. It was kept sealed in the yellowish envelope. Any signs of tampering might blow up the mission. Tom knew we had to act fast.

"We got to go then," Tom said to him.

His eyes widened. "Where?" For a moment, he probably thought he'd done his part and it was over.

"You're going back in."

"No way, I'm not crazy."

"You'll go," he said. "You'll carry the letter to the next guy as planned." Uncle looked over at the Iraqi officer who was giving him a dead-man stare.

This was our plan: we'd take Uncle to the drop off and have him hand off a flowerpot containing the letter for the sheiks, tagged with a tracking device. The flowerpot was how it was always delivered.

The Iraqi element we were working with, however, had different plans for Uncle—they only wanted to capture the next courier, and were extremely reluctant to consider what we call an "IMINT [imagery intelligence] follow"—essentially using a drone to follow the entire chain of couriers up to the top. They didn't get it.

Negotiations were always delicate with the Iraqis. They were reluctant, but we were convincing. When we got them to come around, Uncle was sweating bullets. He kept shaking his head. If the man he was meeting sensed something out of place, he'd kill him, and his family. "We're all dead," he said, drawing his hand across his neck.

"Better be Hollywood," I said.

He didn't understand.

"Just be a good actor."

We washed his clothing to get rid of any evidence that he'd been in custody and gave him muscle relaxers to ease his anxiety. That didn't help. But it was time to go.

We swept Uncle into a chopper with Tom and the operators and they raced off to another safe house, closer to the exchange spot in the city of Samarra.

That afternoon, the team bought new flowers and a random pot from a local store and got a blue bongo truck, which was out-fitted with our geo trackers. Uncle's cover story was that he'd been in a car accident and was borrowing someone's truck (the blue bongo).

We worked all night. Because the initial courier meeting site was far away from my location and closer to Jack's battlespace, he now had control of the drones, which were sent in from Boxes across Iraq. When Uncle headed out at 7 A.M., we had three drones stacked in the sky.

It took some time to find the meeting site. Uncle was unclear of which way to travel, since he was coming from the north. The meeting was supposed to occur soon and if we missed it the whole thing was shot.

After a flurry of direction requests and instructions, we finally found the spot. Two support sedans containing the Iraqi special force staked out the drop by faking car trouble on the side of the road. Within minutes of Uncle arriving at the location, we watched from our eye in the sky as the next courier arrived.

Jason's team stood off while Uncle passed off the flowerpot to the new courier. We paid attention closely to every little movement—how the men embraced each other, the handoff. Our three drones stacked above them, feeding the images back to the wall of TVs. Other days we might have had a dozen different missions up on the screens. Today this was the main event on every monitor.

I remembered being worried that Uncle might tip him off, and we watched closely for any sign of that, but the exchange was made without incident, and now we were in pursuit of the second courier, whom we nicknamed Charlie, with the drone.

YOU'D THINK WE HAD THIS IN THE BAG NOW, BUT THIS WAS WHERE YOU COULD EASily and suddenly lose control over an operation.

We were following a guy who didn't know he was being followed, but we had no eyes on him except for the birds. Sure, the tracking devices were worth something—up to a point. But our enemy could swap cars, flowerpots, and everything else with tags and they'd be nearly invisible.

Preds were technological marvels, but they're still technology, and I knew that at any second something could go wrong. The camera could malfunction for no reason or the Pred's wings could start to ice because of cold temperatures, forcing it to return to base. A mission like this brought stress into high definition. One wrong move or technological mishap and we were back to zero.

We followed Charlie as he traveled north up the main highway, farther into the desert, where goats and sheep were scattered about. A mission like this could go on for hours. Time tended to bend and you'd lose track of the hours. But at least for this leg of it, Charlie only drove for about thirty minutes before pulling over to the side of the road.

We could see another vehicle arriving from the opposite direction.

"Center up on that," the message came over the chat lines.

"Roger that."

This was another messy junction. Depending on who and how many people popped out, and where they went from there, the fact remained that we only had enough drones to follow three targets.

A heavy quiet fell over the Box. I held my breath as the scene unfolded.

The second vehicle arrived and a man exited the white truck to meet Charlie. They greeted each other, the new guy gave Charlie a tire, and Charlie in turn took the flowerpot from the back of his truck and handed it to the new guy.

While this happened, we logged every action taken by every individual as well as details about location and time, both for review later and for the record should we come back on another op.

Once they traded items, the new guy climbed back into his truck and headed north along the highway. We called this new courier Precious Cargo. On the radio, he was just PC.

Charlie headed back south along the highway toward Uncle. As soon as he arrived back at the original meet-up site, he was detained by our Iraqi support element, who had begun frantically calling over the radio that they were being trailed by armed militants. That turned out not to be true—just paranoia.

We had to keep everyone calm because news could travel fast, and any visible blowup could result in word—somehow—getting up the chain.

With Charlie taken care of, the Pred trailing him peeled off and rejoined the operation following PC as he continued farther north.

We were guessing—maybe also hoping—that PC was the last

guy in the chain. The one who would lead us to two of the most wanted men in the world.

PC DROVE AROUND FOR HOURS. HE STOPPED AT A NUMBER OF DIFFERENT LOCATIONS— various houses and stores. He traveled out to the middle of the desert, and then back into little villages.

Each place he stopped, we took notes. These sites—especially any houses—would be targets of strikes later. All the while, the drone cameras were snapping hundreds of photos of each location, cataloging them, along with every GPS point—streets, neighborhoods, mosques. The sophistication of special operations had increased exponentially in part because we were literally mapping the earth.

In the afternoon, PC took his white bongo to a car dealership that had thirty or forty identical white bongos. Turned out PC thought something was up and was trying to ditch his car for another. The dealer didn't take it, though, lucky for us, and PC was stuck.

This was a screwup. PC had been trained to abort the delivery if he thought he was being followed, and clearly he thought he was, since not more than an hour later we saw him throw a large object out of his window into the desert—the flowerpot with the message.

"Something's wrong," I chatted up Jack on our internal chat system.

"It doesn't make sense what he's doing. He keeps stopping in random places and now he just threw the plant out the window. Are the birds too low?"

"They're low. But any higher and we'll be blocked by cloud cover."

"Damn, this is a good sign, though. It means he's up to no good."

"Yeah, you're right," Jack replied.

PC kept going. But soon the weather began to turn. I saw the clouds building in the sky on the monitors. A dark, rolling ocean. "This isn't good," I said to Jack as our birds headed straight into the storm.

We all strained at the monitors, as if that might push back the clouds. But soon enough the clouds had blacked out the cameras and one of the bird's wings began to ice up. That drone had to be brought back to base before a mishap occurred.

Ten more minutes passed and then—PC was gone.

Where the hell did he go? None of the drones had him.

My gut dropped, as I stared at the now totally blackened TV screens. The cameras just streaming back clouds. No bongo. No PC.

Everyone was freaking out.

Some members of the team were cursing the screens, as if fate somehow was not on our side. The odds stacked against us. Why now?

Our internal chat lines were overflowing with new orders and actions needed to reestablish visual.

If PC was completely lost, there was a contingency. The operators were prepping from the safe house to take the first two original couriers, Uncle and Charlie, into the desert to see if they had any idea where PC was going.

The mapping analyst located up north supporting the mission had an idea. Quickly he began to calculate a bunch of different predictions of where the bongo might be if and when the clouds cleared, based on the speed of the truck at its last known point coupled with the speed of the drone.

Once the coordinates were received, the bird's thermal camera sensor was directed there—and we hoped for the best. Five more minutes passed and it felt like hours.

Where was he? Everything building to this moment could be

lost. Now we could see small breaks in the fast-moving weather, like a fuzzy cable channel crashing between crystal clarity and black and gray lines. Each time a break appeared, nothing was showing between the desert floor and our bird thousands of feet up.

The seconds that followed almost stood still.

It was as if someone had heard our prayers, because suddenly the bongo appeared back on our screen. Brian nearly collapsed right in front of me in relief. The bet paid off. We were lucky.

OUT AT THE MAIN COMMAND SITE, DEEP IN THE DESERT, MILES AWAY FROM THE BOX, the operators were ready to go. Jason and his men were suited up, armed to the teeth and closely monitoring the live drone feeds with their Black Hawks on standby.

Day turned to night and soon PC was turning down a desert road, heading deeper into nowhere. Was this his ultimate destination? The top brass at our higher HQ were now tuned into the drone feeds from their main command center. The most senior commanders back in D.C. and in different combat zones were also tuned in to the feed. "Kill TV" was what we called the drone channel.

Even though we didn't know for sure where PC was headed, there was a thrill in the air because five years of hunting was about to come to an end. What was unfolding now could result in one of the most important discoveries in years.

The road was straight as a razor and eventually led to a very small dirt compound with nothing in either direction for miles. On the screen, I could see a few animals mulling around outside. Goats.

"Z in one," Jack told the camera operator. He wanted to see the hut and there it was: body heat signatures, little black ghosts, leaked out of the north side of the dark building. No guards with weapons around or anything from what I could tell.

"What do you think? Could this be it?" Jack chatted me up.

"Well, if I was on the run, that's where I would be—in the middle of fucking nowhere," I replied.

PC came to a stop and climbed out of the bongo. But then he did something that suddenly got everyone uneasy. Instead of entering immediately into the compound, he walked a few hundred feet out into the desert and looked upward. We could see him looking hard into the black night sky. Like he'd heard something. Was he looking for us?

PC FINALLY ENTERED THE HUT AFTER HIS WALK OUT TO THE DESERT. AFTER ABOUT thirty minutes, it was clear he wasn't going anywhere else for the rest of the night. Jason made the call to proceed, and he told the operators to get ready. "Kit up, we depart within the hour."

As the drone scanned the hut, we couldn't be certain how many people were in there, but if this was Manhattan and Brooklyn's location, then at least some of them were going to be heavily armed and would not be taken alive.

Brian got to work right away at mapping out the hut and annotating the maps of the area. Everyone worked with absolute focus, as if our lives depended on this moment working out. Radio chatter interrupted long seconds of working silence.

The commander controlling the operation had ultimately decided against bombing the site. It would have to be a raid. It was just impossible to know who exactly was in the hut and we didn't want to kill a house full of women and children. We couldn't confirm that Manhattan and Brooklyn were in there.

But a raid involved a human risk on our side. Whenever the raid team was sent in, there was an understanding that the target was worth the risk.

The operators always relied on my team, as much as I relied on them to finish the mission on the ground. We were all brothers in this.

I remembered the operator who came back after a mission with blood all over him, asking me who he had just killed.

As the team suited up with their weapons and planned the chopper routes, they also closely studied the layout of the hut through the drone feed: two or three rooms, a carport off to the side, where the bongo truck had parked, and the whole property surrounded by a six-foot mud wall.

The usual target cards were passed out containing the photos of other bad guys that they might find at the various sites. I also got on the phone with Jason and reiterated to him the historical intel we had on Manhattan and Brooklyn.

"These guys wear suicide vests like we wear socks," I told him. "If they're in there, odds are they won't come out alive."

Along PC's route, there were seven separate houses that he had stopped at on his drive through the desert. All would be raided almost simultaneously. The leaders could be in any of them.

Given the number of locations and the distance between them, the operation was too big for our team to carry out alone, so Jason had decided to hit the main courier house and bring in Army Rangers to hit the other six locations.

Jason's initial entry plan was simple. They would take the choppers right to the top of the main target site, where the guys would fast-rope down and storm the place.

"You're set," I said. "Good luck."

"See you when we get back."

THE WEATHER BEGAN TO TURN BAD AGAIN. MORE STORM CLOUDS ROLLING IN THE sky, sharp winds blowing around sand, making it hard for everyone to see.

When the Hawks lifted off at 2 A.M., we had three Preds circling the compound, watching the empty desert for an ambush. The extreme high winds combined with the dust made the visibility for Jason's team almost zero—dangerous conditions for flying choppers, even for the best pilots in the world. But the team was pushing through it either way. There was no turning back now. This was one opportunity we couldn't afford to wait on.

And then word of tragedy hit. As our choppers began their descent at the main site, an urgent call shot over the radio: "Eagle down, eagle down." A chopper with a Ranger team had gone down on the way to one of the courier station sites. A wind gust knocked it off balance and its rotors went spinning into the desert.

We didn't have visibility on it so the call was immediately made to redirect one of the drones from the main house to the crash site.

Soon the wreckage came into stark and terrible view in black and white on our TVs. The chopper was lying on its side and burning while half the Rangers scrambled to secure the area and recover the injured.

More bad news immediately followed over the radio.

"We have one friendly KIA." One Ranger had died.

"Roger that, stand by for medevac," came the call back from the commander, who had also redirected another chopper to the crash site.

Jason, now the commander on the ground, made the decision to press on. There was nothing more to be done about the fallen Ranger and there was no time to slow down. That's a tough thing to admit, but the mission always came first, no matter what. From the moment we signed on to the unit, that message was burned into our heads—the target or the precious cargo over everything else, even when your own is dead. All of us learned how to compartmentalize, which is something that would haunt me later.

Back at the main site, I watched our team race out of the Hawks toward the mud hut. The drone was now sparkling the target house to ensure they saw its exact location through their night-vision goggles.

I watched them enter the house. We all expected gunfire, explosions. But it was surprising because there was no pushback at all. They walked right in and did a full sweep.

"We got PC, no sign of the leaders," Jason radioed. They turned up two children and a woman. "Dry hole."

You gotta be fucking kidding me. Where the fuck were Manhattan and Brooklyn?

The guys on the ground pressed PC, but he was defiant. He'd die before he'd tell them anything.

After the initial sweep, Jason and some of his team climbed back onto the choppers and went to help secure the additional sites that were being raided by the Rangers.

Now only four members of the team remained with PC, the two children, and the woman outside of the house.

But there was something strange about the woman.

She looked familiar to one of the operators on the ground, like he had seen her before. The team snapped her picture and sent it back to the Box. We plugged her into our database.

All the different intel personnel involved tapped away at their computers and ran through family pictures we'd collected over the years of the two men. Dozens of snapshots taken from different target sites over the last decade instantaneously appeared on our TVs, drawing from our databases of thousands of raids and photos from various government agencies.

She looked like Manhattan's wife.

JASON AND HIS TEAM RUSHED BACK TO THE MAIN COMPOUND. HE ORDERED THEM TO grab the courier Charlie and fly him over, too. He might have some answers.

When the courier arrived, he clearly recognized the residence. As he stepped out of the chopper, he instantly became nervous, visibly shaking, while adjusting his kaffiyeh to hide his face.

The five operators laid into him, and in short order Charlie coughed up that he thought there was a secret hole that Manhattan sometimes hid in, and that PC had told him once that he'd bought a particular kind of toilet for the bathroom, specifically for the purpose of creating a cover for the hole.

Jason then went to the door and brought out the woman we suspected to be Manhattan's wife. He asked Charlie if he recognized her. He did but couldn't positively identify her or said he couldn't.

The operators began to pressure the woman. They asked about her husband and told her they believed he was hiding in a hole. "You know about that hole, don't you?" they said. "If he doesn't come out, he's going to die."

She shrugged, like we were talking about the weather. She said her husband was in Baghdad and that if there was a hole, she wasn't aware of it. The team pressed the issue more, at which point she replied, "If he's in there, then you'll have to kill him."

Jason radioed back to HQ. "Whisky Zero One, this is Bravo Zero Four."

"Roger that."

"She said he'll never come out alive. We think he is here hiding."

He wasn't going back into the house without more men. He needed guns on all four sides; otherwise they risked an escape and there was no telling how big that hole was and how many guys were in it. "Send the team back," he radioed urgently. "Over."

The place was a ticking time bomb now. The operators stood around the house with their guns pointed at it, not knowing what to expect. I kept an eye on the house, which was motionless like the desert around it. Other insurgents could show up at any moment. Who knew if the people in the hole had set off some kind of alert.

It was a long thirty minutes before the rest of the guys showed up. While the children and the mother were escorted far away, the operators walked the courier Charlie into the house.

Inside it was dead silent, like the desert. But at the bathroom, Charlie became very excited, as if the whole thing now made sense. He pointed at the toilet—the hideout. "That's it," he said.

This was particularly funny because the toilet had been totally functional and one of our guys had taken a shit in it during the first sweep, hours earlier.

Standing in the house now, the team discussed several courses of action, including placing a large charge on top of the toilet or tossing a thermobaric grenade in it. Eventually they settled on an M67 grenade to ensure that it would fit down the hole, causing the most possible damage to whoever was inside without collapsing the place.

It didn't take long.

Tossing the grenade down the hatch, one of the operators yelled out: "Merry Christmas, motherfuckers!"

Muffled gunshots came from the direction of the toilet after the detonation. Everyone took cover. They were in there.

Pulling a slow retreat, the operators poured gunfire into the house and I kept an eye out for squirters.

Just then, Manhattan's wife broke free from the soldiers and tried to run toward the house—suicide by crossfire. But another soldier grabbed her in time and put her on the ground.

From our birds, the gunfight looked like flashes of black, flocks of cicadas in the dark desert. Strange to say, but even after years of doing this, I still found it beautiful from 16,000 feet up—the snaps of light black against an even blacker desert night.

As the smoke from the grenade cleared, the volume of fire only increased. Stepping back some more, the operators concentrated fire on the door, but at least one person from the hole had crawled out and was now trying to work his way to a room off the bathroom. Two more got out and began shooting at a high rate as they moved through the house.

I was nervous for the operators on the ground, but another part of me was relieved it was happening—because a gunfight meant we were in the right place.

It didn't last long. One of our guys threw another grenade into the house, where the enemy had been hemmed in. About three seconds after that explosion, two other massive explosions went off. Suicide vests. From the drone I could see the whole hut collapse inward almost instantaneously.

The shooting stopped and about fifteen minutes of nothing passed. The assault force moved slowly back into the hut, their guns pointed forward. Groaning sounds were coming from the toilet hole.

One guy pointed his laser down the hole and called out, receiving groans in return. A few moments later there was silence again: the groaner was dead.

When the battle ended, the quiet persisted and the night sounds of the desert returned. The rubble was cleared from the hole and one of the biggest surprises of the mission came to light.

Four men were found dead: Manhattan was in there. And so was Brooklyn. They must have been hiding in the hut together. Wrong night to be together. Both had detonated their vests. Along with Brooklyn was his twelve-year-old son, who was killed when his father detonated. Another senior ISI operative had also died from the grenade dropped in the hole.

Later, when the body of the senior operative was transported back to our main base, the doctors would find a live grenade lodged into his armpit from the blast. They had to call an explosive ordnance disposal (EOD) team to remove it.

The official call finally came over the radio from Jason miles away, sealing the night: "Jackpot, Manhattan and Brooklyn EKIA."

I didn't know what to say at first. I couldn't find words. I turned around from the screens and looked at Mark. He was one of the first guys I had met and he, Bill, and Jack had trained me from the start. He nodded his approval.

Lisa, one of the Pink Mafia girls, jumped on my back, hugging me from behind. It was one of the first times I had seen the room snap out of their serious professional stance and lose a bit of their cool.

It was hard not to celebrate that moment. We had just been a part of arguably the most devastating blow to the network since the war began, and everyone in the world would know it once it hit the press the next day.

Brooklyn in particular was largely regarded by ISIS as the original founder and to this day is still celebrated as the original leader, his photo regularly sent out in propaganda. We had just killed him. When we showed his dead photo to Dark Horse later, he collapsed to the cold cement floor in his holding chamber and just asked for a Koran, clutching it as he rocked back and forth on the ground. It was over and he knew it.

But any celebrations, such as they were, were short-lived. This wasn't the World Series. This was war. All any of us cared about was the next target—not a party for the last.

It would be a few days before the assault team got back to base. They spent hours pulling up debris and collecting whatever was leftover: documents, laptops, DNA, and identifiable body parts. Once everything was gathered, it would be sent back to another secret site for others to analyze. And then weeks and sometimes months of debriefings would follow, with all the new information—newly found associates, safe houses, money trails—layered into our files.

I sent the drones home.

I wasn't tired so I headed for a shower. I stunk because I hadn't taken one in probably weeks. There was a designated trailer with ten stalls and sinks and mirrors to shave. It was probably four in the morning and I had the place to myself so I turned on the hot water and stood there for a long time under the steaming stream, just enjoying the momentary calm. It was probably the greatest shower that I've ever taken. It was like the water was washing away years of anxiety, fatigue, all the emotions of hunting these guys.

I slept that night deeper than I'd slept in months. I needed it. Of course, it was never long enough. My pager started buzzing before the sun rose. HQ was on the line.

21

DOGS OF WAR

HQ called an urgent meeting within hours after we took out Manhattan and Brooklyn and all stations jumped on a teleconference. You'd think we would have been given time off for killing the most wanted men. But there were never breathers. As the video screen of the others flickered live, my team and I huddled around the long table. This had to be important to bring us all together.

The night before had been a lot of ups and downs, the high of taking down Manhattan and Brooklyn running through my veins, and the low of losing a man in the chopper crash. The early morning had dragged a bit, like I was pulling a weight behind me. Sitting there now, I had never felt so tired. My bones ached. My neck felt like it was being dragged down by a fifty-pound weight.

To fight the fatigue, I slugged one energy drink and another, just as the overall commander came online. There was no hello or celebration over the night before. He got straight to the point. "We need to keep the network on the run," he said. "I want you to take down all the targets you've been following, every target you have in your back pocket, all the low-hanging fruit, even if you don't have much on them." At this stage we had taken out twelve of the twenty on our original list of leaders.

I looked over at Mark. Both of us knew what this meant. My chest tightened.

It was the equivalent of unleashing one giant Hellfire on our enemies. The commander had just set us free, weapons cleared hot. With Brooklyn and Manhattan dead, the most dangerous terrorist network in the world was headless and unraveling—and we needed to keep it that way. We were being told to bring them to the brink of extinction.

I edged closer to the table, gripping my drink. The fan spinning away behind us didn't seem like it was working and the air felt hotter than ever, thick with the stink of too many bodies.

"Tell me what we got," the commander said.

We went around to the different intel heads across the country, each one going over who was left, who could be taken out.

Jack was first. "Sir, I've got two we can go on."

"Tonight?"

"Roger that."

"We have a few we can immediately take action on at our location as well," said Travis, another team leader in the north.

"Sir, I've got one big target and a bunch of lower-level guys we've been sitting on," I added.

The meeting was quick and to the point. I could feel the anticipation of things to come, as if a grenade pin had just been slipped out. There was no time to think now. Our deployment was coming to an end and the United States was moving out of Iraq. It was time to finish things.

The commander moved close to the screen. His face blown up in front of all of us, like he was too close to the camera.

"Crush everything," he said, right before signing off. "We go now."

THE SAME AFTERNOON OUR MISSION TO CRUSH EVERYTHING BEGAN. I SENT UP three drones and our operators began to hit the streets.

We grabbed one guy out of a taxi full of stunned people in downtown Baghdad while he was on his way to work. We snagged another as he left a market where he had been distributing propaganda videos. Another was hunkering down at home. Our strikes were more brazen; we were sending them a message in broad daylight in some cases. We wanted the network to know we had been unleashed.

There were more than a dozen missions playing out on multiple screens at once—some drones watching targets, others watching captures and kills. The command center was at full staff, everyone ramped up and ready to help.

It was as if the dogs of war had been let free. Each station was doing its own missions. Night after night. Sometimes two or three at one time. No more patience or hand-wringing from above. The more missions, the more the network was unsteadied. We pored over our list, anyone we had leads on. That first day our teams killed eight targets. By the end of the week, we'd grabbed more than double that.

We even had the Air Force pull the Hellfire missiles off our drones so they didn't weigh the aircraft down as much. That gave each bird an extra few hours in the sky to hunt. More drones were brought in from other battlefields to support our teams. We had them stacked on top of each other in the sky, blanketing major cities across the country.

The scramble led to our last major hit, but it also led to our last major mistake: killing an innocent.

One night we were following a target in an old white Toyota Corolla around the city when I decided it was time to take him out.

We didn't have time to keep following him because we had bigger missions to deal with. The guy was a small-time emir in the network—low on the totem pole of terror—and hiding out in a southern suburb of Baghdad. I didn't have a photo or even know much about what he looked like. Instead I had only one source who had led us to the white Corolla and eventually to a mud house.

As the drone orbited overhead, my gut felt something was off, but I didn't listen to it. I watched the man get out of his car and go inside the hut. The village was well outside Baghdad and made up of a cluster of huts, all of them in complete darkness.

Soon after, I watched a SEAL team show up. Our team's operators had been pulled away for another mission. We thought it would be a quick and easy raid—in and out in a few minutes—and we watched them get to work.

Wearing night-vision goggles, they climbed out of their vehicles and spread out enough to cordon off the outer perimeter of the village. That's where things went wrong.

As they moved in, a man stepped out from one of the other huts and began firing in their direction. The SEALs killed him almost instantly. "Contact!" the commander yelled over the radio, indicating that they had taken fire.

They then proceeded at lightning speed to the actual target's hut. We expected more firing, but the SEALs' commander radioed back within seconds with disturbing news: "Dry hole."

They'd checked his ID, swiped all the information from his cell phone, and talked with others in the village. The man we'd been following was just a regular guy. No connection to the network.

My stomach fell out. It was the worst phrase one could hear in my position. It was basically another way of saying, "You fucked up, Intel."

To make matters worse, the man who'd come out of his hut shooting was also a civilian. He had a family and was just protecting his house, worried that the men were coming for his wife and kids. Now he was dead.

We should have spent more time confirming the target. But we didn't have the time. The network was changing fast, with new, unknown people replacing the guys we'd killed off. There were a lot of things we should have done differently. But we were scrambling to wrap things up.

In the moment, I didn't think much of his death, though. Mistakes happened and we considered it collateral damage. The thing about a drone-related kill is that there are a lot of people involved in the operation and it is easy to distance yourself from any mistake. The SEAL who shot the guy could say, "Well, the intel guy put us there so it's his fault." And I could say, "Well, I didn't pull the trigger." Same thing with a Hellfire strike. These are the new realities of networked wars. Success has a thousand fathers, while failure is an orphan.

But the truth was, I could not escape it then, and cannot escape it now: His death should not have happened. And I'm responsible for it.

22.

THE ONE WHO GOT AWAY

There was always one elusive target on every tour. One guy we hunted and chased but somehow kept slipping away. Every team had its archnemesis. Mine during the summer of 2010 was a man we called Abu Dua.

We hunted Abu Dua for months, pressured sources and captives, put more drones in the sky for extra eyes that never blinked. Maybe it was luck. He'd probably call it divine intervention. Something Allah did for him as thanks for all the mass killings he called holy.

In the spring of 2010, Abu Dua was one of the most wanted men in our covert world—at the top of our target list—but he was largely unknown to the public.

Abu Dua was connected to everyone at the top of ISI and he had his own fiefdom. Among thousands of brainwashed followers, he was known as the Wali of Walis, a title usually reserved for the top three ranks in the network's broader hierarchy. After we killed Manhattan and Brooklyn the month before, we kept hearing that he was taking over. And soon he did.

Not only did he take over the ISI network, but he would help them eventually become ISIS, morphing into an even more murderous and twisted offshoot, swallowing up parts of Syria and Iraq in 2014. He was probably the smartest terrorist I ever hunted.

Most people know him these days as the most wanted terrorist in the world: Abu Bakr al-Baghdadi, the leader of ISIS.

The U.S. government had placed a $10 million bounty on his head.

He didn't know me, but he definitely knew my work. Through my deployment, our team conducted more than thirty-two raids that specifically aimed to uncover him. Most were chasing leads to his whereabouts or capturing people in his inner circle, attempts at tightening the noose around his neck. He had to see some of the closest people in his inner circle, people he met with every day, getting picked off around him. We would get word that he was running around with some target of ours during his daily terrorist duties, meeting at a gas station or some safe house somewhere, then, boom, that other guy with him was suddenly gone, in our custody or dead. Imagine everyone in your circle of friends and family that you always met the same time every week, slowly disappearing one by one over the course of a couple of months. His tight-knit group of the most brutal animals within the network slowly vanishing around him. I forced him underground and got closer to ending his reign than anyone else. But we were always just one step behind him.

There were a lot of reasons that he probably escaped our team's grasp. He was surely better at hiding than any other man on our list. His operations security—OPSEC—was the best in the business. He was paranoid that we were getting close. He would be somewhere and then disappear without a trace, like a weather pattern. He knew, one little slipup and we had him. No doubt our team made him the security-obsessive psychopath he was today. Paranoia kept him alive.

Usually we got the guys we hunted. Maybe not that first tour, but eventually we got to them—and if I didn't, another team did. My team was always followed by another team, which was followed by another, all of us hunting around the clock. But this time was different. With U.S. troops pulling out of Iraq, with fewer of our guys likely to be looking for him, I wasn't so sure there would be another chance to get Abu Dua.

When we first started hunting him, it was because we needed a path to Manhattan and Brooklyn and we were worried that Dark Horse was dead and wouldn't pan out. Abu Dua was one of the only other commanders who knew their whereabouts. So we hunted them both.

Abu Dua was a big fan of an ice cream shop in downtown Baghdad that had an outdoor seating area where many locals socialized all day long. Our sources told us that he met his fighters there on Thursdays and used it as a letter drop for couriers. He didn't seem afraid of being recognized by locals at the time, only because they didn't know about him then.

One summer day we got intelligence that he was going to the ice cream shop for a drop and we put a bird up to check it out. We watched the shop for days and days.

"What a sick joke," Megan said as the monitors streamed back images of families eating ice cream cones. "A terrorist who loves a good ice cream sundae." I imagined him talking to his hired killers about the next massacre over strawberry milkshakes and getting the ice cream foam on his beard.

We had our local informants—the Cobras—on the street, casually mulling around and looking to snap pictures. But nothing stood out. Just families coming and going for dessert. They must have snapped thousands of photos that we sorted through back in the Box. But none of them were him. He never came. Or maybe he did and we just didn't see him.

Pursuing Abu Dua was mostly like that.

I never understood how he rose to the top so fast. Typically, it's hard to climb the ranks because of how Al Qaeda and ISI structured their networks, favoring the rise of longtime followers. My guess was that it had to do with his stretch in prison (for fighting U.S. troops during the second Fallujah war in 2004), the jihadis he met there, and the fact that we were destroying the bigger network so quickly, which forced leadership gaps to be filled. He also seemed to have this oddly close connection to former military officers in Saddam's Ba'ath Party. Many of the guys who had worked with him had similar backgrounds and filled senior officer ranks within former Iraqi intelligence circles.

Usually ISI was mistrustful of newly released prisoners, fearing they had been turned into spies. They kept them on ice for months before bringing them into the mix. But Abu Dua was different. He came right out of prison and was soon one of the top commanders.

Few knew this history at the time. Before the spring of 2010, no one outside of our team knew much about him at all or where he came from. Even the Iraqi government was in the dark.

When we had first started to hunt him, all we had to go off was the nickname Abu Dua. That changed one night when Megan was digging into some old files and his secret history suddenly opened up like a book.

"Look at this," she said. Megan had a bunch of files open on her desktop. We had two drones up over another target that we were about to take out.

She discovered Abu Dua's real name in an old prison file: Dr. Ibrahim Awwad Ibrahim 'Ali al-Badri al-Samarrai.

"This is gold," I said, excitedly. "You hit it."

That name for us was a key to his past. From his name, I

could tell that his father was Awwad Ibrahim, and that he was from Samarra and his subtribe was al-Badri. He had a daughter named Dua.

The Box shot into action. Plugging the names into our databases, we were immediately able to trace his lineage to al-Jabriyah, al-Thaniah village in the Iraqi city of Samarra. He was probably in his early forties, had three brothers and five sisters.

As we pressed on, more of his history began to shake out and a picture emerged.

Abu Dua received a doctoral degree in Islamic studies from Baghdad and preached at numerous mosques, including some in al-Anbar and Samarra. He had multiple wives, Asma, his current wife in the north, and Sumayah, the wife he had met while studying at the university in Baghdad. His mother was Ali Husayn. At first I went after his wives, sending birds to watch over his first wife Asma's parents' house in the middle of Fallujah. But after a few days there was no sign of her there and I quickly decided that she'd probably gone off with Abu Dua before we could find her.

He moved quickly and had the foresight to know that his families would be targets of ours at some point. At the same time, he hadn't been afraid to get in the trenches, showing his face to the fighters he commanded. This was why he appealed to other fighters. He fought in both Fallujah battles in 2004, which were probably the bloodiest battles for American forces in Iraq. During the second battle, U.S. forces grabbed him and sent him to Camp Bucca, the largest prison run by the military.

He was locked up there for years. That prison was a cauldron of hate. Many of the current leaders of ISIS spent time there, alongside Abu Dua. When he finally got out of prison, he seemed to largely go dark as he plotted attacks around the country and recruited soldiers. He was always on the go and we'd only hear about him occasionally from guys that we captured.

Along with his favorite neighborhood ice cream shop, he

stayed at a house in a wealthy part of the city and owned a small Islamic bookstore in downtown Baghdad, where we heard that he had begun conducting meetings. But even with our drones overhead day after day at each of these locations, we never saw him there. It was like he sensed us, knew our game. There was no doubt that word about our raids was getting back to him.

Abu Dua really got to me. More than any other target, I felt something twisting inside me, eating at me, as we flew drones and looked for him over those days and weeks.

The drone feeds of the places where we tracked him burned deeply in my mind: a crumbling tower in downtown Iraq; a mud hut in the north; a packed apartment building in the south; a white truck bumping across the desert, filled with explosives. The feed of Abu Dua churned through my head like a bad song I couldn't shake.

He was clever and cunning—part of me deep down probably had some begrudging respect for Abu Dua, even though he was so clearly one of the most evil men on earth. Competition with a guy like him was what I now lived for.

There were nights where I sat up in my dust-covered bunk and stared at the knotty plywood ceiling, filled with anxiety. My body wouldn't stop sweating. *Is this air-conditioning even working?* It surprised me that the wood and sweat smell of the tiny room hadn't bothered me until now.

I began to get this intense creeping fear that I was losing myself. That the hunt was slowly killing me. Why had I become so obsessed with this war?

I remembered 9/11 and how that had sent me down this road, how I thought I could help the fight. Be a man. An American. And a warrior. Nothing else mattered then. Over the years a lot happened. I had done everything that I could do. And that made me proud, kept me going.

But in those fleeting moments, I thought more and more about my future—something I hadn't done in a long, long time. Ten years from now, I wondered, would I look back and say, where the fuck has my life gone? The questions bubbled up in my head. Who are my friends? Where's my family? Who really cares about me? I had left a lot of people behind. Would anyone even remember me? This war had gone on too long.

The Box was like being freeze-dried—as the rest of the world went on, built relationships, got married, had kids, had other adventures, other lives, all I had was the Box. All I had was my enemies, like Abu Dua. I loved the Box, loved what I could do in there. But it was still a box.

The questions were starting to mess with my head, popping up sometimes and then burrowing back in like a temporary ache. It was easier to ignore it and go back to hunting.

One night our team hopped in Black Hawks with our computers and guns and made an unusual trip up to a small outpost in Samarra. I had discovered a house belonging to Abu Dua's brother Jawwad. Usually we would have done the operation from the Box, but Jason wanted to coordinate this one with the local security forces—a decision that would come back to bite us.

Abu Dua had three brothers. All of them were linked to his terrorist activities. Like a mob king, he liked to keep the business close to his family. Along with Jawwad, there was Ahmed and Lafi.

The outpost was a small Iraqi camp with a few metal trailers and old Iraqi military vehicles parked around it. There were concrete barriers and big mounds of dirt. It looked like a big sandbox, except with people living on it.

We set up inside the trailers and got the bird up right away. In no time, the images were streaming back in black and white. The brother's house was located on the southern end of the city, two stories tall with a small fenced-in yard pressed up against a dirt road.

The images we saw over the days showed a house packed with people. About twenty were living there. We couldn't figure out if Abu Dua was one of them, but we did identify Jawwad and Ahmed. That was all we needed to go in.

But just as the assault team headed out that night to raid, something unexpected happened at the house. I watched a man climb into a car and drive away. Where was he going?

We had only one drone up and had to make a choice, so we kept the bird on the house.

It was the wrong move.

When our guys arrived at the house, Jawwad was gone. We found many members of Abu Dua's extended family there: his daughter, his uncles, aunts, cousins, and his ill grandfather. No Abu Dua.

We found out later that the local Iraqi police forces working with us had tipped off the family, allowing Jawwad to escape minutes before. They had tribal ties, commonplace in the northern half of the country, and those ties always came before some greater notion of justice; it was why the Iraqis couldn't come together as a country. Our only recourse was to compartmentalize our operations even more, keep the security forces in the dark about our next move. I had as much distaste for some of them as I did for the enemy. The thought that they didn't want to protect their own didn't sit well with me. At some point they needed to take control of their country. We couldn't do it all for them. The security forces regularly chose the terrorists within their local districts over us; it was safer for them.

Although the raid on Abu Dua's extended family's home didn't net him, we did arrest his brother Ahmed that night and kept him in a Baghdad prison for months after, hoping that he would tell us something about Abu Dua that we could use. But he gave us nothing.

Abu Dua was actually one of the reasons that we were able to track down and kill the original leaders of the Islamic State—he personally set up the courier network that we used to find Manhattan and Brooklyn. He'd handpicked each of the couriers and switched them out every three months. I spoke to some of these couriers personally after we'd captured them and they genuinely didn't have any idea about the other couriers in the network—the only link between all of them was the man himself.

We found out later that we'd actually almost gotten Abu Dua when we raided Uncle's house. He had spent three hours there writing the letter that was meant to go to Manhattan and Brooklyn in the flowerpot but had slipped out just before we arrived. Uncle told us that we'd missed him by only ten minutes. Knowing that Abu Dua was there inside the same house only a few minutes before the raid would always haunt me.

I spent the last few weeks of my deployment poring over files, talking to sources, turning over everything that might give up a lead.

Part of my obsession for Abu Dua now is due to the fact that we never found him. Because he got away. We wouldn't even realize how truly important he was until years later.

After the deaths of Manhattan and Brooklyn, Abu Dua vanished for a long stretch. Rumors came to us that he'd died. But we knew better. I'm almost positive he went to Syria during this time to get away from the stress of always being targeted by our teams and to rally the troops for a new war.

We knew that he told his fighters to "lay low and wait for the U.S. to leave." And that's what they did. He returned to Iraq in early 2011, as U.S. forces pulled out, and our powers to hunt him dwindled.

By then Abu Dua had taken on his role as the leader of ISIS and had begun stringing together territories in Iraq and Syria. Bin Laden had been killed and tens of thousands of fighters were joining his ranks.

One of my mentors, Jack, and his team had him in their sights at a house in Baghdad in 2011. As most of the troops got on transport planes out of the country, they'd stayed behind, partly to make one last-ditch effort to knock out Abu Dua.

They had information suggesting that Abu Dua was in the city for an important meeting at a house we had visited previously. Jack's plan was to take him out that night, but the State Department had changed the rules for raids and a planned raid on the target was delayed.

Jack's team was now operating under different authorities of law than the year before, because the war had officially come to a close. Before a raid could happen, multiple levels of suits from Washington had to sign off. Days passed by, often weeks, before a raid could be put into action. Lawyers were now running the unofficial war.

Jack tasked a drone over the house and watched as a man, exhibiting the exact signature and description we always had for Abu Dua, arrived in a vehicle and proceeded inside.

When they zoomed in on him, there was no doubt in Jack's mind. It was Abu Dua.

Jack told me about it months later, after I'd left the unit. "The suits screwed us," he said. "I had the guy that night, and still have the old drone feed to prove it."

Few knew the story. It certainly was never made public. No one wanted to talk about it. The world's most wanted terrorist could have very well met his maker that night before he truly took the reins of ISIS years later.

Except there was a problem. This time around Jack didn't have his assault team. The operators had gone home, too. In their place, he relied on a local hit squad—a group of local Iraqis trained by a special branch within the agency. Which wasn't saying much.

Jack's drone team now fell under the suits at the agency and

State Department instead of the Department of Defense. So he had to convince them to move on the target. But his request to strike that night passed from empty suit to suit as he watched Abu Dua at the house.

He called his bosses multiple times, pressing them to make a move, knowing that Abu Dua was in the house at that very moment.

But it was a week before they approved the mission. By that time it didn't matter.

Who did the Iraqis get that night when they finally went in? They grabbed up a gang of ISIS members. And guess what those fighters confirmed? Abu Dua had been there—seven days before.

Guys from our team talked about it for months after. How could the suits fuck up like that?

After that night in 2011, Abu Dua disappeared for months and then years again—when he came back, he was leading the charge across a broken Iraq—and ISIS was the new Al Qaeda, version 2.0. He had established an Islamic terror state and the United States was still trying to track him down.

"We were so close, man, I can't believe we missed him out of all the people we went after," Jack said over drinks one night.

"It's a new kind of war," Jack lamented. "The rules have changed. Our hands have gotten more and more tied by the damn suits."

PART THREE

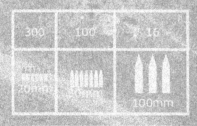

23
GONE

I left Iraq in late July 2010. When the other team arrived to replace us, it was a quick handoff, as always. "Did you leave anyone for us?" one of them joked as we gathered our gear. Word of our exploits had spread fast back home.

Collectively over those four months, our teams across the country had taken out 14 of the 20 targets on the kill list. We'd conducted over 160 raids, captured more than 400 enemy leaders, and killed more than 20. Tens of thousands of flight time hours had been logged. The team who replaced us would kill another four from the list and the last two guys, one being Abu Dua, would vanish. ISI was on the run—for now.

It felt pretty good. Iraq was getting better. Civilian and military casualties were at the lowest point they'd been in years. The drone teams helped. But it was also a testament to the sacrifice and persistence of the greater military.

Still I worried that important targets lurked out there. The enemy could easily regroup and come back with double the force.

I never had this grand view that we were going to take out all the top leaders, instantly solve everyone's problems, and win the war. In the end, all drones really did was help us degrade the enemy and create the time and space for our allies—the Iraqis, especially—to gain the upper hand.

U.S. forces handed Iraq to Maliki's government on a silver platter. And the Obama administration did what they could to maintain a skeleton crew of forces in the country, to keep the heat on the network. Prime Minister Maliki thought his security forces could handle it alone.

What a joke.

As my team prepared to leave, Maliki was already screwing up. Word had begun to trickle down that he planned to release a large number of prisoners—many of the guys we'd captured—as a signal of good faith to the opposing religious sect. These weren't just people who stole a pack of gum. These were some of the worst human beings on earth.

There were arguments about it. But Maliki was committed and, days before we left the country, he asked us to come up with a list of the top fifty bad guys in prison. He'd be sure to keep them behind bars. But fifty was a ridiculous number. There were literally thousands of murderers, rapists, explosives experts, thieves, and failed suicide bombers that our teams had helped put away over the last decade.

Good soldiers over the years had died locking these guys away and those fanatics were just going to be released? It made me sick to think about all the men and women who fought to make this country safe again only to see their efforts discarded for politics. Many of them would in fact eventually reappear in the ranks of ISIS. I couldn't help thinking that we should have killed all of them, rather than letting them go free. But it didn't matter, it wasn't up to us anymore.

On our last day, I ducked through the rotor wash and into the chopper. Running almost. It was around midnight and the Iraqi air was still baking hot. It felt like two hundred degrees. The summer was a killer and I was happy to be leaving the Box, its stink of sweat and wood and coffee, its boxed cereals, its energy drinks, all of that.

The only memento I took from that deployment was the photograph of the kidnapped woman. I still thought about her. I'd heard she was back home and getting better. That kind of thing made me feel that we'd made a difference. It took the edge off the other uncertainties we were leaving behind.

What I'd do next was less clear as the chopper lifted off into the Iraqi sky. The nagging of what the future held had picked up inside me the night before like a drumbeat in my head. I couldn't stop thinking about what was on the other side of the world. What was at home? I hadn't spoken to my mother in what seemed like months. I didn't even know my girlfriend Sarah anymore. Our conversations by phone had basically stopped happening. We lived on different planets, had become different people. I both dreaded and wondered a lot about what I would say. Who did they even see these days when they looked at me? Was there any evidence of my old self anymore? That guy who came from Katy, Texas, and wanted to save the world? There were rumors of other deployments already. Maybe Afghanistan or Yemen, where a new front on the war was opening up, drawing the birds away from Iraq. Part of me wanted that right now. To get away from this sandbox and go somewhere else. A new adventure. The other part of me wasn't sure what I wanted. That part of me felt like I was about to step off a cliff.

The chopper landed at a large forward operating base and our C-17 cargo plane was waiting on the tarmac. Jack and Travis and their teams arrived on choppers around the same time. We'd all be on the same flight out.

It was great to see everyone. We shook hands and patted

each other on the backs without reliving too much of the last few months. Jack was especially happy. I had never seen him give praise before. He'd seen everything in his time so it took a lot for him to show emotion. "This was the greatest Iraq deployment in our history," he said.

As good as it was getting his approval, it also felt like the end of something.

24

LIFE OUTSIDE THE BOX

As the tailgate ramp lowered, we all stepped out with our gear into the night. It was 3 A.M. A scattering of lights on the massive airfield showed the other military planes that had been locked up until morning, not many people around. As I looked across the open space, a feeling of loneliness came over me.

I said goodbye to the team on that quiet, barely lit tarmac in North Carolina, grabbed my gear, and headed for the back lot. After sitting there for the last few months, my car was covered in a film of dust. I turned it on and drove through the midnight streets in a daze, the sleeping pills still in my head.

When I got home, I stumbled in the door and dropped my two big black bags in a pile on the wood floor. I couldn't lie still that night or the next night, either. My mind kept on swirling, thinking I was still in the Box, running through what seemed like hundreds of leads and strategizing about the hunt.

It took me hours to fall asleep. For days I slept and woke and slept again. I lost track of time.

One early morning, padding groggily to the fridge, I caught my reflection in the bathroom mirror. It was terrible. I had dropped a bunch of weight, my face paler than ever. A few gray hairs had formed on my beard along the way. My eyes were bloodshot, like an addict's. I looked like the worst kind of hell, like I'd been living in a crypt.

I stumbled out the back door with a bucket of golf balls to the thirteenth hole on the golf course that my backyard bordered, and spent the next hour driving balls down the fairway. I hardly spoke to Sarah, who came and went from the condo and had begun to expect my post-deployment silence. I couldn't get up the energy to feel for her or anyone else back home. I tried going out to dinner and eating everything that I had been dreaming of eating in the Box. But nothing had much taste this time. "You okay?" Sarah asked one night when we were eating burgers. "Just tired," I said, having a hard time looking at her. It wasn't long before our relationship would end.

The following week I returned to the office, needing a connection to war, and immediately pulled up the drone feeds and started sifting through reports. What could we do to keep pounding the enemy? I sifted through some of the dead guy photos from the replacement team's recent missions and that helped pump me up. It was like hooking up to a feedbag, my blood flowing again.

Still, no matter how much I tried to ignore it, the thought that had been simmering in me over the last few months started to heavily boil inside me again—that this job was slowly swallowing me, that it was turning me into someone else I didn't recognize anymore. Watching those monitors day and night, the stress of the missions, the targets that we took out—all of it had gutted me, erased my emotions. People always thought of the operators when they thought about trauma in the field. I saw a lot through them and all that I saw was pushed down into some deep hole in me where it wasn't thought about—until now.

The key to a job like mine was dividing up my life into two neatly kept worlds: my world in the Box and my world at home. But part of what I found now was that I couldn't separate the two anymore. One had started to bleed into the other and the bleeding felt like it was about to get worse.

My family had no idea what I'd been doing the last few years . . . and they still don't, really, years later. I tried calling my mother a few times, but decided against it, and then I avoided her calls. I knew my family wouldn't be able to grasp the decisions I had to make overseas. How would they understand Dark Horse? Or Manhattan? Or any of them?

One afternoon, I went to the funeral of a fellow soldier in Arlington National Cemetery. He'd died in Afghanistan during battle. It was a warm day, the wind blowing across the field. It was a big crowd, with lots of soldiers I knew from years of coming and going to war zones. He was young like me.

As I looked around, I watched as most of the others bowed their heads and rubbed away tears. Jets flew overhead and soldiers fired guns in salute. As I stared at the American-flag-covered casket, I kept thinking, *Why aren't you feeling anything? What the hell is wrong with you, man?* I didn't shed a tear, no matter how hard I tried. I squeezed my eyes shut, but there was nothing. It was like dry heaving on the bathroom floor, badly wanting something to come out to relieve the pain but just feeling the insides of your body ripping apart.

What I realized that day as I sat in my car long after the other mourners left was that death didn't mean anything to me anymore, no matter who it was, even me. It was one thing to not care about the death of a terrorist who had killed thousands, but another not to think twice about the loss of a fellow soldier or a family member. All the death I'd witnessed through those flat-screen monitors had drained my emotions over hundreds of missions. In the pixels I'd become desensitized to death and, by extension, desensitized to everything around me back home. I lost my heart somewhere along the way. I had basically flat-lined.

On the screens my targets were glowing red. It wasn't hard for me to know who they were. My mind was trained to know what the enemy thought and did every day, not what they felt. Feeling was irrelevant in the drone hunt. My life of watching people die behind a monitor changed how I viewed the world. I might as well have been dead.

It's hard to explain or even recall all the conversations that went on in my head. It wasn't straightforward at all or easy to leave the unit. My enlistment was up and I had to make a decision to reenlist for another three years or not. I flip-flopped about it over a few weeks. One day I was staying, the next I was out. These were some of the hardest weeks for me.

Around that time, I remembered a buddy who had left the unit close to when I'd joined years ago. "I want a dog. I want a wife," he said to me on his last day. "I want something outside of this place." I didn't get it back then and simply shrugged it off. Why would he leave such a respected role? Who would ever give up this job?

Now it made sense. He craved what I had forgotten—what it felt like to be normal. He no longer wanted to know about or experience the horrors of the world, the death and all the evil that existed in dark corners. He craved the simple decency that was home.

Even though I felt a great purpose in what I was doing, I started to battle with the long-term value of my actions. When I'm gone from all this one day, the unit would forget about me, forget about all of these successes. They'd move on—and do just fine without me. As if I didn't even exist. After a new generation of soldiers filled the ranks to help hunt down the next generation of terrorists, what would I be left with? No wife, no kids. Family and friends who moved on without me. Was this what really mattered most in life?

When my cousin died, I didn't go to his funeral. He was family. But he was also my friend. And I didn't even say goodbye. I used to talk to my mother. Now I couldn't even pick up the phone to call her. I couldn't even remember the last time we talked. I had ruined relationships and been absent from those who actually cared about me, because of my own selfishness, because of this never-ending war. In the end, those people were the ones who would be around for me.

One night I dreamed about my own funeral, looking down at it, as I lay in a shiny black casket. The pews were empty and there was no priest. The church was completely silent and I was all alone.

For as long as I was on this earth, there would always be that next target, that next terrorist group that hated America for whatever reason they believed justified their atrocities. The war would never end.

I knew it was time to go.

When I finally brought it up with Jack and Bill, they seemed surprised. "What are you thinking? This is your home now," they said.

I tried to explain that I was gutted, that I needed something else. It was painful talking to them about it. It cut right into my heart. We were friends and brothers. I still remembered when I went through training with them. All those years in the Box. I felt like I was betraying my team, letting every single one of them down.

Jack and Bill tried to get me to stay and even offered some incentives, including time off and a break to finish college. They talked about this being the only life, that there was nothing outside of it. Jack told me how boring the civilian world was when he lived it for a few years. And a piece of me knew that was true. The war, wherever it went, was a life. A good and honorable one that most guys stuck to until they retired. There was no better place to work in the Army. Jack was like that. So was Bill. It was one of the few places in the Army where it happened.

But in the end, I didn't reenlist. I was out. It was the winter of 2010. I was twenty-six years old and I felt two things that day: one great world had now been shut off, and another world was suddenly wide open.

The last day I walked out of the office, I climbed into my car and drove home the usual route, out the backside and the secret way through the woods. I didn't want to see anyone. I walked into my condo and sat on the couch with the TV off and the living room quieter than I ever remembered it being. And that's when it hit me: This was real. I was out. All of these questions started to bubble up in my head. *What will I do with the rest of my life?* I'd always had the Army as my purpose. It defined me. *Now what?*

CIVILIAN LIFE CAN BE A DIFFICULT CHOICE FOR ANY SOLDIER. IT'S A SCARY THING. Like walking to the edge of a cliff and wondering what's below and if your parachute will work. A lot of guys avoid the uncertainty of the change, enlisting over and over all the way to retirement. Some soldiers find comfort in stability and always following a daily regimen. Other soldiers get out only to realize that they don't belong in the real world and so reenlist. Then there are those who fight the harsh realities of a world that doesn't understand them. Fighting a new battle internally to figure out their place and purpose—until they emerge victorious. It's impossible for the public to grasp the realities of war let alone the loneliness that soldiers face while deployed, whether they see daily combat or not.

For me, there was no direct line between coming home from war, leaving the unit, and what came next. It was messy and I didn't experience one big revelation or lightbulb moment where I changed from one thing to another or looked in the mirror and knew exactly what I was going to do. It took a long time to figure things out and if there was one way to describe the next year or so it was anxiousness.

As a transition out, I moved to Washington, D.C., where the unit hooked me up with a contracting job for a special operations organization, working with different intelligence agencies on the war on terror. I wore a suit and tie every day, and it came with a cushy six-figure salary. I sat at a large circular desk in a secured room and managed a team of guys within the Beltway. Our job was more strategically focused, like briefing other intelligence and law enforcement agencies on how special ops did business and convincing seniors in big government positions who knew nothing about terrorism that there was still a war going on. It was a lot of handshaking, patting each other on the back for, say, a great video teleconference or a meeting with federal agency X where nothing truly got accomplished. I mostly dealt with the bureaucracy that is D.C.

When I wasn't in meetings, I sat behind my desk, watching emails come in, one after another, piling up. What amazed me was how many of them said absolutely nothing at all or were about setting up more meetings.

This was a big change for me. In the Box, time didn't exist. It blurred out of shape because there was always something going on, pulling you one way or the other. We weren't just talking, we were *doing*. Now I felt every single minute of the day. As if there was a seconds hand in my head, ticking loudly to remind me how slow time was going. I started feeling like I needed to find something to get my heart beating again.

Those first weeks, I didn't sleep much. I came home and lay on my bed and stared at the ceiling. My new apartment had little in it yet, just a bed, some furniture, a computer, and bags of clothes. Nothing on the walls. Anyone could have lived there, like a hotel, for someone passing through, with no intention of staying.

ONE WEEK MY MOTHER CAME TO TOWN TO SEE HOW I WAS DOING. I HADN'T SPOKEN to her much since I had gotten back and left the unit for a new life in D.C. She wanted to catch up and I was suddenly looking forward to it. But when I walked through the door that night, I found a complete mess.

Tears were streaming down her face as she sat on the couch.

"Why didn't you tell me?" she asked.

"What do you mean? What's wrong?"

"About all these medals and awards."

She pointed at a cardboard box on the floor. It was filled with a bunch of the military awards that I'd received over the years. Usually I kept the box hidden in the closet, except when I wanted to remember things about those days. Recently I had been pulling the box out a lot.

"You earned a Bronze Star," she said, picking up one plaque.

"Yeah, so?" I said.

She turned it over in her hands and then just stared at it.

"It reads here that you were directly responsible for arguably the most devastating blow to the enemy since the insurgency began in 2003."

I nodded.

She had this look of pride on her face behind the tears running down. It was as if all these years she knew deep inside I was doing something important, but never really knew for sure until now.

It validated pride she'd held on faith. This was the proof for her after all the years wondering where I had been.

"Why didn't you tell me this?"

"I didn't think it was a big deal."

She shook her head and wiped away a tear with her sleeve.

"It's just a piece of paper," I said. "The memories are worth more to me."

"It's much more than that," she said. "Don't you see that?"

I didn't.

"This is your life," she said.

That's what was killing me.

I TRIED NOT TO THINK ABOUT THE BOX. I TRIED TO QUIET THE DEMONS OF THE screens that kept saying, Go back, you're still needed out there. I went out at night, looking for something else, anything, to feel alive. First that meant getting in my car and driving fast and recklessly on the 495 interstate, which circled the city. I liked to drive alone late at night down long stretches of the freeway, weaving in and out of traffic, with no particular destination in sight.

Later I started gambling online, thousands of dollars a night. The risk gave me the slight feeling I was back in the combat zone. On my home computer, I had two monitors flipped on, playing eight poker tables at once, just like all the screens in the Box. This time my targets were the other players. I would even research the players' names, using poker analytic software to help understand my enemy better to try to turn the odds in my favor.

I was taught to fight, not to show weakness. The U.S. military had spent millions of dollars teaching me how to deal with the anxiety of fighting. Being in the moment of a mission and knowing how to keep your head on straight. What it didn't teach was how to keep your head straight after you left. That was hard for a lot of people. It was hard for me. I had no idea.

Weeks passed and I began to feel a lot like the main character in the movie *Crank*, who has to keep his adrenaline going to stay alive. Even though I didn't tell anyone about my night life I began to wonder if they could tell. I had gained some weight back and color had returned to my face after coming home from Iraq. But now I was losing weight again and going pale. Casper was creeping back.

One day I left work and drove out to the countryside. I took the freeway heading toward West Virginia, well outside of D.C., and didn't care about the speed limit or the cops who might have been waiting for a guy like me going 100, 110, 140. I was feeling reckless, like nothing could hurt me, like I couldn't crash if I wanted to. I might have gone for hours if I hadn't seen the sign that took me back to the Box in the nowhere hills of West Virginia: "Speed Limit Enforced by Aircraft."

I had to pull over. Open farm fields stretched forever on either side of my car. Immediately I thought of a Predator enforcing that speed limit with a Hellfire missile.

Over the last few weeks, when I sat staring at my work computer screen, I'd called Jack and Bill to check in, but they were always too busy. It took them days to get back to me, even after a text message. I missed them.

As I sat there on the side of the road now, I suddenly had this terrible feeling that hit me like a semi coming in at top speed from the other direction—that the life I wanted to live outside of the world of the unit might not be as good as I had imagined. Somehow I found myself falling deeper into a state of apathy. This was the low point of my confusion. What had I done? Where was I?

THE ONE GOOD THING THAT CAME IN THIS TIME WAS JOYCE.

I met her at Duke University's business school, where I'd applied after getting my bachelor's degree—done online over the years between deployments. The MBA program was internationally focused and involved studying abroad in the top financial hubs around the world. So we were in China one month, Russia the next.

Business school was the first time since joining the unit that I interacted with anyone outside of drones and intelligence. I had been trained not to trust people. When you'd witnessed the worst of humanity, watching people do things when they thought no one was looking, you became out of touch with the real world. You lost trust in other humans.

My initial conversations with classmates were short and generic. When we had class gatherings, I felt self-conscious, like I'd landed on another planet and everyone was wondering who I was, and what I wanted to do. I immediately went into my old mindset of being secretive about where I'd been. Most had come from corporate places, like Google or GE or Goldman. A part of me thought they wouldn't understand me anyway. When I met a Muslim classmate, I fought off the battlefield instinct of thinking enemy. My world had been so blocked off and the first few weeks I worried that I wouldn't fit in with these people who had grown up so differently, had not seen the things I'd seen. In a way, I felt like I'd lost my identity somewhere over the past few years. I had no identity now and wasn't sure how to relate to anyone.

Joyce started to change all that a little. During orientation in Shanghai, China, in mid-2012, they'd sat us near each other in a large conference room because our last names were close in the alphabet. I remember sneaking peeks of her from the corner of my eye as the lectures began. She was beautiful and it was hard to concentrate even with the commotion onstage.

When we had a break, I made my way over to her at the edge of the room where a few others had gathered. It was a big hotel ballroom, with more than 150 other students from all over the world. They were passing around trays of little bite-sized sand-wiches and drinks. Even though she had a big name tag dangling around her neck that said Joyce, I said, "Hey, Julie." She smiled at the mistake the first time. And gave me shit about it the second and third times I did it that night.

I managed to collect that she was from Lexington, Kentucky, horse and bourbon country. She was smart, funny, and had a subtle southern accent that hit me right away. She also made me nervous—a feeling I hadn't experienced since I was in the Box, tasking drones over a moving target. Sometimes that night I just didn't know what to say to her and found myself searching for the right thing. I liked the nerves, an electric shock moving through me again. I needed more. I asked her out the next night. We went out until midnight—and pretty much every night after that for a week straight.

Shanghai was just the beginning. We traveled the world together. Little by little over the school year, as we traveled to different countries, I let my walls down. Sharing things I normally wouldn't talk about. After a few months, I told her my secret: the life I lived before. It was the first time I talked about it openly with someone outside my closed-up community.

I told her stories, not all at once, but in pieces. She was always saying, tell me more. She wasn't from a military family and the stories might as well have been out of a movie. I told her about the missile strike where I'd almost died. I told her about the Pizza Hut in Baghdad.

Those sixteen months at school with her were like an island that appeared out of nowhere. The more time I spent with her, the less I felt disconnected from reality. There were even times when my past slipped away like a great big balloon let go into the sky and I hoped it would never come back.

"WE ARE JUST WAITING TO BE CLEARED HOT," THE WOMAN CHATTED OVER THE computer.

My tie hurt my neck. I loosened it and undid a button on my shirt but kept my eyes glued to the drone feed in my D.C. office.

I felt my heartbeat click up a few notches as the Reaper's camera suddenly zoomed on top of the motorcycle, giving us the point of view of riding with them.

When a target was on the move in the desert, a strike sometimes made the most sense. It meant less collateral damage because these dirt roads were miles away from the city centers and the target was largely out in the open.

Now, as the Reaper circled around the target, like a hawk eyeing its prey, it turned into its attack orbit. It was time. It headed straight for the two men on the motorcycle.

"Ten seconds time on target."

Those seconds between a Hellfire launch and the impact on target always slowed down. The men on that motorbike had no idea they were about to die.

But just before the Hellfire hit, the motorbike did something unexpected. The men started following a small curve in the road that took it around a four-story building that appeared to rise out of nowhere.

Boom.

I couldn't tell what type of building it was, maybe residential, possibly abandoned. It had been hit along with the motorcycle. Civilians soon began appearing in the road from around the corner, cautious at first, looking into the sky, before a few men finally dragged the bodies away.

I turned my screen off that morning and just sat there for

what seemed like hours as the day went on around me. Emails coming in as usual. Meetings taking place. I didn't move and left the office early in a bit of a trance.

That afternoon I got a call from a close friend, Mike Stock, who owned Bancroft, a nonprofit involved in military training. He was working with African troops to fight the Al Qaeda–affiliated terrorist group al-Shabaab. After just returning stateside, he had filled me in on some of his work in Mogadishu, Somalia. His stories of their progress pushing al-Shabaab fighters farther outside the city and the rampant war in the region was starting to get my interest again.

"It's no-man's-land out there, just enough danger to get your heart beating again. You should come out and see it for yourself sometime."

I talked to Joyce at dinner. I didn't tell her about the strike days before. It wasn't about that anyway. It was everything leading up to it. The strike probably just brought clarity: I couldn't figure out life outside of the Box. My mind was racing thinking about the possibility of going back. *What purpose do we have sitting back here when there is so much evil out there? It's like people here have forgotten how lucky we all are to live this way.* Fighting for something greater was my world. I couldn't take it anymore and had already convinced myself I needed to be there.

"I need to go back," I said. "They need my help." We were sitting at the kitchen table. We'd grown even closer over the last few months and I trusted her. She'd told me before that she never wanted me to return to war. But I couldn't shake it.

"What are you talking about?"

"I'm going to Somalia," I said, making the decision right then and there.

"What?" It was like she'd eaten something radioactive. Her mouth curled up.

"It's not a big deal. It's a secure base."

Joyce stood up and walked across the room and then looked back at me. "Do you even love me?"

"Of course I do."

"Say it then."

"Of course I love you."

"Would you cry if I died?"

"What?" I laughed this off. She'd brought this up before and I'd done the same thing.

"You don't tell me things," she said. She was from a big, emotional family that shared everything. "You don't hug me. You don't tell me 'I love you.' It's like you're cut off."

I tried to tell her that wasn't true, but she wasn't hearing it.

"Would you cry if I died?" she asked again.

"Oh babe, I'd cry."

"I don't know," she said. "It's like sometimes I wonder if you feel anything."

In a corner, she noticed my old black bag—the one I took around with me before. On it was my bulletproof vest.

"And you need that for a secure base?"

She resented that I chose another war over her. I tried to explain that this was who I was. That I needed it. I had a hunger that wouldn't quit. I had been through a lot and saw a lot and I was better. "You don't understand," I said.

But it was me who didn't understand. That reckoning wouldn't come until later.

DAYS LATER IN THE SPRING OF 2013, I WAS ON A PLANE TO NAIROBI, KENYA. THERE I crammed into a chartered Cessna on my way to Mogadishu, the bullet- and IED-riddled capital of Somalia—another front on the war on terror.

One of the first things I did was take a walk. I ended up on the beach at the edge of the airport, looking down a cliff at the blue crashing water. In the distance, Mogadishu rose up in a jumble, one of the most dangerous cities in the world. The only thing separating us from all the forces fighting al-Shabaab was a chain-link fence.

I stood there, taking in the sea as a plane landed, swooping right past me and dropping onto the tarmac—a drug delivery that happened once a day. It was a massive cargo plane filled floor to ceiling with khat—the drug chewed by the locals that made them high and took them away from their troubles. Which was disturbing when you realized that nearly every man walking around Mogadishu had an AK-47 strapped to his chest. It was a city where anything could happen, where violence could erupt at any moment. And yet, standing there, I felt calm and completely in control. Something about it all was simply beautiful.

In Mogadishu, I slept in a converted trailer in the city's heavily fortified airport and spent the next few weeks teaching the African Union what I knew about intelligence gathering and flying handheld drones like Ravens to locate targets. It was just like the old days. One week we located a suicide bomber looking to attack the main military base in the capital, another day we nailed a guy making IEDs to blow up convoys. Then we crashed a drone.

I was working with a group who'd come into the country to provide local support to the Ugandan army fighting al-Shabaab. The drone went down in the middle of the night during a reconnaissance mission. We worried the drone was lost and that it would soon emerge on the black market—only to be used against us later.

It was one of the handheld Puma drones, which were about a hundred grand a pop. At first the GPS locator pinged back but then it quickly went dead. It could have been anywhere.

The group flying it weren't legally allowed out of the airport so we took a team of Ugandan soldiers working with us, got suited up, and went to check out the last ping location we'd seen for the drone.

We snuck out the backside of the airport. The streets were dead silent, only the sand and dirt crunching under our feet. We were in full body armor, MP5 submachine guns pointed outward with our flashlights, eyeing shadows for movement. The streets were a mix of falling-down shacks and buildings bullet-ridden or blown up from the war. This was the kind of situation that could go south fast.

When we got to the ping location, about a quarter of a mile out, there was nothing there: the drone was gone.

But in a few minutes, the Ugandans found three local men up late who had seen what had happened. They pointed at the sky, mimicked a bird falling, and waved down the street, toward the sea. "The police took it," the older one said. Now they could be anywhere.

We retreated to the base but eventually got a tip from another source—the drone had been handed over to a Somali general within national intelligence. You'd think that would be good news for us, but it wasn't.

As we stepped into his compound in the middle of Mogadishu during daylight hours the next day, there was definitely a feeling in the air that we were out of our element. Somali soldiers gawked from the wall ledges as me and another guy from the airport walked in. It was rare for them to see Americans strolling around.

The general greeted us at the end of a large stone courtyard and led us into his office. He was a fat man, with a gray mustache and a patch of hair covering his chin. He wore glasses with a bright gold watch.

"So you men are here to talk about what exactly, some device that fell from the sky?" he said, leaning back in a wood chair, fan blowing nicely on his face. "I'm not sure what you are talking about."

No need for pleasantries.

"The drone that crashed and was eventually picked up by

your men, we know you have it," I replied, not wanting to waste any time. It was never good to stay in a place too long in Mogadishu. Word quickly spread of your presence and the next thing you knew you were living out in the desert being ransomed off to the highest bidder.

"Oh yes, that," he said, as if he didn't know exactly why we were there. "I have received numerous calls from different groups telling us it is theirs."

"Different groups?"

Clearly he was lying. He leaned back and watched us squirm a little. "How do I believe it is yours?"

I drew a diagram of it on a piece of paper on his desk. "It's probably broken in a few pieces right now, isn't it? You can't turn it on, can you?"

The general looked at his deputy in the corner of the room and then looked back at us, smiled. "I still don't know if I believe this is yours. And even if it was, we don't have it here."

The Somalis were experts at this game. But I had something up my sleeve.

"General, can you come with me outside for a second?"

He and his deputy looked at me skeptically, but then got up and followed me to the courtyard.

As we walked into the courtyard, no translator was needed. I drew his attention to the sky.

"Now do you believe me?" I said pointing to the exact same Puma drone hovering overhead. I had asked the group back at the airport to do a flyover with their backup.

I'll never forget the look on the general's face. He could have dropped dead right there, his eyes popping out of his head with excitement. It was priceless as he and his deputy watched the drone glide just above us, about five hundred feet up. He was in awe, as if a magic trick had just changed what he believed to be true in the world.

I radioed to the group that they could return the backup drone to the airport. When it disappeared, the general invited us back inside. We'd won. He told us he had the crashed drone. It was in a separate office, all the pieces there.

But the general had one more card to play.

He leaned forward and looked me right in the eye.

"We should give a reward to the Somali local citizens who found it," he said.

"Of course, of course," we said, laughing inside about this proposition. Obviously he was thinking of himself. "How much do you think is appropriate, General?"

I could see the general's lips curl upward, his eyes blinking dollar signs like a cartoon character thinking about a pot of gold.

"Five thousand dollars U.S.," was his quick response.

"We're only prepared to give you one thousand today," we came back.

"Fine," he said, without blinking.

We got $1,000 in hundred-dollar bills from the base and gave it to him in a brown paper bag—pennies considering what the drone was worth.

Not everything was that exciting. Most wasn't at all.

I stayed for three months in Somalia and the whole time I thought being there would feed my urge to be back in action and get my heart beating again. But it didn't do that.

When I was away before, I never thought much about home. It was just the mission around the clock. But in Somalia, things weren't like that. I talked to Joyce more and more then. For hours at a time, I sat on my bed with my computer flipped open to Skype, her blurry image coming in.

It was always after midnight, the air conditioner rumbling away in the window of the shipping container. We talked mostly about what she was up to, staying away from talk about the war that was going on a hundred yards or so over the wall. And she didn't press me much—until one night she did.

"I don't understand it," she said.

She moved up close to the screen so I could see her hazel eyes clearly. They looked a little glassy. I could tell that she was upset.

"What?"

"Don't do that."

"What?"

"Why does this make you happy," she said, "being over there in such a dangerous place?"

I tried to explain as best I could, but all that came out was "I needed to do this. It was important."

She let that sit between us and for a second I thought she'd drop it, but then she said, "I didn't sign up for this, for your old life. You know that? I don't want this kind of thing forever." Then she turned away from the screen.

It took a second for this to sink in and for a moment my stomach got this terrible pain. Like I'd been swung at. I hadn't felt this feeling before.

"It won't—" I started to say before she cut me off.

"I know others do this life." Her voice was shaking a little. "They're okay with going off and disappearing but I can't."

She paused, as if she'd been planning this out. "I don't want that life."

I let her finish and then waited for her to turn back to me. The conversation ended with both of us quiet with heavy hearts—both conflicted in a different way.

In the weeks since I had left, I'd begun to realize that this war action fix just wasn't enough for me anymore, Somalia wasn't enough, no war zone would ever be enough.

Days later, I had some time to digest our conversation. As I sat there looking at Joyce on Skype, I could see how this was affecting her. It was about more than just me now. I felt more than any other time that I needed her, I needed something more tangible, something that I could hold on to. This is why I originally left the Army; I asked for a normal life and now I was creating my own barriers keeping me from it. Being home, laying the foundations for a family and good friends—and not being in some distant place fighting an enemy that would always hate us.

I tried to tell her some of that over Skype that night.

"I heard what you said the other night and I'm sorry I made you feel that way. You're right . . . it's not fair."

She stayed quiet and let me go on. Probably because I was showing emotion and she knew I was trying.

"I didn't think I would ever say this, but the feeling of being here isn't good—because I miss you. It's weird for me. But I think I'm ready to come home."

Her face lit up just knowing she was missed and her words were heard.

"Ready to come home?" she said with a confused look on her face. "Are you done with everything you have been working on?"

"I am going to complete what I came out here to do. But I'm done."

Both of us were finally on the same page. It's like the conversation bonded a new part of us. Though it was short, it was exactly what we both needed.

Soon after, the connection went bad and I couldn't get back online. The Internet sucked in Somalia. But one thing I knew as I sat there alone in the shipping container with the air conditioner fan beating back the sea's humidity from outside: This was the woman I cared about. This was the woman I wanted to marry and I wasn't going to lose her. I needed her.

That could have been the end for me. I could have left drones and war behind once and for all and the story might have ended right there with Joyce and me living happily ever after. Except life is never that neat.

I WAS SIPPING COFFEE ONE MORNING WHEN BRAD, AN AIR FORCE INTEL GUY, WALKED over to my corner desk and asked if I had a second to talk. "Can we do this privately?" he said.

It was about a year after leaving Somalia—spring of 2014. For the last few months, I'd been working as a consultant for the Silicon Valley software company Palantir. They'd sent me to Stuttgart, Germany, to help implement new software at the main U.S. military command center that handled Africa.

Months had passed and I had kept to myself. No one in the office except Brad knew what I'd done before. (We'd crossed paths in the intel world while I was running some drone missions.) Working there felt so far away from what I'd been doing before—like I'd gone to the other side of the moon. And I liked it that way. I was finally comfortable not needing that old adrenaline-fumed life.

Joyce and I had grown even closer. There had been moments over the last few months since Somalia when I finally thought I had escaped my past. Joyce had come with me to Stuttgart and we had a two-bedroom apartment on the top floor of a new complex overlooking downtown. On the weekends, we traveled all over Europe, jumping in a car and not thinking about anything much, just enjoying the time away and being together. One weekend we would drive to Prague, the next to Milan or Zurich. It felt like one big vacation that I never wanted to end.

But now that was all about to get upended.

"Do you know the girls who were kidnapped in Nigeria?" Brad asked.

Of course I did. It was all over the news in May. More than two hundred girls had been kidnapped from a school in Chibok, Borno State, Nigeria, by the terrorist group Boko Haram.

#BringBackOurGirls was the headline on all the news channels. A search had been launched but the group and the girls seemed to have melted away into the dense jungle of the countryside without a trace. I didn't pay too much attention to it. Worrying about those kinds of things wasn't my job anymore.

Brad was a stout guy, tall, black hair, and with a commanding presence. He threw a shadow. He sat down on a plastic chair across from me and looked me right in the eyes. "We've just been tasked with finding the girls," he said. "We could use your help."

Boko Haram had been locked in a fight with the Nigerian government for years and security forces had largely ceded them the eastern part of the country. The United States saw them as terrorists—they were affiliated with Al Qaeda and would later pledge allegiance to ISIS. The United States had a $7 million reward for the head of the group's leader, a lunatic named Abubakar Shekau.

Shekau frequently posted videos online dressed in dark camouflage, like he was some military figure, waving an automatic weapon, threatening to attack the United States and preaching about his jihad against Christianity. There were stories of him reciting verses from the Koran that didn't exist, to justify his atrocities. His men rampaged through Nigerian villages, hacking away with machetes at any man, woman, or child who refused to join them. With the kidnapped girls, he said he'd be converting them to Islam and marrying them off to his fighters. We worried some of them would also be used as suicide bombers, just as he had done previously with girls he had brainwashed.

Brad must have seen the doubt written all over my face. "I know you're out," he said. "But this is a big deal."

My days working for Palantir had been mostly the same, just troubleshooting the new software and banging my head against the wall when new glitches turned up. It was an easy nine-to-five job, a cakewalk compared to what I was used to, and I was sleeping again.

My first inclination was to say no. They could figure it out on their own. This wasn't my fight and Joyce had asked me after Somalia to never go back to the person I was before. I knew that if I flipped that switch on again, she probably wouldn't like the person I became and then I'd lose her.

But when I got home that night, I couldn't stop thinking about the girls. It didn't help that it was all over CNN, which Joyce had turned on while we ate dinner.

"You are giving me that same look you gave me right before you told me you were going to Somalia," she said, putting her fork down. "What's going on?"

I waited a second before answering.

"I can't say right now, but these guys are asking for my help on a mission."

"Well you said *no,* of course, right?" she asked. "You're done with that!"

I thought about it more that night. But the other side of me won out. It would only be a month. I could help guide these guys, share with them some of my experience, and I'd be out when they had to give the Pred back. Maybe it was stupid. But I thought, *What the hell?* I was at a better place in my life. I couldn't resist. I was in.

NONE OF US SLEPT THE FIRST TWENTY-FOUR HOURS. WE WERE A GROUP OF FEWER than ten, all of us bent over laptops, staring at TV screens, just like the days when I was running the Box in Iraq.

Everyone supporting the mission was crammed into a small windowless room on the top floor of a secure military facility. It felt like a bank vault. The room was barely big enough, with the computers, screens, and desks nearly stacked on top of each other.

A heavy steel door, locked with secure codes, separated us from the rest of the place.

We'd gotten official clearance to fly into Nigerian airspace, something they'd been against until now, with all the media attention.

We worked fast: combed through intelligence about the group, dug into national and international databases of maps and old files, and analyzed videos of the girls that had begun circulating on YouTube and other social media sites.

The northeastern part of Nigeria, where Boko Haram had taken the girls, was about the size of New York State and bordered by the countries Chad and Cameroon. Boko Haram didn't acknowledge the borders.

From our sleuthing, we soon came up with about forty different startpoints—mainly places where the group had been seen or known to hide. My gut was that the girls had been broken up into three different groups—that's how they'd operated before—with one group likely in the Sambisa Forest, just outside of Maidiguri, another near the Lake Chad Basin, across the border, and another perhaps in the southeast near the national parks on the Nigerian side near the Cameroon border.

It was showtime now with the drone. In a sense, we were literally mapping the earth, where few Americans had even traveled. It was a lot to soak in at first. The ground was mostly sporadic trees with patches of wide-open grassland. Everything was so green below, except for the bright brown dirt roads that wound around everywhere like something undone. Many people lived under trees instead of houses because it was cooler than inside. Others lived in the open land, entire families set up in fields just off the roads.

There were people everywhere. On foot and dirt bikes. And the Boko Haram foot soldiers didn't even hide. It was clear that the group felt invincible there, not a care in the world.

Within the first two days of hunting, one of the first start-points we added to the list paid off—in the Sambisa Forest.

At first it was hard to tell if it was the lost girls. The tree was taller than anything else around for miles, with a thick trunk and huge branches that extended over everything below it like one big umbrella. We called it the "Tree of Life."

There wasn't much around for miles except a few small villages, some thick bush, and a dirt road that curved around the Tree of Life like a ribbon.

It was early in the morning there, late night for us. There was a lot of confusion at first as the scene happened and the room erupted into an urgent conversation.

"Wow, there's a lot of people under there," someone said.

"Yeah, that tree is huge."

"Can we tell if those are females?"

"The sensor operator thinks they might be."

After prayer time ended, the people were quickly corralled back into the tent. It took us a full day of these prayer sessions to know for sure. Others in the room, including a bunch of the military officers, went back and forth about what they were seeing. Trying to make sense of it all, not knowing if their rank could handle telling their superiors what we had just discovered in the event someone got it wrong. But I knew better. I knew 100 percent. We had found them.

WE NEEDED TO KNOW EVERY SQUARE INCH OF THE SAMBISA FOREST BEFORE ANYONE went in.

One day we saw what we believed to be one of the girls running away from the group during prayer time, only to have two of the men in the group chase after her with AK-47s in hand and drag her back.

When one of the targeting officers, who had personally traveled to the U.S. embassy in Nigeria, finally delivered images of the Tree of Life to the Nigerian security forces, they were surprised that we'd found them so fast. They said they would go in. The Nigerians were still trying to gather their own information on the girls' whereabouts, at this point they had nothing really credible. They did a great job of pretending that they had it all covered, though, as we watched news outlets interviewing various senior Nigerian officials assuring the public that they knew way more than they actually did.

But then an odd thing happened after a lot of back-and-forth with their forces. They didn't act.

Weeks passed and we waited for a rescue mission and watched the Tree of Life through the monitors. It wasn't like the days of the Box when I could just send in the operators.

The Nigerians never sent troops. It seemed that they were worried about going in, afraid of a firefight. Weeks later, instead, they sent one fighter jet to swoop low and over the Tree of Life, as a show of force to the Boko Haram fighters. It couldn't have been a dumber decision. They showed the public that they knew one of the locations of the girls, as the cameras captured it, but they also alerted the abductors.

A day or two after the flyby, it was over. Bad weather moved in and we had to bring the Pred down. When we got it back up and panned over the patch of forest, the girls were gone.

As we orbited the Tree of Life, there was no sign of them below. It was just the tree now and nothing around it. They had likely been moved because of those jets.

It killed us.

It was a perfect example of why drones are nothing without a finishing capability. Whether that was a Hellfire or assault force, somebody on the ground had to be proficient enough to act on what the drones saw.

As far as we could tell, the Nigerian leaders didn't want to find the girls. For example, with the information we gave them they could have done something. The kidnapping was a political tool and they embraced it like a politician suddenly supporting an agenda to win votes and for the wrong reasons. All they wanted to do was figure out how other countries could give them money, how America could give them drones. The Nigerians used it as an opportunity to ask for Predators and Reapers from the U.S. government. Like they were somehow pros at using them and all they needed were the drones and not the infrastructure behind it. They wanted the expensive ones with the Hellfires, and they wanted the U.S. government to buy them.

We only had the Pred for another two weeks before it went back in its box and was sent home. In that time, we found a bunch of other sites with a confirmed Boko Haram presence, but we never saw the missing girls again.

A few months passed and news of the kidnappings in the mainstream media subsided, as did the interest in the U.S. government to commit any more aerial assets. That's what happens when you're not in headlines anymore: people forget.

Boko Haram was and still is one of the biggest threats to the region. It was depressing to think about how we'd missed the girls, how the Nigerians had messed it up after we'd tracked them down—and how many of those girls are still missing today.

I walked out of that room after weeks of not sleeping, beat up and tired, just like the days in the Box. But I could see clearer than I'd ever seen.

I'd been fighting the pull of drones, trying to find another way forward in the world. Arguing with that feeling. Believing that to go on meant giving them up. But that changed for me as I left the ops center that night and took a break back home. It had taken a long time, with a lot of pain, to finally realize that drones didn't only have to be about counterterrorism and killing bad guys. I had the power to use drones for more important things than war. Before I hadn't even thought about that sort of thing. In the military, I'd been completely under its spell. I had blinders on to the rest of the world. Now I saw something else entirely.

25

A NEW BEGINNING

As an elephant family grazed in the grassy plain of the Great Rift Valley in northern Kenya, I zoomed the drone camera back out to the perimeter of the wildlife conservancy—until I saw three men crawling slowly through the bush toward them in the darkness.

We had received intel from the local wildlife service that a small campsite had been discovered in a cave nearby the day before. With the embers still cooling, I knew any wildlife in the proximity could be in danger.

I switched on the drone's thermal camera to get a better look. The men were carrying AK-47s and large machetes. They'd come for the elephant tusks, a prize that could bring them tens of thousands on the black market.

"We're tracking hostiles near the eastern fence line from above, push out the Rangers to the site immediately."

"Roger that," a voice came back over the radio.

It was early evening, the sun just down. In a glowing white, the drone feeds lit up the small ops center that we'd set up in the middle of the conservancy. It wasn't the Box. It was different now.

All around us were tens of thousands of acres: mountains, valleys, and lakes. Crazy wildlife that made you feel like we were in *The Jungle Book*: elephants, rhinos, leopards, and hyenas. Creatures from an earlier age before man.

"We can't wait any longer," I called out. "If they make it through that perimeter those elephants are good as dead. I'm moving another drone to protect the family and will keep this one on the perimeter threat until you secure it."

The choppers were winding up just outside my tent, the rangers on the move to take them out. "We're in route to intercept," the voice said.

I'D BEEN WORKING OUT THAT PLAY-BY-PLAY FOR MONTHS NOW—WHAT A DRONE operation would look like if it were put into action in Kenya, home to some of the world's most famous wildlife parks and reserves.

It all started when two Silicon Valley entrepreneurs got in touch with me and said they had an idea that would change my life. Before we met, I thought, *What could live up to that?*

They flew me first-class out to Paris one weekend in the spring of 2014 and we met at an upscale, swanky hotel bar. Reza was in his forties, with an aura of mystery and excitement about him. His family was from Iran, but he had grown up mostly in America and France. He had built a fortune out of a handful of Internet companies in the United States. But over the past few years he had roamed the earth in search of a deeper calling.

Jory, his partner, had roots in telecom. A slightly older man, he exuded cool and calmness. After a successful career working at multinational U.S. firms, he had crossed paths with Reza while on a similar quest to help Haiti after its earthquake. They'd bonded over the potential of doing humanitarian projects.

"What these wildlife conservations are doing out there is not working," Reza said to me that night, as techno music hummed in the background. "They need a game changer."

We connected right away.

Their idea was straightforward. Animals were dying at alarming rates in parts of Africa and innovative new technology was needed to actually do something about it. They felt that drones could fight that war—and win.

The goal was simple but ambitious. Start a program that would work with the government and wildlife conservations that oversaw much of the land, to patrol them with drones and use the rangers as the assault team. Basically, set up an operation like I had in Iraq.

We talked for hours at that bar about the different technologies being developed by U.S. companies.

"Do you think drones could help solve this issue?" Reza asked.

"It's possible," I replied. "I just need to get on the ground and see the terrain to be sure."

"Well, that's why you're here. We want you to lead the expedition. Are you in?"

I smiled, pausing for a few seconds to take it all in. The well-dressed people swanned around us with their drinks and I felt like an island with these guys and this new idea. Together they were poised, and yet in them burned an agitation that made me feel very much empowered, enthusiastic, and alive.

"Of course I am," I said.

A week later, we were flying into Kenya.

OUR TINY CESSNA LIFTED OFF FROM SMALL WILSON AIRPORT IN NAIROBI, KENYA, heading south toward the Kenya–Tanzania border.

The seats were cramped, but it didn't matter. I was heading into the Maasai Mara, one of Africa's greatest wildlife reserves.

The Mara cuts along the southwest Kenya border and spills over the Tanzania border, connecting with Serengeti National Park. The massive reserve was home to the legendary Maasai warriors, a group of people who lived off the land. There is a symbiotic relationship between the Maasai and the wildlife there, and it has been that way for centuries.

Landing on a dirt airstrip a few hours after leaving Nairobi, the Cessna bumped to a stop. There, in the open grass plains around me, I got my first glimpse of the remote area. Wildlife was everywhere: antelopes, wildebeest, hyenas, hippo, elephants, zebras.

It felt almost prehistoric when I set foot there—like an explorer experiencing a new world for the first time. The open grassland alternated with hills and the land reached for hundreds of miles around us.

The terrain was perfect for drones to operate in, with hundreds of miles of open land and few trees. With the cameras it would be easy to distinguish between animal and man from three to four thousand feet up.

That day, I got my first up-close view of an elephant in the wild. We climbed into jeeps with a Kenyan ranger who was waiting for the three of us and began to drive. Soon an elephant family walked in front of us. Two big ones and three smaller ones. A couple hundred yards away, just grazing. They were some of the most peaceful, majestic animals I'd ever seen—except they were dying.

I WAS STILL ADJUSTING TO LIFE OUTSIDE OF THE MILITARY, BUT IT WAS GETTING easier. I had done a lot of soul-searching.

Joyce stuck with me. Even though I still didn't know how everything would end up, I took out all the money I had in the bank and bought her a diamond ring. We got engaged and moved into an apartment in downtown D.C. It had started to feel a lot like home—something I hadn't had in a long time.

We talked about the past a lot. It was like getting things off my back. Sometimes Joyce said that when I talked about the terrorists I'd hunted, I still acted like they weren't real people, like they didn't have souls.

I saw a kill or capture as business. It was my job and it was transactional. And because of the good I believed—and still believe—it did, it consumed me and made me cold.

I tried for some time to explain this to her. But I got that it didn't make much sense to someone normal. These days I did less explaining about that. I didn't need to anymore. I was slowly losing the coldness day by day.

And then I surprised myself—and Joyce. It was early one night and I was watching TV news when there was a story that came on about an old man and woman who had been married for more than fifty years. I don't know what happened inside of me but watching them talk about their connection to one another over the long decades got to me. Joyce was trying to say something to me, but I didn't hear her so she came over. "Brett, you're crying," she said.

I put a hand on my cheek and it was wet. I hadn't even noticed. "It's nice," I said.

Joyce laughed. "After all of what you've been through, this is what you shed tears over?"

I hadn't cried for my cousin. I hadn't been able to cry at the funeral of the soldier who had died. I hadn't been able to cry ever since I began my life in the Box. But this was a start.

THE MORE TIME I SPENT OUT OF THE MILITARY, THE MORE I STARTED TO SEE THAT drones were a part of me now and could play a role in my life.

I could still use them—just differently and to help humanity. I started a company to that end.

I realized that the knowledge I had was unlike any others' in the field of drones. I could use that knowledge for greater purposes than simply counterterrorism. I could use drones for good. As I looked around, I didn't see anyone who was helping businesses and people understand how to effectively deploy them in the skies, what you could do with them if you used them right.

The way that they could be used to monitor farm crops or to augment disaster recovery sites or even help search for missing children. Consumer drone technology was starting to take shape. Some of the same equipment I had used in the government world was trickling down into the private sector. Around the same time that I got the call about Kenya, I also got a call about using drones to monitor fisheries off the coast of Somalia. Drones could bring stability in a region plagued by poverty and piracy. The world was changing fast, and Jory and Reza showed me how business could be aligned with a deep sense of purpose. We shared the same conviction. Inspired by that philosophy, I started my own company: Dronepire Inc.

The new company meant that I would sometimes have to get into a suit and go to an office. There were spreadsheets and other paperwork. Things I didn't do or like to do in the Box. But this was my first step. I didn't need the gambling. I didn't need the fake adrenaline. Using drones to promote good—which is just as important as preventing evil—was what started to get me up in the morning.

I DON'T HAVE ANY REGRETS ABOUT MY LIFE IN THE BOX AND HOW WE USED OUR drones to fight a brutal enemy. Very few people understand just how sick our enemies can be—we haven't seen the worst of them yet. The stuff that shows up on CNN about ISIS every other day is only scratching the surface.

Hunting terrorists was a rough existence. It was a stressful job and I had to give up a lot to do it right. It taught me patience and the importance of being persistent against the enemy. Stress these days, though, was nothing. I learned to trust in my gut, because it was backed up by years of experience combating terrorists in different settings.

I saw how effective teams can be when they are devoted and love what they do, and are given the right tools and freedom to achieve their potential. Few have ever experienced what it's like to have a full arsenal of drones backing you up and leaders giving you the leeway needed to truly fight the enemy.

When Mr. White brought me into the unit, I had no idea what the life would be like. I wondered sometimes if Mr. White followed what I did over those years, if he ever checked in on me. There's no way of telling.

I'm amazed by the devotion to country my old friends from the unit still have. Jack and Bill taught me more life lessons than they will really ever know. When people ask me about the years of service, I still don't talk about much of it. Most of the people around me today still have no idea. They don't understand how the last few years truly shaped me into who I became. They are probably just as surprised as you reading this now. Some guys said that we did bad things to bad people, but that's what it took to fight them. The one thing I know for sure without question: I'd do it all again.

EPILOGUE

"Where are all the animals?" I asked Kuki Gallmann, as we both stared off across the Great Rift Valley from a mountaintop on her property one late afternoon.

Surrounding us were miles and miles of forests, mountains, and valleys spread across western Kenya in the Gallmann Wildlife Conservancy. The beauty of the landscape didn't even seem real; it was like being in an IMAX. But there was little movement at all, very few signs of life, as if we were the last people alive.

"What you're seeing now is the greed of man," said Kuki. "The work of poachers."

The Great Rift Valley was considered by many to be the cradle of civilization because so many ancient human remains had been found there.

After flying into Kenya, we'd been jetting all over the country, meeting people and businesses to discuss poaching and explain how we could bring our idea of drones to the world.

Kuki Gallmann is a world-renowned wildlife conservationist, a legend in the conservation world and the subject of the movie *I Dreamed of Africa*, which followed her family's travels from Italy into Kenya in the early 1970s.

Kuki was in her seventies now but didn't look it. She had blond hair thrown around by the wind, and was fit. Colorful bracelets dangled off her wrists. She still had a bit of an Italian accent. Her daughter Sveva, who had brought us here, looked like a younger version of her.

The nearly hundred thousand acres of conservancy had been a part of their family's blood for decades—and it was one of the largest privately owned reserves in the world. But a lot had changed in that time.

"It wasn't many years ago when we had one of the largest populations of black rhinos," she said.

"What happened to them?" I asked.

It was late afternoon, the sun of January burning on our faces. She looked down at her feet, then back up at me.

"I just recently flew our last rhino out by helicopter," she said. "He wouldn't have survived here much longer. They would have killed him."

The poacher gangs came for the animals with poison-tipped spears and darts, she said. It was the story of Kenya, what we'd heard all over on our travels. The gangs came across the borders in 4x4 trucks, hid in the hills, where they could see plenty of land, and waited for the elephant families to come. They left trailing rivers of blood.

The cradle of civilization was now the cradle of death.

The Gallmann reserve was one of many private parks in Kenya, along with the famous government-run wildlife reserves like Nairobi National Park and Tsavo East and West. But the miles and miles of land were impossible to fully police. It was remote and rugged. Some villages had taken up to fighting the poachers like militarized neighborhood watches. In other places, loosely organized rangers mostly financed by Western donors hunted the gangs. Still, the body count kept climbing.

More elephants were being killed every day in Africa than were being born. Hundreds of them were killed every year. More than 100,000 African elephants had been killed in the last three years alone. At the current rate, the species was on the brink of extinction. The ivory from their tusks was channeled to the black markets in Asia. An elephant tusk: $1,500 per kilogram. Rhinos were even worse because there were so few left. A rhino horn could command as much as $60,000 per kilogram on the streets of Beijing—each horn worth more than its weight in gold. Wealthy buyers drove up prices. The horns were added to expensive antiaging lotions. Some thought the shavings cured cancer. Millionaires in Asia sprinkled them in their martinis.

This was what we were up against—a different kind of terror. But still terror.

Illegal trafficking is big money—some say more than $20 billion a year. The profits spread around the world like a tangled bloodline—some go to corrupt government officials in on the action but more money ends up with international crime syndicates and terrorist groups like al-Shabaab in Somalia, just to the east. Wildlife trafficking is in the same camp as drugs, human trafficking, and weapons: it is a worldwide epidemic with all kinds of dangerous ripples. No wonder the United States recently called it out as a national security threat. Those dollars could end up funding attacks on our country.

When I talked to Kuki that day, she described it all the same way a war would be described. With winners and losers. When the poachers got caught, they paid bribes to get out of jail. The government recently passed a law allowing people to shoot the bad guys if they had guns, but that didn't slow things down. The poachers still operated with impunity. The animals were losing. Kuki didn't have helicopters or planes. Only a few reserves had even those resources. She just had rangers.

The rangers fought by hiding in the bush and trying to spot poachers as they set up. As we bumped along the back roads of her conservancy that afternoon in an old Land Cruiser, her rangers would just appear out of nowhere. Their war wasn't very coordinated. For the most part it relied on luck, being in the right place at the right time. They were no match for the poachers.

"The elephants used to take no interest in anyone that traveled through my conservation," Kuki told us as we traveled farther into the Rift Valley that day, as if to explain why we weren't seeing many animals. They didn't think much about humans then. "Now they keep their distance. They know that we're going to bring them harm."

"The problem is bigger than just us now. It's about saving the species."

"Your drones will change this?" she asked.

THIS WAS THE FUTURE OF DRONES.

Missions would work just like they did in the Box: gathering intelligence on poacher networks and grazing patterns, where and when an elephant family, say, had been killed before. We would be going on the offense this time, stopping poachers before they could get close enough to the animals.

Drones would do the jobs of one hundred rangers, scouring the massive stretches of remote territory for the hunters. As they stalked the skies, they'd also map swaths of land and count herds.

We'd identify hotspots with drones from our local intelligence on the ground and that's where the targeting would begin. As long as you sighted the poachers a couple of miles out, there would be time for the choppers to swoop in and cut them off. Boom. They'd be toast.

But there was one important point to all this. The drones had to be military grade. Not something you'd find under your Christmas tree.

When we were in the Maasai Mara reserve earlier in the week, we met the head of the elephant project there, Marc Goss, who for years had been banging his head over how to innovate in his fight against the poachers.

Marc's group worked out of a small compound miles away from any of the tourist areas. He lived there with more than fifty wildlife security rangers who patrolled the place with old Toyota Land Cruisers and rifles. The compound they based their operation from was a series of huts hidden away in the bush. His own house was a large tent he shared with his wife, overlooking the Mara.

Marc was a military guy, too. The BBC had done a story about him attempting to get support for drones a year or so ago. He'd bought a drone online to help his fifty rangers. But the experiment hadn't worked, the drone technology available to the public wasn't capable enough yet for his teams' needs. He was excited that I was there. "Look at this," he said as we walked out of his headquarters and into the reservation.

It was midday. Marc wore an old camouflaged military uniform with the name of the reserve knitted on the front pocket. He was tall and his hair was starting to go gray in places. He was jumpy with enthusiasm and had the build and energy of a guy who could run up a mountain.

From a storage area, he pulled out a Parrot AR drone—basically four tiny plastic propellers attached to a video camera controlled from your iPhone. You could get them at Brookstone for about two hundred dollars. Parrots could fly for only about twenty minutes and barely cleared some of the highest trees.

Marc started it up and it sounded like a nest of bees that had been kicked. When he got the thing off the ground, it flew about fifty feet before a gust of wind grabbed it and threw it into a tree. He had to climb up and get it.

"I GOT SOMETHING ELSE YOU SHOULD SEE," MARC SAID.

We walked around the compound to the backside in the shade of some trees. I stopped dead in my tracks before Marc could even say another word.

Damn.

It was a massacre. On the grass were dozens of leopard pelts, the skin of a python that was probably fifteen feet long, and a trove of elephant tusks. Over the last few months, Marc's rangers had recovered all of it from poachers.

Why would somebody do this? I just couldn't understand. For some reason I had this feeling of disgust and disdain for the poachers. It reminded me of feelings I used to have in the Box for my targets.

Marc walked over to the collection of tusks. They were covered in dirt and you could still see blood in places. "That's hundreds of thousands of dollars in tusks there," he said.

I picked up a few of the tusks and held them in my hands. I was surprised by their weight. They were heavy.

"What do you do with them all now?" I asked.

Marc shook his head.

"Everything will be burned," he said.

These were guys in the bush who wouldn't know what hit them if I was out there hunting them down.

Just then, Marc got a call. He gets a lot of calls all day long from his rangers who are out in the field, hunting and working their own intel networks. In this case, a GPS collar on an elephant they'd been tracking had stopped moving, close to the Tanzania border.

Marc put the phone back in his pocket and sighed. "It's probably been killed," he said. At this point, there wasn't much they could do about it. It would take too long to get out there right now in trucks. They needed to wait for a plane to come back.

"Want to go on a ride with us?" Marc asked. He was going with a few rangers to check out a rumor of poachers in the northern edge of the reserve—about sixty miles away.

We got in 4x4s and bumped along the grassy plains deeper into the Mara for hours. Sometimes we'd encounter Maasai people walking between remote villages, but mostly it was us and the animals.

When we came to the hills, we couldn't travel by truck anymore, so we got out and walked. This was poacher territory. Far from people, hard to reach. As we climbed higher through the hills, the views of the land below began to open up. You could see for miles out. It took us about thirty minutes to get to the top and soon we spotted a cave.

The cave was about ten yards deep, with a jagged ledge where you could watch miles of the massive, open land below. Nearby I saw the remnants of a recent fire. Some crushed-up charcoal and a plastic bag hanging on a tree, where the hunters had hung their things. Water bottles were scattered about.

"They could have been here last night," one of the rangers said to me. "At least this week."

It was amazing that they didn't even hide. A fire on a high hill. It's like a signal asking for someone to find out. Rangers wouldn't have been able to see this at night very well, but I would.

From my point of view, this was the perfect startpoint. If I had a drone in the air, these poachers would have been done before they even got the chance to stalk an elephant family. With the drone's infrared camera, I could have seen that fire from miles away.

We stood there in the poachers' camp and stared out over the grasslands below. The Ranger pointed out to the distance.

"When they find the elephants they want to kill, they come down from the hilltops and hide in the bush with poison-tipped spears and stab the elephants late at night," he said.

He explained how they watch the elephant die in agony over the course of twenty-four to forty-eight hours as it stumbles through the fields, eventually losing all strength to continue. After the elephant finally collapses, the poachers rip out the tusks one by one.

"It is usually a very slow death."

The sun was going down now on the hilltop. No sign of anyone. The poachers were long gone. We'd never catch them now.

THE ONE THING THAT BECAME CLEAR OVER THE MONTHS WE WORKED ON THE DRONE project: it wasn't going to be easy. There were obstacles all over the place and getting around them was going to be a lot like going around IEDs.

The biggest challenge was that government corruption was deep and some officials secretly benefited from the killing. Kenya was nervous about opening its airspace. To them, drones were foreign eyes in the sky. Few had even seen drones outside the news and movies. They didn't get how they worked. When we walked into the offices of a few government officials, they wondered if we were CIA. "Are you going to use your drones to spy on us?" they asked at different times.

"No, we are going to use drones to protect your livelihoods. Do you think tourists will come out here to stare at grass all day?" I said.

African governments tend to be skeptical of foreigners coming in, even when one is legitimately trying to help them protect their country. It took time to build relationships with them and the American style of business typically didn't fare well.

The other issue was funding. At the start, the business was

running off investments by Reza and Jory. Corporations were beginning to offer support. The military spec drones were perfect for the remote terrain we would be operating in. The wrinkle was that we needed the State Department to sign off on exporting them. The suits. And that sort of thing took time. You can't just buy a bunch of military-grade drones with infrared cameras and throw them in your suitcase on the next flight to Africa.

We had our eyes set on launching from the private Lewa Wildlife Conservancy in the country's Laikipia district. It was famous for the celebrities who went there on safari; Prince William and Kate Middleton had visited when they got engaged. The owners were game when we spoke to them, as long as the government opened the airspace. They also began to introduce us to the right people to make that happen.

The great thing about Lewa was that they already had an ops center, an army of rangers with military experience, some intelligence people who acted as spies inside the poaching world, and Little Bird choppers. These were key elements the foundation needed for the reserves to make this drone war work.

All it took was one success story. We'd show the government and conservancies how a drone operation could work and hope that they would eventually put up the money to fund it with our people. It was a gamble. But even with some of the bigger obstacles out there, I liked our chances. In my eyes, drones were unequivocally the answer to this problem. I knew that with the right drones and the right people, who knew how to use them correctly, we would reduce virtually overnight the percentage of illegally killed elephants and rhinos. I had never been so sure of anything in my life.

That feeling got me up in the morning now. It felt bigger than myself. In the long run, we even saw the possibility of making some money. Drone feeds streaming to classrooms back home the live migrations of elephant families. Educating others on the opposite side of the world about wildlife conservation and the lasting effects of environmental crimes.

It was at Lewa that I saw one of the last northern white rhinos in the world. The owner of the conservancy, Batian, was trying to breed them, to save what was left of the species. Batian told me that this one had come to them from a zoo in the Czech Republic a few years ago.

When I walked up, the rhino didn't move away from me. I touched the rhino's back and the skin was thick and rough, like what I imagined a dinosaur's skin might feel like. I'd never seen or felt anything like it before.

Batian told me the rhino was one of only two breeding male northern white rhinos left in the world. There were only four females left.

That was one of the last times anyone would see that rhino. Not too long after I flew out of Kenya, he died. Another female died months later. Now there were only four left in the entire world.

THE DAY WAS COMING TO A CLOSE. WE SAT ON THE GRASS AND WATCHED THE SUN as it fell across her land, shadows stretching oblong from trees. The sun seemed gigantic, all yellow and red. We'd been talking for hours and I could see how passionate Kuki was about doing something to protect these animals. As far as she was concerned, the dying animals were one of the greatest threats to the world. She had spent a lifetime trying to save them.

As the sun disappeared finally beyond the horizon, we sat there in silence for a stretch. Sitting there, overlooking the breathtaking landscape, I couldn't imagine anything more perfect. Everything I had done in my life up to this moment had led me here. This was what I was born to do.

ACKNOWLEDGMENTS

There were many people who played a role in the making of *Drone Warrior*, and they deserve my utmost gratitude. It's hard to know where to start. What began as something that I thought could be written in just a few months, turned into a nearly three-year exhausting endeavor. The idea for the book was brought to me while I was working in Somalia by a highly regarded *Wall Street Journal* investigative reporter I came in contact with. My apprehension to talk about my experiences at the time couldn't be overstated. I first told him absolutely not. It's tough for someone like me that worked within the special operations community to speak on the intimate subject, let alone to believe his story is worth telling. We are taught quite the opposite in fact. You simply don't talk about fight club.

What finally did it for me was driving past the headquarters of the CIA months later in McLean, VA, only to find hundreds of protesters outside hoisting up fake Predator drones on their shoulders and carrying signs that said things like "when drones fly, children die!" and "drones equal war crimes." How wrong they are, they couldn't be more ignorant about the truth. The men and women behind America's drone program are the utmost professionals, doing this work every day to protect American lives. They don't ask for credit, but I can assure you that each of them understands the great importance of what they do and the trust the American government and the American people have placed in their hands. Those men and women don't take any decisions lightly, every decision that is made behind closed doors is carefully considered. There is no secret agenda to assassinate random civilians, political opponents, or to purposely hurt women and children as some try to allege. We go to great lengths often to ensure innocent women and children are not injured in the process, even to the point of allowing the actual targets to get away so as to protect them. So while this book is written by me, it's actually about their sacrifices and the others behind this work. Thank you to all those still serving in various intelligence and operational capacities required to ensure the drone program's success.

To the operators, words can't describe how honored I am to have supported you downrange. You put your lives on the line every day and go violently into the line of fire while I sat back behind a computer in the safety of the Box, none of what I did was possible without you. There is no other band of soldiers in the world I would want kicking in the door, the American public has no idea. Thank you to all of the military officers, non-commissioned officers, soldiers, sailors, Marines and airmen from the various units I had the pleasure of serving with over time. To the unit for shaping me into the man who I am today. To my mentors and other intelligence analysts I worked with, names I can't release because most are still involved in this work, you know who you are. I am forever in your debt. I know that members of my old team there are still downrange, hunting the enemy like ISIS every day, never letting them sleep. Don't let up, Abu Bakr al-Baghdadi and his ISIS henchmen are still out there afraid of you, he knows you are inching closer every day. I'm confident you will find him soon, and he will die at the hands of American forces just like all the other leaders who came before him.

As for the many people and organizations behind the physical making of this book's success, I couldn't ask for a better team.

Thank you first and foremost to Christopher S. Stewart, my co-writer, for convincing me and others that my experiences were worth telling. Thank you also for not getting me killed that one time chasing your story outside Mogadishu, although it probably would have made for a good time. Thank you to my agent, Eric Lupfer, formerly of WME and fellow MBA classmate, for your guidance through the process and unrelenting support to get this book published. To my agency, William Morris Endeavor (WME), we have had an incredible run. You've taken *Drone Warrior* to another level, and I appreciate how so many people at the agency have gotten behind the project. Big shout out to Ashley Fox, formerly of WME for getting Hollywood excited and securing the movie rights to the book. To Anna DeRoy of WME, for her continued work from the movie side and wisdom navigating the entertainment world.

Thank you to Paramount Pictures and Michael Bay, Matthew Cohan and their team at Bay Films for optioning the movie rights to the book, can't wait to see this come to life on the big screen.

To my editor Julia Cheiffetz and the Dey Street/HarperCollins team for seeing the vision and the potential of what this book can become. Also, thank you for letting me fly drones inside your office in NYC. I'm going to go out on a limb and say that was a first for the both of us.

To my lawyer Alan Enslen with Maynard Cooper & Gale, your guidance on legal and national security matters and perseverance working with the Defense Department's security review office deserves a ton of credit for making this book see the light of day and for making it legally possible for my story to be told. Your background as a former Special Forces Officer with 10th SF Group goes to show I had the right man behind me trying to tackle this tedious job. Thanks for navigating the DOD's exhausting security review process and keeping up the constant pressure over the past years so we could finally receive approval from the (last time

I counted) thirteen separate government organizations that had to officially sign off (including the Special Operations Commands, my former unit and all the intelligence agencies I worked with that were required to see the manuscript prior to publication).

While the government review took nearly a year and a half longer than expected, the process is necessary and important to protect national security; that being said, I should also thank the security personnel at the various agencies for their time spent reviewing this book. I appreciate you allowing me to talk about my experiences even at all especially knowing the special programs I took part in.

Finally, to my family back home in Texas and elsewhere. I've spent too many years overseas without contacting you, I hope to change that going forward and be the family member I should have been. Thank you for always being there for me. Especially to my mother, Kathleen Zaccaria, you are kind, beautiful, and raised me to be who I am today. I hope this book makes you proud of me. My friends back in Katy, "the Herd," thanks for keeping me humble and being the same down to earth group every time I come back to visit.

Most important, to my wife Joyce. My mother once told me that when you find a woman better than you, marry her. So I did. You have always been my biggest supporter and sounding board, not sure what I would do without you next to me. Can't wait to grow old with you.

It feels a bit odd to write a memoir at my age. I'm thirty-three now and feel like I'm just getting started with my life. I know many more adventures await. This is only the beginning.

THE ARSENAL

I have seen nearly every drone in the U.S. government's arsenal. I used a lot of them—and had access to pretty much any one I wanted. These are the models my team controlled the most—that I can talk about.

MQ-1 PREDATOR

For most of my time in special operations, this was the team's go-to drone. I saw one for the first time on my first deployment to Baghdad. It had wide wings (48 feet) and a narrow, startlingly black body.

The Predator is a single-engine, medium-altitude, long-endurance UAV capable of long-term surveillance. It's equipped with 2x AGM 114 Hellfire missiles, the warheads varying based on the target. You can remove the Hellfire missiles to get a few more hours of time in the air.

The bird is a day/night camera capable of allowing it to use its sensors to loiter over our targets even when there is no light around. The MQ-1 is outfitted with an electro-optical (daytime) sensor in the nose fuselage that is mounted in a forward-looking fixed position, which essentially is the view you'd see from the cockpit on an airplane.

The UAV is capable of flying a max of 25,000 feet. With a flip of a switch, the camera can be toggled between day and night-time views. Often we'd use the infrared camera during the day because it provided a different perspective on the target and the surrounding area. The infrared camera is also better for following targets when they go dynamic, or move.

The MQ-1 is slow, which may be surprising to some people. UAVs are not fighter jets; they are there to provide us with a persistent surveillance capability first and foremost. The MQ-1 typically orbits at a speed of 70–80 knots—about 80–90 miles per hour. The MQ-1 has a twenty-hour max endurance. The launch/recovery element location and the drone's proximity to the targets we followed determined how long we had the UAV over our targets, what is called "on station" time.

MQ-9 REAPER

This bird is an advanced version of the Predator. At a cost of close to $15 million, it's also the most expensive UAV on this list. It looks similar to its older brother—with a few major upgrades. It can operate at a higher altitude, watch a target longer, and its speed is nearly double the Predator's, at about 300 miles per hour. Its payload is also gigantic and can rain down all kinds of god-awful force if needed: four Hellfire missiles and two 500-pound GBU-12 laser-guided bombs. In this way, the Reaper is probably the deadliest in our arsenal. It was also the most highly sought after when I was deployed. There were too few to go around and typically they were reserved for agency missions in Pakistan. There weren't many when I was in Delta, but now the Reaper is basically all they fly.

RQ-11 RAVEN

When I first joined the Army, there were very few Ravens in the military. Typically they were only handed out to special forces teams in the field, mainly in Afghanistan and Iraq. But by the time I left that had changed. It became the most widely distributed handheld bird in the U.S. military. Most combat units had them. Even the infantry teams used them.

I almost always had two of them with me wherever our team set up the Box. It is handheld—the size of a toy glider you had when you were a kid. Ravens are very lightweight and fly at low altitudes; they are ideal for the battlefield when you need real-time situational awareness. You throw it up and you can see your enemy hunkered down across a clearing and make better decisions about how to attack.

Even though our team had the Raven on hand at all times, I didn't use it a lot over the years. The video from the cameras is shaky, and the winds blow them around. The aircraft was designed to break apart upon recovery and essentially crash land, which meant that it was constantly in the repair shop.

The Raven wasn't ideal for most of my situations—long-term surveillance in particular. I never used it to follow around bad guys because it has a 60–90 minute flight duration, a typical operating altitude of 100–500 feet, and a very short range from its launch station—no more than six miles. At that max range we sometimes lost our link to the UAV, losing it forever to the unknown. It just disappeared.

Plus, you can hear the Raven's persistent buzzing coming from miles away. I saw Ravens shot at during battle because the enemy knew that it was swarming above them like an army of bees.

PUMA

The Puma is one step up from the Raven, but in my opinion a completely different aerial platform altogether. It is one of the better tactical UAVs I used: handheld, one man operated, and waterproof so it can fly in both land and maritime environments.

The bird has a flight endurance of nearly three hours and

its optimal operating altitude is anywhere from 500–1,000 feet. At such altitude the Puma can barely be heard by those on the ground. When we didn't have a long-endurance asset such as a Predator at our disposal, the Puma was a good alternative for surveillance or to assess battle damage after a suicide bombing. Its main limitation was its eight-mile range, which meant that it couldn't go too far from the control station.

On a few occasions, I used it to follow me around a city as a force protection measure—like a guardian angel. It watched me and if something happened there were silent eyes that could alert the others to come in force.

There were few Pumas in the military during my time. While the Raven cost about as much as an entry-level BMW, the price tag on the Puma was north of $100,000.

I-GNAT

The i-Gnat is the same class as the Predator, but has a longer endurance and higher operating altitude. The i-Gnat that I used actually had better optics and was closer to silent than the Predator. We flew it at lower altitudes because it was also smaller than the Predator and had a lower signature to the enemy. The difference is that the i-Gnat isn't armed, making it simply a solid reconnaissance bird. We only had one of these in our arsenal, but I could call in an extra from the agency when we needed an extra set of eyes. They were best for cities. I used them in Baghdad a lot because they could be flown at a lower altitude than the Predator without the enemy seeing or hearing it.

THE SHADOW

The U.S. Army has employed the Shadow for more than a decade and it was one of the original surveillance drones procured to support U.S. forces in multiple combat theaters, from Iraq to Afghanistan. This platform was typically used to support as a kind of cover over more conventional military forces, such as an infantry brigade.

The Shadow is a capable surveillance aircraft. It has an endurance time of approximately nine hours, a typical cruising speed of 80 miles per hour, and max range of approximately 70 miles from base. The platform requires a significant amount of personnel to operate it and the data systems that go along with it. When it lands, the platform needs a runway and is caught by a wire, similar to how a fighter jet may land on an aircraft carrier. These UAVs were housed out of the larger U.S. bases throughout Iraq and Afghanistan. As I was on my way out of special ops, there was talk of arming this aircraft to give it strike capability.

SCAN EAGLE

The Scan Eagle is a gasoline-engine, medium-altitude UAV with a typical cruising speed of 50–60 knots. It is relatively small in size compared to UAVs with similar endurance (about 20 hours) and altitude (2,000–3,000 feet) capabilities. We kept a few of these parked at our larger bases in Iraq.

One of the great things about the Scan Eagle is that it doesn't need a runway. It launches out of a pneumatic catapult called a SuperWedge and is recovered by a skyhook system, which basically reaches up and grabs the drone in midair.

The big problem with this bird is the unexpected crashes. One time we lost a satellite link to one and it went nosediving into a police station in Mosul. Luckily the police knew it was ours and gave it back before it could be sold off to the highest bidder.

Most times it was a backup for us when another Predator was on a higher-priority mission or being serviced. I didn't like to rely on it fully without the help of another drone because it failed us on a number of occasions when tracking vehicles.

During one mission, three mornings in a row, the Scan Eagle lost sight of a vehicle in heavy traffic—something we referred to as going "nadir." That happened when the drone camera was zoomed in on a vehicle and, just at the right angle, the camera would begin to malfunction, spinning around.

RQ-4 GLOBAL HAWK

The Hawk is the unmanned version of the U2 plane. It doesn't kill. It doesn't have any bombs. It is pure spy craft: capable of providing reconnaissance at an altitude of up to 65,000 feet, endurance of about 35 hours, a range of nearly 1,000 miles, and a cruising speed of over 300 knots.

It is the second-largest drone in history, only to be outdone by the Heron, the Israeli equivalent. We didn't use the Hawk like we might use a Predator or Scan Eagle to follow bad guys around all day with full-motion video. We deployed the Hawk to take snapshots of huge swaths of territory we deemed of interest to a mission, similar to a satellite photo but a lot faster. For example, we used the Hawk to take photos of training camps in Africa, just to see if they were still occupied by extremist groups.

So while a single Predator takes a while to look at specific locations on the ground that are spread across an entire country, the Hawk can simply snap photos of all those locations within minutes. If we wanted to find a needle in a haystack, the Hawk could see the entire haystack.

Personally, I believe the costs to maintain and deploy this drone heavily outweigh the benefits. Advancements in current UAVs such as the MQ-1 and MQ-9, coupled with improvements in the U.S. government's satellite technology, could quickly make this drone obsolete.

ABOUT THE AUTHORS

Brett Velicovich has over ten years of experience conducting counterterrorism and intelligence operations globally. As an intelligence analyst within the U.S. military's elite 1st Special Forces Operational Detachment—Delta, his work was directly responsible for countless missions leading to the successful capture and kill of terrorist leaders. Serving five combat tours to Iraq and Afghanistan, he also worked in Somalia and received numerous combat medals for his service, including the Bronze Star and Combat Action Badge. Regarded as a world-renowned drone expert, he left the service and earned an MBA from Duke University and helped start an initiative that looks to employ unmanned aerial vehicles in support of wildlife conservation in East Africa. He lives in Virginia.

Christopher S. Stewart is an investigative reporter at the *Wall Street Journal,* where he shared a 2015 Pulitzer Prize for Investigative Reporting. His work has appeared in *GQ, Harper's, The New York Times Magazine, New York* magazine, *The Paris Review, Wired,* and other publications, and he also served as deputy editor at the *New York Observer* and is a former contributing editor at *Condé Nast Portfolio.* Stewart is the author of *Hunting the Tiger* and *Jungleland.* He lives with his family in New York.